Based on the latest research and recommendations from the American Academy of Pediatrics, this essential handbook answers common questions parents have about attention-deficit/hyperactivity disorder (ADHD), including

- How is ADHD defined today?
- How can I tell if my child's problems are due to ADHD and not some other problem?
- What is the best way to work with my child's teacher?
- What types of medications are used to treat ADHD?
- What steps can I take to help my parenting be as successful as possible?
- Should I involve my child in the treatment plan?
- Are there classroom structures and school policies that will best support my child?
- How can I help my teenager manage social and emotional pressures?
- Can I trust the information available on the Internet?

…and much more, to help improve the quality of life for your child and your family.

Also available from the
American Academy of Pediatrics

**Caring for Your Baby and Young Child:
Birth to Age 5**

**Caring for Your School-Age Child:
Ages 5 to 12**

**Caring for Your Teenager:
The Complete and Authoritative Guide**

Your Baby's First Year

**Guide to Your Child's Symptoms:
Birth Through Adolescence**

**Guide to Your Child's Sleep:
Birth Through Adolescence**

**Guide to Your Child's Allergies and Asthma:
Breathing Easy and Bringing Up Healthy, Active Children**

**Guide to Your Child's Nutrition:
Making Peace at the Table and Building Healthy
Eating Habits for Life**

New Mother's Guide to Breastfeeding

Guide to Toilet Training

THE AMERICAN ACADEMY OF PEDIATRICS

ADHD
A Complete and Authoritative Guide

Michael I. Reiff, MD, FAAP

with Sherill Tippins

American Academy of Pediatrics

DEDICATED TO THE HEALTH OF ALL CHILDREN™

AAP Publishing Staff

Director, Department of Marketing and Publications
Maureen DeRosa, MPA

Director, Division of Product Development
Mark Grimes

Manager, Consumer Publishing
Eileen Glasstetter

Director, Division of Publishing and Production Services
Sandi King

Manager, Editorial Services
Kate Larson

Manager, Print Production Services
Leesa Levin-Doroba

Manager, Graphic Design
Linda Diamond

Director, Division of Marketing and Sales
Jill Ferguson

Manager, Consumer Product Marketing and Sales
Susan Thompson

Library of Congress Control Number: 2003106045
ISBN: 1-58110-121-X

The recommendations in this publication do not indicate an exclusive course of treatment or serve as a standard of medical care. Variations, taking into account individual circumstances, may be appropriate.

Reviewers/Contributors

Editor in Chief
Michael I. Reiff, MD, FAAP
Associate Professor, Department of Pediatrics
Division of Pediatric Clinical Neurosciences
University of Minnesota School of Medicine

AAP Board of Directors Reviewer
Ellen Buerk, MD, MEd, FAAP

American Academy of Pediatrics
Executive Director
Joe M. Sanders, Jr, MD, FAAP

Associate Executive Director
Roger F. Suchyta, MD, FAAP

Co-Director, Department of Practice and Research
Ed Zimmerman, MS

Director, Department of Marketing and Publications
Maureen DeRosa, MPA

Director, Division of Product Development
Mark Grimes

Manager, Consumer Publishing
Division of Product Development
Eileen Glasstetter, MS

Reviewers/Contributors

Reviewers and Contributors
*ADHD Diagnosis and Treatment Guidelines Implementation
Project Advisory Committee*
Carole M. Lannon, MD, MPH, FAAP, Cochairperson
James M. Perrin, MD, FAAP, Cochairperson
Jane M. Foy, MD, FAAP
Charles J. Homer, MD, MPH, FAAP
Kelly J. Kelleher, MD, FAAP
Karen J. Miller, MD, FAAP
Jerry L. Rushton, MD, MPH, FAAP
Martin T. Stein, MD, FAAP
Thomas J. Sullivan, MD, FAAP
Mark L. Wolraich, MD, FAAP

Additional Reviewers and Contributors
Howard Abikoff, PhD
Robert W. Amler, MD, MS, FAAP
Ronald T. Brown, PhD, ABPP
Harlan R. Gephart, MD, FAAP
Ross Greene, PhD
William E. Pelham, Jr, PhD
Karen Pierce, MD
Francis E. Rushton, MD, FAAP
Howard H. Schubiner, MD, FAAP
James Swanson, PhD

Reviewers/Contributors

Writer
Sherill Tippins

Illustrator
Anthony Alex LeTourneau

Editors
Robin Michaelson
Kate Larson

Additional Assistance
Michelle Esquivel, MPH
Brent Heathcott
Holly Kaminski
Lisa Miller
Veronica Laude Noland
Noreen Stewart
Karen Wanatowicz

Dedication

▲   ▲   ▲   ▲

Listen to the Mustn'ts, child, listen to the Don'ts
Listen to the Shouldn'ts, the Impossibles, the Won'ts.
Listen to the Never Haves, then listen close to me.
Anything can happen, Anything can be

Shel Silverstein

To Dylan and Jess who have taught me about the rich journey through childhood and adolescence.

And to all the children, adolescents, and their families who struggle daily to turn the Don'ts and Won'ts of ADHD into the Anything Can Bes.

Please Note

▲   ▲   ▲   ▲

The information contained in this book is intended to complement, not substitute for, the advice of your child's pediatrician. Before starting any medical treatment or medical program, you should consult with your child's pediatrician, who can discuss your child's individual needs and counsel you about symptoms and treatment. If you have any questions regarding how the information in this book applies to your child, speak to your child's pediatrician.

This book has been developed by the American Academy of Pediatrics. The authors, editors, and contributors are expert authorities in the field of pediatrics. No commercial involvement of any kind has been solicited or accepted in the development of the content of this publication.

Table of Contents

▲ ▲ ▲ ▲

Foreword

▲ ▲ ▲ ▲

The American Academy of Pediatrics (AAP) welcomes you to the latest in its series of books for parents, *ADHD: A Complete and Authoritative Guide.*

This book will help readers apply the most current evidence-based and best-practice approaches for finding solutions for children with attention-deficit/hyperactivity disorder (ADHD). Many important topics are addressed in this book, including the diagnostic process, behavior therapy, medication, and advice on management techniques for school and home. We encourage its use in concert with the advice and counsel of our readers' pediatricians and hope that it serves to strengthen collaboration among parents, children, primary care professionals, and school personnel.

What separates *ADHD: A Complete and Authoritative Guide* from other reference books on this topic is that pediatricians who specialize in this have extensively reviewed it. Under the editorial direction of Michael Reiff, MD, FAAP, the material in this book was developed with the assistance of numerous contributors from the AAP.

The AAP is an organization of 57,000 primary care pediatricians, pediatric medical subspecialists, and pediatric surgical specialists dedicated to the health, safety, and well-being of infants, children, adolescents, and young adults. *ADHD: A Complete and Authoritative Guide* is part of the ongoing educational efforts of the AAP to provide parents and caregivers with high-quality information on a broad spectrum of children's health issues.

Joe M. Sanders, Jr, MD, FAAP
Executive Director

A Note on Gender

▲　▲　▲　▲

A good deal of discussion went into the use of pronouns ("hes" and "shes") for this book, particularly when describing different subtypes of attention-deficit/hyperactivity disorder (ADHD) or different problems faced by children with ADHD. Although boys and girls can have any subtype of ADHD or any of the related problems, the number of boys diagnosed with ADHD is about 3 to 1 over girls, and the combined type of ADHD with all 3 key elements—impulsivity, hyperactivity, and inattention—is diagnosed about 2½ times more frequently than the predominantly inattentive type. However, if all the children in a school system were evaluated, it is likely that the inattentive type would be found to be about 1½ times more common than the combined type—this inattentive type is just more likely to go undiagnosed, and girls are more likely to have this subtype than boys. With this as background, we have attempted to balance the "hes" and "shes" in this book in an interchangeable way.

Introduction

▲ ▲ ▲ ▲

Why Another Book About ADHD?

Almost all children have times when their attention or behavior veers out of control. However, for some children, these types of behaviors are more than an occasional problem. Children with attention-deficit/hyperactivity disorder (ADHD) have behavior problems that are so frequent and severe that they interfere with their ability to function adequately on a daily basis. Attention-deficit/hyperactivity disorder is the most commonly diagnosed behavioral condition in children, affecting approximately 6% to 9% of the school-aged population. It is a chronic condition whose symptoms continue in 60% to 80% of adolescents and, in some individuals, even into adulthood. It can have effects on children's learning, ability to regulate their behavior, social skills, and self-esteem.

Attention-deficit/hyperactivity disorder is the most researched of all childhood behavioral disorders, with more than 1,000 scientific articles published yearly. Yet a great deal of controversy still exists in the media and in the general public about the nature of ADHD and the best means of treatment. You are probably already aware of the variety of books on ADHD dominating the "parenting" shelves of your local bookstore. Web sites also abound with an enormous amount of information for parents, ranging from carefully researched to highly irresponsible. This glut of advice can be mind-boggling for parents to sort out. Attention-deficit/hyperactivity disorder is reported by the media to be overdiagnosed and underdiagnosed, and overtreated and undertreated all at the same time. Descriptions of the same new medication can range from "groundbreaking" to "dangerous." How can a responsible parent sort through this quagmire of seemingly contradictory data? Helping parents to answer this question is a major goal of this book. Why all the confusion? If only ADHD was as easy to diagnose as, say, diabetes or asthma. But unfortunately, as you will learn in chapters 1 and 2, there is no laboratory test for ADHD, no urine or blood test, x-ray, or brain wave study that can tell you definitively whether your child has ADHD. Instead, your child's treatment team—consisting of you, your child, his pediatrician, teachers, and others who know and work with him—will work together to analyze your child's *functioning*—that is, whether and how his symptoms seriously affect his behavior, learning, social skills, and/or self-esteem at home, at school, or in other situations. This is done through careful observation, exchange of information, the completion of behavior-rating questionnaires, and other steps as outlined in the latest research-based guidelines developed by the American Academy of Pediatrics that you will read about in chapters 1 and 2. The diagnostic process can be complicated by the fact that some other conditions, such as anxiety or depression and behavior disorders, can seem quite similar to ADHD and often accompany, or "coexist with," the condition. These will be reviewed in detail in Chapter 8. With this information in hand, it is certainly possible to accurately diagnose ADHD in a way that can lead to effective treatment.

What do we know about treatment? Physicians and psychologists are constantly juggling and integrating several levels of information in their attempt to help you and your family find the best solutions and outcomes for your child with ADHD. The most reliable and consistent information is what we call *evidence-based.* Evidence-based medicine unites the unique clinical expertise of your child's physician with the best clinical evidence from systematic research studies in making decisions about the care of your child and family. In chapters 3 through 7 you will learn that the only 2 treatments for ADHD that are strongly evidence-based are medication and behavior therapy. The good news is that these treatments have been found to be effective in rigorous clinical studies. The challenge is that some of the procedures and routines used in these clinical studies are not easily available in real-life situations. This is why it is so important to work with your own child's clinicians and educators to adapt as many of the principles of "ideal management" described in this book to your own family circumstances and to the unique needs of your child. Although monthly visits for medication management may be ideal (but not practical), for example, you and your child's pediatrician may decide that many of the same goals can be accomplished by carefully planned visits every 3 to 4 months. Likewise, the type of systematic parent training described in Chapter 6 may not be readily available in your community, or may not be covered by your insurance plan. Still, you can adapt many of these principles after reading the chapter, and may find it even more useful to work with a child therapist to modify these techniques even if it is not in the exact systematic approach described here. The types of summer school and camp programs described in Chapter 7 also may not be readily available in your community, but their principles can be adapted to many classroom and other group situations. These programs also can be used as models by parents when advocating for needed community services that have been proven effective.

In some cases, especially with ADHD and related disorders, not enough studies have been done to indicate an effective, evidence-based approach to a given problem, even though the need for help is clear. In these cases, a best-practice approach is the best alternative. A best-practice approach is based on a consensus of what experts consider the best advice in the absence of definitive studies. Many of the suggestions in chapters 5, 7, 10, and 11, especially those on effective management techniques for home and school in addition to behavior therapy, are based on this best-practice approach.

If sorting out the material for parents written by recognized experts (some of these are included as recommendations in the Resources section of this book) is difficult, knowing what to make of other books, material from Web sites, information from parent chat rooms, etc, can be daunting. Some of the more controversial, unproven, and alternative treatments proposed for ADHD are reviewed in Chapter 9. Consumer beware! Some of these treatments, like eliminating sugar from the diet, have been shown to be ineffective. Others, such as biofeedback, are time-consuming and costly, and have not been studied systematically enough to be able to recommend them. In Chapter 9 you will find information on how to judge claims of treatment success by analyzing the evidence and considering the source of the information, whether there is a scientific basis for the claim, and whether an unstated motive (such as making a sale) may underlie claims for a particular theory or treatment plan. Your child's pediatrician can be an excellent resource in helping to evaluate ADHD-related information and likely has had experience with many families who have applied a wide spectrum of approaches to help their children with ADHD.

This book strongly recommends that you consider evidence-based or best-practice approaches as the mainstay of any evaluation or treatment plan, and that alternative treatments be tried only after a critical discussion with the professionals on your child's treatment team. So read this book and any other materials on ADHD diagnosis, evaluation, or treatment critically! Always ask yourself if the material presented is evidence-based or reflects best practice, sound expert advice, someone's belief based only on what they did for their own child, an opinion criticizing established treatments for some political agenda, an attempt to sell an unproven product, etc, and draw your own informed conclusions.

Finally, will following the advice in this book lead to a better long-term result for your child and your family? Surprisingly, the number of long-term studies are extremely limited—especially those using the types of evidence-based approaches to treatment that we recommend. Such studies are costly, require large numbers of families, and can be difficult to interpret because of all the ways that real-life considerations impose themselves on individual children in different ways over a long study period. In addition, as you will read in this book, the last few years have led to major advances in our knowledge about ADHD, and it will take several years to be able to see how these advances translate into better outcomes over a long period. Having said that, we remain optimistic that by using the information contained in this book, you will be applying the most current evidence-based and best-practice approaches for improving the life and functioning of your child.

CHAPTER ONE

What Is ADHD?

▲   ▲   ▲   ▲

Andrew Scott had always been an active child. From the time he learned to walk he was "into everything." His parents were surprised at how eagerly he participated in preschool beginning at age 3 years—throwing himself into playground activities and peppering adults with questions. In fact, Andrew's teachers frequently commented on how active he was. Kindergarten and first grade passed without any major problems, though Andrew's kindergarten teacher observed that he was "quite a handful" and that his level of activity seemed to overwhelm some of the other children during playtime. In third grade, however, Andrew began to fall behind in arithmetic and reading. His teacher said he was too restless to pay attention. During class time he pestered and provoked the children around him, and seemed unable to focus on a learning activity for longer than a few minutes. On the playground he was "over-physical" with his peers, invading their space and then over-reacting when they pushed him away.

Around the middle of the year, Andrew's teacher arranged for a conference with his parents. She informed them that she believed Andrew's inattention, high activity level, and troubles with schoolwork might indicate the presence of attention-deficit/hyperactivity disorder (ADHD). She explained that ADHD often goes undetected until the child enters school and academic performance and social relationships begin to be affected.

Despite the teacher's positive attitude, Andrew's parents were stunned by her recommendation that their son be evaluated for ADHD. They had always been challenged by their active child, but they had never considered his behavior out of the ordinary for a healthy young boy. As Andrew's father always liked to point out, Andrew was "just like me when I was in school"— eager, excited, and always on the go." While both parents agreed that Andrew could use some extra attention to his social skills and needed help with reading, they did not see how these behaviors could be construed as a medical condition. "I think his teacher just cannot handle him in class," Andrew's mother told her husband later, when they were back at home. "She has a discipline problem and she calls it ADHD. I think it's the school that should be evaluated."

Three blocks away from the Scotts, the Keller family was experiencing similar confusion. Their 12-year-old daughter, Emma, was also having problems. Emma's personal style, however, could hardly be more different from Andrew's. If anything, she was on the quiet and somewhat anxious side. Since early childhood, she had been a "dreamer" whose thoughts tended to drift easily, who frequently forgot things she had recently learned or been told, and who spent much of her time alone. In recent years, her "randomness" and lack of organization had begun to seriously affect her school performance, social life, and family relationships. At present she was having trouble completing tasks and was messy and careless about her schoolwork. Her parents noted that she is often forgetful and at times it seems as if her mind is elsewhere and that she is not listening. In addition to her schoolwork these issues also affect her friendships and meeting her responsibilities at home. Still, Emma's parents felt that her behavior was typical of many adolescent girls, and was nothing that a little maturation and help with organization could not cure. Was it really necessary, they asked Emma's pediatrician, to consider this a medical issue or to start an evaluation for ADHD as he had suggested?

As different as Andrew's and Emma's situations seem to be, both are typical for children with ADHD—a disorder in which children are significantly limited in their ability to filter out irrelevant input, focus, organize, prioritize, delay gratification, think before they act, or perform other so-called executive functions that most of us perform automatically. In children such as Andrew, with hyperactive-impulsive elements to his ADHD, the disorder presents itself as an inability to control impulses or regulate activity, even when the child knows how he is expected to behave. In those with inattentive-type ADHD, including Emma, an inability to filter information means that the peeling wallpaper on a classroom wall can claim as much attention as the teacher's lecture, and that a date with a friend can be forgotten in a flood of unregulated input.

Because these behaviors—short attention span, forgetfulness, inability to sit still, unusually high activity level, and a tendency to act before thinking— are so common in children with and without ADHD, many families are surprised when their child is referred for an evaluation. Adding to their confusion is the fact that all of these behaviors occur in children throughout their development, though children with ADHD exhibit more extreme and immature forms of these behaviors and do not outgrow them at the same pace that other children do. Because, as you will read later on in this book, other disorders, such as learning disabilities, oppositional defiant disorder, and anxiety or depression, can resemble ADHD (and, in fact, often accompany it), it can be difficult to tell whether a child has another condition, ADHD, or both. Finally, the fact that ADHD is diagnosed through a methodical description of carefully defined behaviors and their consequences—rather than the types of laboratory procedures used to diagnose such disorders as diabetes—leads some adults and the popular press to question whether ADHD exists at all.

Yet more and more evidence suggests that ADHD is a biological, brain-based condition that typically, especially if untreated, can lead to poor performance in school; failed friendships; plunging self-esteem; and continued social, emotional, and performance difficulties through adolescence and into adulthood. In fact, the scientific research on ADHD is more thorough and compelling than for most behavioral and mental health disorders, and even many medical conditions. In 1998 the National Institutes of Health, responding to public concern and debate about ADHD diagnosis and treatment, assembled a group of experts for a consensus conference on ADHD. They then published their conclusions affirming that ADHD is indeed a legitimate disorder. According to recent estimates, it is among the most prevalent chronic childhood disorders, occurring in 6% to 9% of school-aged children (second only to asthma), and currently accounting for as many as 30% to 50% of child referrals to mental health services. Many people believe that the incidence of ADHD has increased significantly in recent decades, perhaps due to environmental factors, but this is not the case. The number of children who have ADHD has likely remained roughly stable, but the number of children diagnosed with the condition has increased as more clinicians have become familiar with its symptoms and the criteria for diagnosing ADHD have been refined.

While there are no confirming medical tests for ADHD, a generally reliable method for diagnosing the condition based on the child's behavior and functioning has been established. Parents whose children have been adequately evaluated for ADHD, and who have implemented appropriate treatment as a result, frequently report that the difference before and after their child's treatment is "like night and day." While ADHD cannot be cured, children can be helped to compensate for their problems so that progress at school is affected as little as possible and social relationships improve. With adequate treatment, many will get to the point where they appear indistinguishable from classmates without ADHD. As a result, their self-esteem increases, as do their chances for future successes.

In this book, you will learn how ADHD is defined and recognized; how it is evaluated; and how, according to the latest reliable scientific research, it can best be treated. Particularly in recent years, enormous progress has been made in the basic science of ADHD and in identifying which forms of treatment help most children with this condition. Researchers have identified the types of behavioral, academic, and social supports most likely to be useful at school and at home, and courses and therapies have been developed to pass this information on to parents and teachers in the community. It has become increasingly clear how important it is for adults—parents, educators, professionals, and others—to work together to help a child with ADHD, and how vital it is for the child to become actively involved in his own evaluation and treatment. Finally, the changing effect of this chronic condition over time—on the growing child, adolescent, young adult, and mature individual—is being actively studied to provide insight into how your child can improve his experience at each stage of life.

This is not to say that we now know everything there is to know about the nature and proper treatment of ADHD. As you will learn in the later chapters, a number of questions remain to be answered, and there is a great deal of research still to be done. The good news, however, is that evaluation and treatment of ADHD is at a much more advanced stage today than ever before. Armed with the knowledge provided to you in these pages, you and your child will be able to address the challenges of ADHD with greater confidence and optimism than families of any preceding generation.

Before learning about how ADHD is recognized, diagnosed, and treated, however, it is necessary to understand exactly what ADHD is—and what it is not. In this chapter you will learn

- How the view of ADHD has evolved over time
- How ADHD is defined today
- What scientists believe may cause ADHD
- How the condition typically alters a child's experience and what its long-term effects are

▲   ▲   ▲   ▲

MYTHS AND MISCONCEPTIONS ABOUT ADHD

So much misinformation has circulated about ADHD and its causes, diagnosis, and treatment over recent decades that it is just as productive to describe what ADHD is not as what it is. Following are a number of erroneous assumptions about the disorder, along with explanations aimed at clarifying the issues:

- **"He's just lazy and unmotivated."** This assumption is a common response to the behavior exhibited by a child who is struggling with ADHD. A child who finds it nearly impossible to stay focused in class, or to complete a lengthy task such as writing a long essay, may try to save face by acting as though he does not want to do it or is too lazy to finish. This posture may look like laziness or lack of motivation, but it stems from real difficulty in functioning. All children want to succeed and get praised for their good work. If such tasks were easy for children with ADHD to accomplish, and provided rewarding feedback, those children would seem just as "motivated" as anyone else.

- **"He's a handful—or, she's a daydreamer—but that's normal. They just don't let kids be kids these days."** It is true that all children are impulsive, active, and inattentive at times, sometimes to the extreme. A child with ADHD, however, is more than just a "handful" for his parents and teachers, or

▲   ▲   ▲   ▲

a "daydreamer" who tends to lose herself in thought. His or her hyperactivity and/or inattentiveness constitute a real day-to-day functional disability—that is, it seriously and consistently impedes the ability to succeed at school, fit into family routines, follow household rules, maintain friendships, interact positively with family members, avoid injury, or otherwise manage in his or her environment. As you will learn in Chapter 2, this clear functional disability is what pediatricians look for when diagnosing ADHD and recommending treatment.

- **"Treatment for ADHD will cure it. The goal is to get off medication as soon as possible."** Attention-deficit/hyperactivity disorder is a chronic condition that does not go away, but instead changes form over time. Many older adolescents and adults are able to organize their lives and use techniques that allow them to forego medical treatment, although a significant number continue various forms of treatment throughout their life spans. Depending on the circumstances and demands as a person matures, this may or may not include continuing with medication or other treatments for ADHD at different times, even through adult life. The true goal is to function well at each stage of childhood and adolescence, and as an adult, rather than to stop any or all treatments as soon as possible.

- **"He focuses on his video games for hours. He can't have ADHD."** For the most part ADHD poses problems with tasks that require focused attention over long periods, not so much for activities that are highly engaging or stimulating. School can be especially challenging for a person with ADHD because the typical classroom lecture, compared with a video game, can be relatively unstimulating in terms of visuals, sound, and physical activity. Assignments can be long and require sustained, organized thought and effort, and the daily routine can be less structured and predictable than a child with ADHD might require. Most children with ADHD are diagnosed during their school years precisely because these conditions are so difficult for them. The difficulties that such children experience may make it seem that the school is the problem (and, certainly, that

▲ ▲ ▲ ▲

MYTHS AND MISCONCEPTIONS
ABOUT ADHD (*continued*)

possibility should be considered), but it is more likely to be a result of the child's struggle to manage in this environment.

Other situations that require much more active attention than a video game—and that can therefore be problematic for children with ADHD—include social interactions, with their constant, subtle exchange of emotional and social information; sports that require a high degree of focus or concentration; and extracurricular activities that require them to sit still, listen, or wait their turn for long periods.

- **"ADHD is caused by poor parental discipline."** Attention-deficit/hyperactivity disorder is not a result of poor discipline—although behaviors that stem from ADHD can challenge otherwise effective parenting styles. Inconsistent limit-setting and other ineffective parenting practices can, however, worsen its expression. In chapters 5 and 6 you will find a number of proven parenting techniques that can help children with ADHD manage their behavior.

- **"If, after a careful evaluation, a child doesn't receive the ADHD diagnosis, she doesn't need help."** Attention-deficit/hyperactivity disorder is diagnosed on a continuum, which means that a child can exhibit a number of ADHD-type behaviors yet not to the extent that she is diagnosed with ADHD. This does not mean she needs no help coping with the problems that she does have. The family of a child who does not meet the criteria for ADHD but has similar problems may be offered pediatric counseling, education about the range of normal developmental behaviors, home behavior management tools, school behavior management recommendations, social skills interventions, and help with managing homework flow and with organization and planning.

How Is ADHD Defined?

The condition now known as ADHD has long been surrounded by controversy in the popular media and among the general public. On television, in magazines and newspapers, and in thousands of everyday conversations, there is ongoing debate around the issue of whether certain "ADHD-type" behaviors lie within the realm of normal childhood experience or constitute a real disorder that requires treatment. As we have pointed out earlier in this chapter, much of the confusion over these issues lies in the fact that the behaviors associated with ADHD are exhibited by all children—only much more so and for a much longer period among children with ADHD. The issue of exactly where and how to draw the line between normal behavior and a clinical condition may become even clearer as increasingly sophisticated diagnostic techniques provide researchers with more information about the nature of the precise brain processes involved in children with ADHD.

For more than a century physicians have been aware of children displaying the behaviors that we now call ADHD. In 1902 British pediatrician George Still first formally documented a condition in which children seemed inattentive, impulsive, and hyperactive, stating his conviction that this was a result of biological makeup rather than poor parenting or other environmental factors. New neuropsychological research in the 1980s supported this hypothesis and led to the use of the term *attention deficit disorder.* In 1987, in response to even more precise information provided by new studies, the term *attention-deficit/hyperactivity disorder* was introduced.

Today ADHD is defined by the American Psychiatric Association (APA) as developmentally inappropriate attention and/or hyperactivity and impulsivity so pervasive and persistent as to significantly interfere with a child's daily life. You will become familiar with the complete "diagnostic criteria" for ADHD in Chapter 2. A child with ADHD has difficulty controlling her behavior in most major settings, including home and school. She may speed about in constant motion, make noise nonstop, refuse to wait her turn, and crash into everything around her. At other times she may drift as if in a daydream, failing to pay attention to or finish what she starts. She may have trouble learning and remembering. An impulsive nature may put her in actual physical danger. Because she has difficulty controlling this behavior, she may be labeled a "bad kid" or a "space cadet." These problems begin to occur relatively early in life (before age 7 years), though they sometimes go unrecognized until later. However, if there are absolutely no indications of ADHD before age 7 years, an alternative explanation for a child's later behaviors should be sought. Although a child's particular behaviors or symptoms may change as she matures and grows, some symptoms usually persist through later childhood and adolescence, and may last even into adulthood. (As you will learn in Chapter 8, ADHD symptoms that begin later in life or last for brief periods may indicate other conditions, such as depression, learning disabilities, or even substance abuse.)

It is easy to see why parents, teachers, and children themselves become confused when experts suggest to them that such "typical" if extreme childhood behavior like inattention, hyperactivity, and impulsivity may indicate the presence of ADHD. But professionals have identified clear differences between the functioning of a child without ADHD and a child with the condition. The presence of ADHD may be suspected if the

- Inattentive, impulsive, or hyperactive behavior is not age-appropriate. That is, if it is not typical of children of the same age who do not have ADHD.
- Behavior leads to chronic problems in daily functioning. A mild tendency to daydream or an active temperament, which may cause occasional problems for a child but is not seriously disabling, is not considered evidence of ADHD.
- Behavior is innate to the child and not a result of inadequate care, physical injury, disease, or other environmental influence. One way to determine whether the problem is environmental is to look at whether the problem occurs in more than one setting, such as at home and at school. If not, then an environmental cause, such as stresses at home or an inappropriate classroom placement, is more likely than ADHD to be the cause of the problem for the child.

For a child's condition to be diagnosed as ADHD, *all 3* of these conditions not just 1 or 2 must be met.

In the absence of any laboratory test for ADHD, the condition can only be recognized by its symptoms, and by the problems that these symptoms create for the child as she gets through the day. This is why it is so important for parents, teachers, mental health professionals, and medical experts to

work together when evaluating a child for ADHD, each con-
tributing his or her own observations, experience, and expertise
to create a comprehensive picture of the child's social, academic,
and emotional progress.

The fact that ADHD can be manifested in such varied ways
in different children has caused confusion in the past. In 1994
the APA addressed this issue by dividing the disorder called
ADHD into 3 general subtypes: *predominantly hyperactive/
impulsive-type ADHD, predominantly inattentive-type ADHD,*
and *combined-type ADHD.* A child with predominantly
hyperactive/impulsive-type ADHD may fidget or squirm in his
seat, have difficulty waiting his turn, and show a tendency to be
disorganized. He may act immaturely, have a poor sense of
physical boundaries, and tend toward destructive behaviors and
conduct problems. A child with predominantly inattentive-type
ADHD, on the other hand, may seem distracted and "spacey" or
"daydreamy," but lacks the hyperactive component of the disorder. She may seem to process information slowly and may also

▲ ▲ ▲ ▲

GIRLS AND ADHD

The fact that many more boys than girls are diagnosed with ADHD—at a ratio of approximately 3:1—has led to the mistaken belief among many parents and teachers that ADHD is a "boys'" disorder that rarely occurs in girls. This belief, along with the fact that girls are more likely to have inattentive-type ADHD that tends to be overlooked entirely or does not attract attention until the child is older, means that girls are less likely to be referred for evaluation and to receive the treatment they need. Even when diagnosis and treatment have been obtained, girls with ADHD are further disadvantaged by the fact that most ADHD research to date has focused on boys, and little is known about potential differences between the genders in the development of the condition over time or response to medication and other forms of treatment. When looked at separately, girls with ADHD have been found to have noteworthy problems in academic achievement and grade retention, an increased incidence of special education placement, significant peer rejection, and a tendency for their parents to adopt authoritarian discipline styles.

If your daughter has been referred for evaluation for ADHD, or if you suspect that she may have the condition, it is important not to discount the possibility just because she is female. Be aware that some sociocultural beliefs about girls (that they tend to daydream, that they just are not interested in academics) may mask a real problem in your child's ability to function; that teachers tend to under-refer girls for evaluation, even when their symptoms are the same as boys', and that girls are less likely than boys to receive sufficient medical treatment once they have been diagnosed. If your daughter is diagnosed with ADHD, ask the pediatrician to keep you updated on ongoing research about the development of ADHD in girls, the particular challenges girls with ADHD are likely to confront, and the different ways in which they may respond to various forms of treatment.

have a learning disorder, anxiety, or depression. A child with combined-type ADHD typically exhibits many of the behaviors of the first 2 subtypes.

These subtypes tend to be diagnosed at different ages and stages of development. Because of the hyperactivity and impulsivity, children with predominantly hyperactive/impulsive type or combined type may be diagnosed as early as the preschool years in extreme situations. Because they do not have obvious behavioral problems, children with predominantly inattentive type often go undetected until fourth grade or even later, when increased demands for sustained attention and more homework lead to significant problems in functioning. In the early grades children *learn to read,* but at around fourth grade they need to begin to *read to learn.* When this transition takes place, children with inattentive type typically begin to have more problems.

While the problems of hyperactivity/impulsivity and inattentiveness may seem at first to be unrelated, they both influence a child's inability to focus and function well in school, with peers, and in the family. Attention-deficit/hyperactivity disorder can be thought of as a spectrum of "attentional disorders" with a number of possible manifestations at different ages and developmental stages.

What Causes ADHD?
Many likely causes have been proposed for ADHD, but no single cause has yet been identified. A number of risk factors have been noted, however, that affect a child's brain development and behavior that acting in combination may lead to ADHD symptoms. They include genetic factors, variations in temperament (a child's individual differences in emotional reactivity, activity level, attention, and self-regulation), medical causes (especially those that affect brain development), and a host of environmental influences on the developing brain (including toxins such as lead, alcohol, and nutritional deficiencies).

One fact of which researchers are certain is that ADHD tends to run in families. Close relatives of people with ADHD have about a 5 times greater than random chance of having ADHD themselves, as well as a higher risk for such common accompanying disorders as anxiety, depression, learning disabilities, and conduct disorders. An identical twin is at high risk of sharing her twin's ADHD, and a sibling of a child with ADHD has about a 30% chance of having similar problems. Although no single gene has been identified for ADHD, research continues in this area, and it is likely that several genes will be found that contribute to ADHD symptoms. Brain imaging studies have found some differences in brain anatomy between children diagnosed with ADHD and those who have not been diagnosed, but no consistent pattern has yet emerged from these studies. The fact that children and adolescents respond so consistently to stimulant medications, and that these medications influence biochemical systems in the brain, suggests that biochemical causes may contribute to ADHD symptoms as well. This remains an area of active research. In the next few years newer brain-imaging tools and more sophisticated genetic techniques will continue to shed more light on the processes underlying ADHD. Still, it is unlikely that a single cause will be identified.

ADHD Over Time

Attention-deficit/hyperactivity disorder is a complex disorder with different challenges arising at each new phase of a child's development. Children who are born with ADHD generally carry some symptoms with them throughout adolescence and even into adulthood. However, as a child grows, her ADHD symptoms are likely to be expressed in different ways. Hyperactivity, for example, frequently takes center stage in early childhood but diminishes and may no longer be a problem by late adolescence or early adulthood. Inattention and impulsivity are likely to persist and can affect an adult's educational experience, work life, and relationships. Learning disabilities that were present during childhood also continue to exist in later years, as can any emotional, behavioral, and social problems that have not been fully resolved. They may just take different forms at different stages of development.

At one time or another all children and adolescents with ADHD may face some challenges relating to family relationships, status among their peers, social skills, academic achievement, self-esteem, self-perception, and/or accidental injury. With help, however, children and parents can learn to manage their symptoms in their early years as well as through adolescence and into adulthood. Early and accurate diagnosis, as you will learn in the next chapter, is the first step toward organizing a plan that can make a difference to your child and your family.

Finally, as you begin to focus on the problems and issues that your child is facing, do not forget to appreciate her unique strengths and abilities as well, and to communicate that appreciation to her. A child with ADHD (like all other children) not only thrives on positive reinforcement and praise, but also desperately needs to know that her symptoms do not make her "bad," "undisciplined," "stupid," or "lazy," as is so often implied. Educating her about what ADHD is—*and what it is not*—will help her cope with whatever discouraging comments or self-doubts come her way. The more she understands, the greater are her chances of success.

Children with ADHD frequently grow up to become successful and happy adults. In the chapters that follow you will learn how to identify, treat, effectively parent, and advocate for your child in ways that will help her minimize her challenges and fulfill her enormous promise.

▲ ▲ ▲ ▲

A PARENT'S STORY
Missed Clues and Lost Opportunities

"I suspected from my daughter's preschool days that she might have ADHD—not because of her activity level but because she could never stay focused on a single activity and she tended to forget things she had just learned. To me it was obvious that she was having real problems, but her teachers did not believe me because she is also unusually bright. They assumed that her restless behavior and underachievement were a result of 'just being bored.'

"It was only in middle school, when my daughter began forgetting homework assignments, not taking notes, and even forgetting her locker combination from one day to the next, that her teachers began to think something serious might be going on. I remember one day when I was at the school for a parent-teacher conference, I saw her standing in the hall looking confused. I asked her what was wrong, and she told me she'd forgotten how to get to her next class. She did not know what to do or where to go."

"That was the day I decided to have her evaluated by a specialist. She was diagnosed with ADHD and is being treated now. Her situation has improved, but I wish we had done this earlier before she fell so far behind. It is a huge relief to her, at least, to know that the problems she had been having at school were not 'her fault' but were symptoms of her condition. My biggest hope for her is that she realizes the potential she had when she was born."

Roberta, Pittsburgh, PA

CHAPTER TWO

Does My Child Have ADHD?
Evaluation and Diagnosis

▲   ▲   ▲   ▲

If only it were as straightforward to diagnose attention-deficit/
hyperactivity disorder (ADHD) as it is to diagnose diabetes.
Unfortunately, this is not the case because of some important
differences. First, the line between having or not having diabetes
is clear-cut because the diagnosis can be confirmed through laboratory tests. In addition, the symptoms of diabetes are not easily confused with routine concerns in children who are well. As
you will learn in this chapter, neither of these advantages exists
in determining whether a child has ADHD.

No laboratory tests—no urine, blood, x-ray, or psychological analysis—can prove objectively whether ADHD is present.
To complicate things further, the symptoms that characterize
ADHD—inattention, hyperactivity, and impulsivity—occur
in most children from time to time. Deciding whether a child's
behavior signals the presence of ADHD is therefore a complex
process that involves comparing a child's behaviors and abilities to function with those of other children his age. To do this,
pediatricians and mental health professionals must rely on parents' and caregivers' observations of how the child is functioning, information obtained from a child's teachers or other
school professionals, and the results of well-designed questionnaires structured to evaluate whether specific problems may be
interfering with a child's life on a daily basis. A diagnosis based

on these types of evaluation procedures can become even more challenging when, as is often the case, other problems exist such as vision or hearing deficiencies, emotional disorders, or learning disabilities. In some cases an evaluation may require a team of professionals with different specialties because some of the accompanying problems are more medical in nature, some are more psychological, and others are related to learning and language processes.

Fortunately, many professional organizations, including the American Academy of Pediatrics (AAP), have developed guidelines in recent years that standardize the evaluation process for ADHD. As a result, diagnosis of the condition has become more consistent. In this chapter you will learn how a child is evaluated for ADHD, from the first recognition that "something may be wrong" through a methodical assessment of all of the specific problems that need addressing. Along the way you will find information about

- The types of behaviors that often alert adults to the possible presence of ADHD
- How your child's pediatrician will evaluate him and arrive at a diagnosis
- How your child's particular subtype of ADHD will be identified
- How clinicians will pinpoint the presence of any accompanying conditions
- How a "team approach" that involves you, your child, his educators, and his clinicians all working together can bring about the best diagnosis and prepare you for planning a course of treatment

Early Warning Signs: When ADHD Is First Suspected
Most experts agree that the tendency to develop ADHD is present from birth, yet ADHD behaviors usually are not

noticed until children enter elementary school. As we pointed out in Chapter 1, one reason for this delay is the fact that
nearly all preschool-aged children frequently exhibit the core
behaviors or symptoms of ADHD—inattention, impulsivity,
and hyperactivity—as part of their normal development, whether they will ever receive the ADHD diagnosis. As other children gradually begin to grow out of such behaviors, however,
children with ADHD do not, and this difference becomes
increasingly clear as the years pass. School settings can highlight a child's problems relating to inattention, impulsivity, and
hyperactivity because classroom activities demand an increased
amount of focus, patience, and self-control from children if
they are to accomplish individual and group goals. These types
of demands are not as prevalent at home or in playgroups, so
in those settings, the child may have had fewer problems.

Usually by the time a child with ADHD reaches age 6 years,
her parents have already become aware that their child's inattentiveness, level of activity, or impulsiveness is greater than
normal. You may have noticed that your child finds it nearly
impossible to focus on a workbook for even a very short period,
even when you are there to assist her. Or you may still feel as
worn out at the end of a day with your overly active 8-year-old
as you did when she was 2. Your child may pepper adults with
questions so relentlessly that you have begun to suspect it is not
"normal," or you may have noticed that she does not seem to be
picking up the nuances of social interaction (respecting others'
personal space, letting other people have a turn to talk) that her
playmates are beginning to adopt. Yet it is difficult for a parent
to tell whether such behaviors are part of the normal process
of growing up ("Plenty of six-year-olds get bored with workbooks!"), whether they result from parenting difficulties
("Maybe I've been too inconsistent with setting limits."), or
whether this child's temperament puts her far to one end of

the spectrum ("She's always been a handful."), but not so far as to represent a disorder such as ADHD. This is why, for a child to be diagnosed with the disorder, the AAP advises pediatricians to gather information about the child's behavior in at least one other major setting besides her home—including a review of any reports provided by teachers and school professionals. By comparing the child's behavior across 2 or more settings, the pediatrician can begin to differentiate among such varied reasons for attentional problems as a "difficult" but normal temperament, ineffective parenting practices, inappropriate academic setting, and other challenges. He can also clarify whether the child's behavior is preventing her from *functioning* adequately in more than one setting—another requirement for diagnosis.

"SOMETHING'S NOT RIGHT…"
What Parents Notice When ADHD Behaviors Emerge

It is sometimes hard to match the behavior we observe in our children with the formal terminology used by pediatricians and other medical professionals. We rarely think of our children as having hyperactive/impulsive problems. Instead, we think, "Why can't she ever settle down?" When reviewing the list that follows of typical remarks made about children with ADHD, ask yourself how many times per day or week you say or think the same things yourself. It is true that all parents make such comments now and then, but parents of children with ADHD continue to see the same behaviors on a daily basis, and for extended periods—long after other children have progressed.

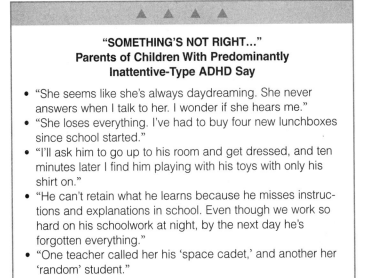

"SOMETHING'S NOT RIGHT..."
Parents of Children With Predominantly
Inattentive-Type ADHD Say

- "She seems like she's always daydreaming. She never answers when I talk to her. I wonder if she hears me."
- "She loses everything. I've had to buy four new lunchboxes since school started."
- "I'll ask him to go up to his room and get dressed, and ten minutes later I find him playing with his toys with only his shirt on."
- "He can't retain what he learns because he misses instructions and explanations in school. Even though we work so hard on his schoolwork at night, by the next day he's forgotten everything."
- "One teacher called her his 'space cadet,' and another her 'random' student."

Parents of Children With Predominantly
Hyperactive/Impulsive-Type ADHD Say

- "He never slows down. You can never get him to sit down to finish a meal or get ready for bed."
- "He interrupts constantly. You can't have a decent conversation when he's in the room."
- "She never thinks before she acts. She knows she shouldn't run across the street before stopping to look, but she does it all the time."
- "She operates out of order—like, 'ready...fire...aim.'"
- "Her classmates don't like her. She's always 'getting in their face.' No one invites her over to their house. She always has to be first and things always have to be her way."

First Steps Toward Evaluation

If you have begun to suspect that your child's poor progress at school, limited friendships, or frequent discipline problems add up to more than the normal difficulties of childhood, schedule an appointment with her teacher or school counselor as soon as possible. These people see your child daily in a group setting, where they can compare her behavior and ability to function to that of many other children her age. In many cases, teachers and counselors are trained to recognize symptoms of ADHD and similar disorders (although it is best not to assume that this is so). Certainly, they can give you a clearer idea of your child's experience at school, where ADHD so often manifests itself and creates problems. In many situations, it is the teacher or counselor who first notices that a child is failing to progress in ways that may indicate ADHD or a related disorder. In these instances, it is important for the teacher to contact the child's parents without delay to discuss the issue. Keep in mind that although teachers may identify more than 15% of their students as exhibiting many of the behaviors compatible with ADHD and recommend those students for an evaluation by their pediatrician, a much smaller number of these students will actually be diagnosed with ADHD after a careful evaluation. Whether your child will end up being diagnosed with ADHD, it is always important to follow up on teachers' concerns. The sooner a child with ADHD symptoms can be evaluated, diagnosed, and effectively treated, the greater her chances of progressing through school with good self-esteem and without losing too much ground.

If you and your child's teacher or other caregiver agree that your child is having clear problems functioning in the areas of difficult-to-manage behaviors or learning at home or at school, the next step is to make an appointment with his pediatrician to begin an evaluation. Pediatricians are accustomed to evaluating

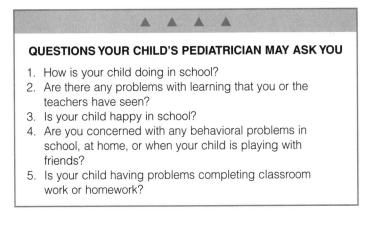

QUESTIONS YOUR CHILD'S PEDIATRICIAN MAY ASK YOU

1. How is your child doing in school?
2. Are there any problems with learning that you or the teachers have seen?
3. Is your child happy in school?
4. Are you concerned with any behavioral problems in school, at home, or when your child is playing with friends?
5. Is your child having problems completing classroom work or homework?

children for developmental or behavioral problems, and because ADHD is such a common problem, they often screen for it during health supervision visits in school-aged children as a matter of routine.

Confirming the Diagnosis and Identifying Your Child's Specific Problem Areas

To create a uniform process for diagnosing ADHD among school-aged children, the AAP recently created a list of standard guidelines for pediatricians to follow in evaluating a child reported to be inattentive, hyperactive, impulsive, underachieving academically, or having behavioral problems. These guidelines are based on a systematic review of the latest evidence about the prevalence of ADHD, coexisting conditions, and the diagnostic procedures most commonly used. As an informed consumer you should expect your child's pediatrician to follow these recommended steps or a procedure much like them. To accomplish this, the evaluation process will most likely require at least 2 or 3 visits to the doctor, possibly longer sessions with the pediatrician than you may be used to, and the filling out of a number of questionnaires, checklists, and other standard diagnostic tools. Your child's pediatrician may also ask you to forward questionnaires or ask the teacher to write a brief statement about your child's behavior and learning in the classroom before your first visit to make the initial interview more productive.

Your child's pediatrician will start by listening to your observations and experience with your child's behavior and the

▲ ▲ ▲ ▲

THE AAP RECOMMENDS...
Diagnostic Guidelines for ADHD

To ensure that children referred for evaluation for ADHD receive the most reliable, thorough assessment possible, the AAP has developed a set of diagnosis and evaluation guidelines, and recommends that pediatricians follow the steps outlined below. Your child's pediatrician may prefer one variation or another of a particular step (talking in person or on the phone with a teacher, asking the teacher to write a brief narrative, for example, instead of or in addition to requesting written questionnaires), but in general each of these steps should be considered.

1. When a child aged 6 to 12 years is described as being unusually inattentive, hyperactive, or impulsive; underachieving at school; or having behavior problems, the child's pediatrician should evaluate the child for ADHD.
2. A diagnosis of ADHD requires that a child meet the criteria for ADHD listed in the *Diagnostic and Statistical Manual of Mental Disorders, Fourth Edition (DSM-IV)*, of the American Psychiatric Association (see box on page 29).
3. The assessment of ADHD requires direct evidence obtained by the pediatrician from parents or caregivers regarding the core symptoms of ADHD (inattention, impulsivity, hyperactivity) in various settings; the age at which the symptoms were first noticed; how long the symptoms have been apparent; and to what degree they interfere with the child's ability to function.

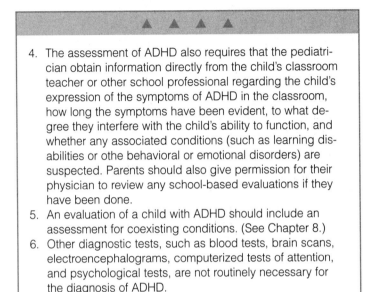

4. The assessment of ADHD also requires that the pediatrician obtain information directly from the child's classroom teacher or other school professional regarding the child's expression of the symptoms of ADHD in the classroom, how long the symptoms have been evident, to what degree they interfere with the child's ability to function, and whether any associated conditions (such as learning disabilities or othe behavioral or emotional disorders) are suspected. Parents should also give permission for their physician to review any school-based evaluations if they have been done.

5. An evaluation of a child with ADHD should include an assessment for coexisting conditions. (See Chapter 8.)

6. Other diagnostic tests, such as blood tests, brain scans, electroencephalograms, computerized tests of attention, and psychological tests, are not routinely necessary for the diagnosis of ADHD.

difficulties that you have observed him having, along with your explanations of why you think (or do not think) that they may be related to ADHD. If she has not already received written reports from teachers, school counselors, or caregivers, she may ask for them now, and she will ask you to relate what you have been told about your child's behavior in school and in his other daily settings outside the home. In many cases, parents' and teachers' opinions about a child differ significantly. This is all right and not unexpected. Your child's pediatrician will be prepared for this possibility and will listen carefully to reports from both "camps." She may ask to speak with other adults in your child's life (your spouse or partner, former teachers, coaches, or others in your community) to gain a broader impression of the types of problems your child may be experiencing.

Do not be surprised if your child's pediatrician seems to rely much more on these reports than on her own observation of your child. Most children with ADHD do not exhibit symptoms of the disorder while in the doctor's office, so she will not expect to see them. (Keep in mind that ADHD, an *attentional disorder,* usually manifests itself in routine or monotonous situations, and visits to the doctor's office tend to be stimulating and outside of a child's usual routines.) Likewise, though she may give your child a physical examination, she will not rely on this to indicate whether ADHD is present because there are no physical findings that by themselves verify ADHD. She will, however, carefully review your child's and your family's medical history for ADHD, related disorders, and other medical conditions that can have ADHD-like symptoms. Because ADHD has been shown to run in families, the discovery that you or other relatives have experienced ADHD-specific or similar symptoms may help point the way toward an accurate diagnosis.

Once your child's pediatrician has collected as much information about your child as you can provide and taken a family medical history, she will move on toward the first of what may be a series of structured questions, checklists, and evaluative procedures to identify his specific problems. She may ask your permission to have your child's teacher speak to her and complete some rating scales as well. Other medical or mental health professionals to whom your child's pediatrician has referred you may also administer parts of the evaluation. The AAP advises health professionals to begin with determining whether your child's behaviors match those considered necessary for making the diagnosis of ADHD. The behaviors comprising the "diagnostic criteria" for ADHD are set out in the manual *Diagnostic and Statistical Manual of Mental Disorders, Fourth Edition (DSM-IV),* developed by the American Psychiatric Association. This manual is presently considered the "gold standard" for any professionals who diagnose behavioral and emotional disorders (see box below). The *DSM-IV* lists 9 typical behaviors that apply to each of 2 subtypes of ADHD: predominantly inattentive type and predominantly hyperactive/impulsive type. A child whose symptoms are significant and match at least 6 of the 9 behaviors described for each subtype is at risk for and may be diagnosed as having that disorder. A child with 6 or more matches in both categories is at risk for and may be eventually diagnosed as having a third subtype of ADHD: combined type. Children are only diagnosed as having ADHD if

- Some of the symptoms were present before the age of 7 years.
- The symptoms have been observed to interfere with the child's functioning in 2 or more settings.
- The behaviors significantly impair the child's functioning in academic or social situations.
- The symptoms have been present for longer than 6 months and are more pronounced than for most children at the same developmental level.

▲   ▲   ▲   ▲

DIAGNOSTIC AND STATISTICAL MANUAL OF MENTAL DISORDERS, FOURTH EDITION (DSM-IV)

The following symptoms are included in the *DSM-IV* diagnostic criteria for ADHD:

Inattention
- Often fails to give close attention to details, makes careless mistakes in schoolwork or other activities
- Often has difficulty sustaining attention in tasks or play activities
- Often does not seem to listen when spoken to directly

▲ ▲ ▲ ▲

DIAGNOSTIC AND STATISTICAL MANUAL OF MENTAL DISORDERS, FOURTH EDITION (DSM-IV) (continued)

- Often does not follow through on instructions and fails to finish schoolwork or chores (not due to oppositional behavior or failure to understand directions)
- Often has difficulty organizing tasks and activities
- Often avoids, dislikes, or is reluctant to engage in tasks that require sustained mental effort (such as schoolwork or homework)
- Often loses things necessary for tasks or activities (eg, toys, school assignments, pencils, books, tools)
- Is often easily distracted by extraneous stimuli
- Is often forgetful in daily activities

Hyperactivity/Impulsivity
Hyperactivity
- Often fidgets with hands/feet or squirms in seat
- Often leaves seat in classroom or in other situations in which remaining seated is expected
- Often runs about or climbs excessively in situation in which it is inappropriate (in adolescents or adults, may be limited to subjective feelings of restlessness)
- Often has difficulty playing or engaging in leisure activities quietly
- Is often "on the go" or often acts as if "driven by a motor"
- Often talks excessively

Impulsivity
- Often blurts out answers before questions are completed
- Often has difficulty awaiting turn
- Often interrupts or intrudes on others

Reprinted with permission from the *Diagnostic and Statistical Manual of Mental Disorders, Fourth Edition.* Washington, DC: American Psychiatric Association; 1994.

Of course, all children exhibit many of these behaviors some of the time. Still, by considering the *degree* to which a child functions in these ways, and to what extent such behaviors interfere with the child's *ability to function* at home, in school, and in social settings, your child's pediatrician or other health professionals can begin to arrive at a better idea of whether ADHD is the best explanation for the problems. As you have learned, it is also necessary to differentiate behavior that is age-appropriate from behavior that strongly suggests a full diagnosis of ADHD. As you and your child's pediatrician consider these detailed descriptions of different types of behavior, you can develop a better idea about whether her behaviors are typical for her age, represent problems that need to be addressed, or signal the likelihood of ADHD. Pediatricians and other experts rely on knowledge about how ADHD-type behaviors are expressed *at different ages*, as described in the following boxes:

▲ ▲ ▲ ▲

COMMON SYMPTOMS OF INATTENTION

Early Childhood (preschool and early school years)

- **Behavior within normal range:** Difficulty attending, except briefly, to a storybook or quiet task such as coloring or drawing.
- **Behavior signaling an inattention problem:** Sometimes unable to complete games or activities without being distracted, is unable to complete a game with a child of comparable age, and only attends to any activity for a very short period before shifting attention to another object or activity. Symptoms are present to the degree that they cause some family difficulties.

▲ ▲ ▲ ▲

COMMON SYMPTOMS OF INATTENTION
(continued)

- **Behavior signaling the possible presence of ADHD, predominantly inattentive type:** The child is unable to function and play appropriately and may seem immature, does not engage in any activity long enough, is easily distracted, is unable to complete activities, has a much shorter attention span than other children the same age, often misses important aspects of an object or situation (eg, rules of games or sequences), and does not persist in various self-care tasks (dressing or washing) to the same extent as other children of comparable age. The child shows problems in many settings over a long period and is affected functionally.

Middle Childhood (later primary grades through preteen years) and Adolescence

- **Behavior within normal range:** May not persist very long with a task the child does not want to do, such as reading an assigned book or homework, or a task that requires concentration, such as cleaning something. Adolescents may be easily distracted from tasks that they do not want to perform.
- **Behavior signaling an inattention problem:** At times the child misses some instructions and explanations in school, begins a number of activities without completing them, has some difficulties completing games with other children or grownups, becomes distracted, and tends to give up easily. The child may not complete or succeed at new activities, has some social deficiency, and does not pick up subtle social cues from others.
- **Behavior signaling the possible presence of ADHD, predominantly inattentive type:** The child has significant school and social problems, often shifts activities, does not complete tasks, is messy, and is careless about schoolwork. The child may start tasks prematurely and without appropriate review as if he or she were not listening, has difficulty organizing tasks, dislikes activities that require close concentration, is easily distracted, and is often forgetful.

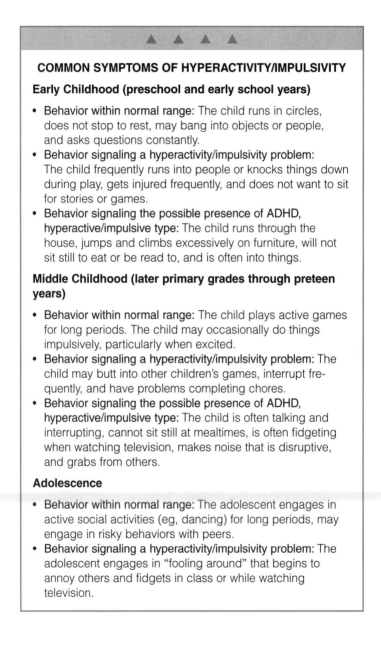

COMMON SYMPTOMS OF HYPERACTIVITY/IMPULSIVITY

Early Childhood (preschool and early school years)

- **Behavior within normal range:** The child runs in circles, does not stop to rest, may bang into objects or people, and asks questions constantly.
- **Behavior signaling a hyperactivity/impulsivity problem:** The child frequently runs into people or knocks things down during play, gets injured frequently, and does not want to sit for stories or games.
- **Behavior signaling the possible presence of ADHD, hyperactive/impulsive type:** The child runs through the house, jumps and climbs excessively on furniture, will not sit still to eat or be read to, and is often into things.

Middle Childhood (later primary grades through preteen years)

- **Behavior within normal range:** The child plays active games for long periods. The child may occasionally do things impulsively, particularly when excited.
- **Behavior signaling a hyperactivity/impulsivity problem:** The child may butt into other children's games, interrupt frequently, and have problems completing chores.
- **Behavior signaling the possible presence of ADHD, hyperactive/impulsive type:** The child is often talking and interrupting, cannot sit still at mealtimes, is often fidgeting when watching television, makes noise that is disruptive, and grabs from others.

Adolescence

- **Behavior within normal range:** The adolescent engages in active social activities (eg, dancing) for long periods, may engage in risky behaviors with peers.
- **Behavior signaling a hyperactivity/impulsivity problem:** The adolescent engages in "fooling around" that begins to annoy others and fidgets in class or while watching television.

▲   ▲   ▲   ▲

COMMON SYMPTOMS OF HYPERACTIVITY/IMPULSIVITY
(continued)

- Behavior signaling the possible presence of ADHD, hyperactive/impulsive type: The adolescent is restless and fidgety while doing any and all quiet activities, interrupts and "bugs" other people, and gets into trouble frequently. Hyperactive symptoms decrease or are replaced with a sense of restlessness.

Adapted from Wolraich ML, Felice ME, Drotar D, eds. *The Classification of Child and Adolescent Mental Diagnoses in Primary Care: Diagnostic and Statistical Manual for Primary Care (DSM-PC) Child and Adolescent Version.* Elk Grove Village, IL: American Academy of Pediatrics; 1996.

Knowing that your child's behaviors meet criteria for ADHD does not necessarily pinpoint the areas that cause her the most difficulties in her day-to-day functioning. Establishing the ADHD diagnosis is just the first step. A second major aim of an evaluation is to describe the problems caused by the ADHD behaviors specifically enough that they can be translated into a treatment plan. (See Chapter 3.) The main problem areas for children with ADHD—the areas of "functional impairment"— include difficulties with family relationships, peer status, social skills, academic achievement, self-esteem, and self-perception, as well as accidental injuries.

As you and your child's pediatrician work through these detailed descriptions of different types of behavior, your own child's problem areas should become increasingly clear. Some of these may fall out of the usual difficulties expected as a result of ADHD alone. Pediatricians, parents, teachers, and other members of a child's support team must thoroughly consider other environmental, situational, and emotional factors that may be influencing or causing these behaviors.

Is It Only ADHD, a Coexisting Problem, or Both?

One of the advantages offered by thorough discussions during the evaluation as well as diagnostic tests and rating scales that you, your child's teacher, and others complete is that they frequently pinpoint other psychological or developmental problems that exist alongside or in place of ADHD. As many as two thirds of children with ADHD have one or more additional or coexisting conditions. The most frequent coexisting conditions include other behavior problems, depression, anxiety, learning disabilities, and language disorders.

Your child's pediatrician may be initially alerted to the possibility of some of these conditions by the reports you or other

adults have provided. For example, a child described as frequently sad and who prefers isolated activities may be at risk for depression. A child who experiences frequent fears or unusual anxiety at being separated from a parent, and who has relatives with anxiety disorders, may have a similar disorder himself. Poor school performance may indicate a learning disability. Oppositional defiant disorder and conduct disorders are indicated by negative, defiant, disobedient, and oppositional behaviors toward authority figures and, less frequently, by persistent violation of others' basic rights or of common social rules.

Coexisting conditions will be discussed in greater detail in Chapter 8. For now, though, it is important to consider the fact that such accompanying disorders can have a profound effect on how well your child functions behaviorally, emotionally, socially, and academically. Your child's pediatrician and others working with your child should carefully consider whether such disorders may be your child's central challenge—that is, that they are the greatest impediment in his ability to function in his environment. To determine this, further evaluation, including referrals to other specialists, may be necessary. These evaluations can be part of the process of further narrowing the field of possibilities to arrive at the most accurate diagnosis for your child.

The Importance of Teamwork

By now it should be abundantly clear that evaluating a child for ADHD and related conditions is not an overnight, cut-and-dried process, nor can it be necessarily completed by your child's pediatrician or another professional alone. Evaluating a child's behaviors and arriving at a diagnosis of the problems or disorders causing them is an undertaking that requires the accurate observation, insight, experience, and even a certain amount of educated intuition on the part of parents, teachers, and medical professionals alike. As you have read, a number of conditions that lead to behaviors similar to those resulting from ADHD must be considered and either eliminated or identified. The functional, real-world effects of each disorder must be carefully considered before an effective treatment plan can be put into place.

There is no question that assessing a child for ADHD requires patience and a great deal of teamwork from all adults involved—and this is good practice for the challenges to come. If the diagnostic process for ADHD seems complex, the process of choosing and implementing treatment may be even more so. For this reason, one of your foremost goals during this period should be to create and maintain clear lines of communication among the members of your child's diagnostic team. If you disagree with a teacher's assessment of your child's school performance, air your concerns now and work toward arriving at a better mutual understanding of some kind. Make sure that your child's pediatrician's findings and conclusions are reviewed with you in detail. This can avoid misunderstandings or unnecessary concerns about diagnoses, labels, or future recommendations. Pursue any questions that you still have. A low comfort level with any of the evaluation or diagnostic information you have received can be the biggest obstacle for you in deciding to begin, develop, and carry out a treatment plan for your child and your family. Keep teachers' reports, evaluation reports, and other materials used for diagnosis together in one file so that you can easily present and review them when necessary. The more professionals you see, the more important it is for you to have your own complete home-based medical record. Diagnosis is only the first step in a long journey that you and your child are undertaking. By making sure that your child's support team is in agreement and that you are all focusing on the important issues, you can look forward with greater confidence to the day when her situation will be improved.

▲ ▲ ▲ ▲

Q & A

Q: *I have ADHD, but because I am high functioning I was not diagnosed until I went to college, when my inability to keep to the task at hand began to seriously interfere with my school performance and relationships. As a child, I was quiet and shy, and because I did not have the hyperactive component of ADHD, no one noticed my condition. Now I am concerned that my daughter, who is in kindergarten, may have the same form of ADHD. But her teacher says she's doing well in school and has the usual number of friends even if she does have more trouble paying attention than most of her classmates. The teacher has discouraged me from having my daughter evaluated. Should I follow her advice?*

A: Children with inattentive-type ADHD are often first identified when the work demands of school start to accelerate—by third or fourth grade. Similar to your own experience, girls are often identified late, or not at all. You have a head start on this by already knowing a good deal about ADHD. The question now is whether your daughter's behaviors are still in the broad range of normal for a girl in kindergarten or whether they are an early expression of ADHD. The positive news from her teacher is that she is doing well in school and with social situations. An evaluation should be considered at any point that her behaviors start to interfere significantly with her school progress or other areas of functioning. As you suggest, ADHD does tend to run in families, so it is especially important to keep carefully tracking your daughter's progress. At this stage you might just want to bring your concerns to your child's pediatrician so that you can both keep a watchful eye on the situation and actively screen for problems at regular intervals.

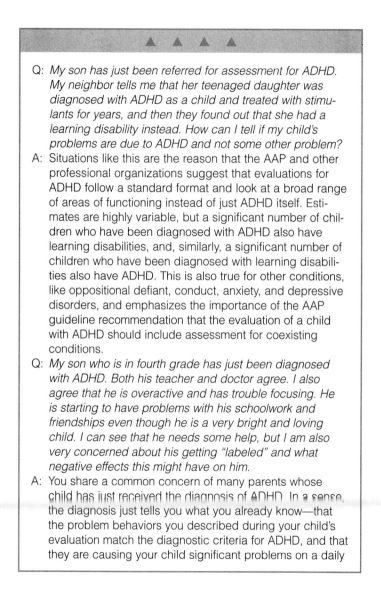

Q: *My son has just been referred for assessment for ADHD. My neighbor tells me that her teenaged daughter was diagnosed with ADHD as a child and treated with stimulants for years, and then they found out that she had a learning disability instead. How can I tell if my child's problems are due to ADHD and not some other problem?*

A: Situations like this are the reason that the AAP and other professional organizations suggest that evaluations for ADHD follow a standard format and look at a broad range of areas of functioning instead of just ADHD itself. Estimates are highly variable, but a significant number of children who have been diagnosed with ADHD also have learning disabilities, and, similarly, a significant number of children who have been diagnosed with learning disabilities also have ADHD. This is also true for other conditions, like oppositional defiant, conduct, anxiety, and depressive disorders, and emphasizes the importance of the AAP guideline recommendation that the evaluation of a child with ADHD should include assessment for coexisting conditions.

Q: *My son who is in fourth grade has just been diagnosed with ADHD. Both his teacher and doctor agree. I also agree that he is overactive and has trouble focusing. He is starting to have problems with his schoolwork and friendships even though he is a very bright and loving child. I can see that he needs some help, but I am also very concerned about his getting "labeled" and what negative effects this might have on him.*

A: You share a common concern of many parents whose child has just received the diagnosis of ADHD. In a sense, the diagnosis just tells you what you already know—that the problem behaviors you described during your child's evaluation match the diagnostic criteria for ADHD, and that they are causing your child significant problems on a daily

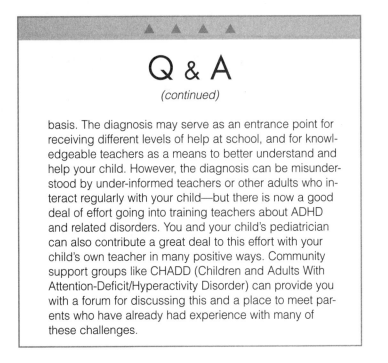

Q & A
(continued)

basis. The diagnosis may serve as an entrance point for receiving different levels of help at school, and for knowledgeable teachers as a means to better understand and help your child. However, the diagnosis can be misunderstood by under-informed teachers or other adults who interact regularly with your child—but there is now a good deal of effort going into training teachers about ADHD and related disorders. You and your child's pediatrician can also contribute a great deal to this effort with your child's own teacher in many positive ways. Community support groups like CHADD (Children and Adults With Attention-Deficit/Hyperactivity Disorder) can provide you with a forum for discussing this and a place to meet parents who have already had experience with many of these challenges.

CHAPTER THREE

What Should We Do?
Treatment Options

▲　▲　▲　▲

"It was a shock, even after all the interviews, evaluations, and reports, when Andy was diagnosed with ADHD," writes a parent about her experience with her 8-year-old son. "On the one hand, I was so relieved to have an explanation for Andy's behavior. On the other, I was concerned that now the teachers and kids at school would 'label' him in negative ways, and I was worried about what types of medications might be prescribed for him. I wondered, too, how Andy would respond to the diagnosis—would he lose even more of his self-confidence now that he knew he had a disorder?"

If your child has been diagnosed with attention-deficit/hyperactivity disorder (ADHD), you have probably asked similar questions and experienced some of the same concerns. Because there is still such a lack of understanding about ADHD among the general public, you may also face a variety of responses to plans for your child's treatment—and much conflicting advice from friends, relatives, educators, your partner, and even your child. Friends who have not been educated about ADHD may insist that your child's behavior is just the result of a discipline or parenting problem. You may feel that teachers who have witnessed the positive effect of stimulant drugs in many children with ADHD are pushing you to put your child on medication. Your spouse or partner may believe that an alternative treatment is the answer, while your child insists that he does not have a problem at all—that others' concerns about him are "their problem."

Such opinions and concerns are understandable given how much inaccurate information about ADHD has been spread through the media, the Internet, and other channels, and it is important that it be addressed. In this chapter, you will find the answers to many of the questions that you and others are likely to have regarding treatment for your child. You will learn

- Which types and combinations of treatment programs have been shown to be most effective for ADHD
- How you, your child, his teachers, his pediatrician, and other members of his "treatment team" can work together to identify specific problem areas—"targets"—that will become the focus of treatment efforts
- How the treatment team can then create a management plan to address these target areas
- How ongoing observation and follow-up meetings of the treatment team can be used to monitor your child's progress and adjust aspects of his treatment when necessary to better address his ongoing needs
- How to help your child understand the treatment plan and become a member of the treatment team at each stage of his development

▲ ▲ ▲ ▲

"WHAT SHOULD I TELL THEM?"

As you move from ADHD diagnosis toward the creation of a treatment plan, you are likely to face a number of questions and remarks from friends, relatives, and others. Following are some responses that may help you through awkward situations and answer some of your questions.

"I have had several students with ADHD in my classes in the past. I recommend that your child be put on medication as soon as possible."

Response: "My child's pediatrician tells me that the most effective treatment plans, which may or may not include medication, need to be designed through a team approach by him, my child, us, and you, his teacher. Your feedback and observations are essential as we start the treatment process. If we make the decision to use medication as a part of the overall treatment plan, your observations and comments will be critical to monitoring and refining it."

"Everyone knows that ADHD is just teachers' excuse to have kids medicated so they stay quiet and the classroom is easier to manage."

Response: "ADHD is a recognized disorder, it is widespread and it is treatable. Medication is just one of the ways that children can be helped to become more manageable from the teacher's perspective, but its real value lies in its ability to help the child attend to daily tasks and thus function better."

"I don't care what the doctor says. There is no way you should give your child drugs."

Response: "Stimulant medications have been shown to make an enormous positive difference in the lives of many children with ADHD. Some experts say that medication in such cases is equivalent to prescribing inhalers for children with asthma—they regulate the child's system enough to allow him to carry on a normal life. Before making up our minds about treatment, we will talk to experts in the field, look at the research, read to inform ourselves, talk to other families with ADHD, and discuss our child's situation with him and with his doctors."

▲   ▲   ▲   ▲

"WHAT SHOULD I TELL THEM?"
(continued)

"She just seems depressed to me. How do you know it's ADHD and not some other disorder?"

Response: "It's true that a number of other conditions (for example, anxiety disorder and depression disorder) can mimic ADHD symptoms, but the evaluation my child just completed was designed to eliminate or identify most of them. Some of the rarer coexisting conditions such as bipolar disorder may start out looking identical to ADHD and only evolve into the specific disorder at an older age. That's why we'll continue to monitor and review her symptoms throughout childhood—to make sure the diagnosis and treatment are still correct, timely, and appropriate."

"There's nothing wrong with me. It's other people who have a problem. My behavior is fine—they just can't handle it."

Response: "I can see how hard it is on you when you feel like your teacher is always singling you out and picking on you, and when we always seem to be arguing about following rules at home. Now that we are finished with your evaluation, we can start learning more ways to turn these things around and make a happier situation at home and school."

Taking Action: First Steps in Developing a Treatment Plan

Treating ADHD is not like treating diabetes and other disorders, where drawing the line between children who have or do not have the diagnosis is clear, and where only children with the diagnosis have problems and need treatment while others do not. It is more like treating wheezing. The symptoms can vary from mild asthma, needing no or minimal treatment, to severe asthma, requiring medication and intensive treatments. In the same way, many children have difficulty paying attention, controlling impulses, and being fidgety. If these become problems, but do not fully meet the criteria for diagnosis, your child's pediatrician may still suggest pediatric counseling, education about the range of normal developmental behaviors, home behavior management tools, school behavior management recommendations, social skills work, and/or help with managing homework flow and with organization and planning. If the symptoms begin to significantly interfere with your child's functioning at home and school on a daily basis, she will work with you to create a more comprehensive and organized overall plan. That plan may include the measures mentioned previously, but also medication management, behavior therapy, and other forms of treatment and support—all coordinated through an individualized and specific treatment plan.

The American Academy of Pediatrics (AAP) has recently developed a set of guidelines to assist pediatricians in developing comprehensive treatment plans for children with ADHD.

▲ ▲ ▲ ▲

THE AAP RECOMMENDS...
Treatment Guidelines for ADHD

Following is a brief summary of AAP guidelines for pediatricians to use in helping parents create a treatment plan for ADHD. You should expect your child's pediatrician to follow these or similar steps as your child's treatment plan is formulated and carried out.

1. A treatment plan should be created that recognizes ADHD as a *chronic* condition—that is, an ongoing disorder that may change expression or form over time but that will probably remain with the child through adolescence and perhaps into adulthood.
2. The parents, child, pediatrician, and other clinicians, in collaboration with school personnel, should identify specific goals or target outcomes on which to base decisions about treatment.

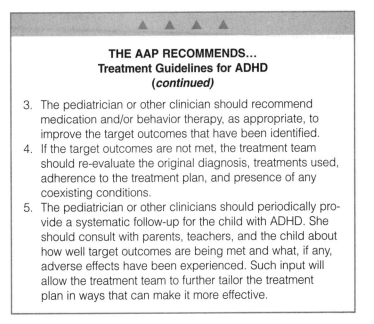

▲ ▲ ▲ ▲

THE AAP RECOMMENDS...
Treatment Guidelines for ADHD
(*continued*)

3. The pediatrician or other clinician should recommend medication and/or behavior therapy, as appropriate, to improve the target outcomes that have been identified.
4. If the target outcomes are not met, the treatment team should re-evaluate the original diagnosis, treatments used, adherence to the treatment plan, and presence of any coexisting conditions.
5. The pediatrician or other clinicians should periodically provide a systematic follow-up for the child with ADHD. She should consult with parents, teachers, and the child about how well target outcomes are being met and what, if any, adverse effects have been experienced. Such input will allow the treatment team to further tailor the treatment plan in ways that can make it more effective.

Identifying the Treatment Team

To successfully develop a treatment plan and put it into action, you will need to create a treatment team. This entails identifying the people most directly involved in your child's care and education. Their combined efforts will lead you to developing and carrying out the most thoughtful, informed, and effective treatment plan. The team will obviously include you the parent(s), your child, your child's pediatrician, and your child's teacher. It may also include other adults at school and any involved mental health professionals. Why a team? It will promote communication and the development of an agreed-on unified approach, and, like all good teams, should be more valuable than the sum of each member's individual contribution to your child's success.

Creating a List: Defining Target Outcomes

Knowing that your child has been diagnosed with ADHD does not necessarily make the course of action for your child and family obvious. Before you, your child, her pediatrician, and other members of her treatment team can create an appropriate treatment plan, you will need to carefully consider which behaviors are most problematic for your child and most in need of attention. The best way to begin this process is to focus on her actual problems with functioning at school, at home, and elsewhere—that is, to think in terms of *treating your child* in the context of your family and community resources, rather than *treating "her ADHD."* Such an approach involves first creating a full picture of your child—including all the problems and accompanying diagnoses that were identified during her evaluation, a sense of how your family functions, a summary of any other major demands on family members that may affect her situation, the resources available in your community, and so on. Only in this broad context can your child's pediatrician decide with you how best to help create a realistic treatment plan that will work in your own unique circumstances.

Once you have mapped out this broad picture of your child's situation and her difficulties functioning within it, your next step in creating a treatment plan is to identify approximately 3 to 6 areas, or "targets," that would most improve her functioning and self-esteem. Such targets may include

- Improved relationships with parents, siblings, teachers, and friends
- Fewer disruptive behaviors
- Improved academic performance, particularly in the volume of work, efficiency, completion, and accuracy
- Greater independence in self-care or homework
- Improved self-esteem and self-perception

- Safer behavior in the community (such as when crossing streets and riding bicycles)
- More thinking before doing and making better behavioral choices

Once you, your child, and the other members of her treatment team have agreed on this list, you can turn these types of broad targets into specific behaviors and criteria that will help you know if your child is meeting the goals that you set. For example, if the broader area is "improved teacher relationships," your target outcomes might be

- Appropriately accepts feedback (no more than 2 arguments per day following feedback)
- Appropriately asks for adult help when needed
- Maintains appropriate eye contact when talking to an adult with fewer than 2 prompts to maintain eye contact
- Respects adults (talks back fewer than 2 times per period)
- Complies with 80% of teachers' requests with fewer than 2 noncompliances per period

Adapted with permission from William E. Pelham, Jr, PhD. School-Home Daily Report Card packet available for down-loading at no cost at www.CTADD.com and http://wings.buffalo.edu/adhd.

Note how specific each item has become. Also be aware that if you use words like "appropriately," you will need to define what it means for you, your child, your child's teacher, and other adults who will be involved with the treatment plan.

After you have defined these targets, you can arrange them in order of priority to make sure that you are not taking on too much at once. Highest-priority issues will be those that most impair your child's functioning to the greatest degree at school, at home, or with her peers; those that impede her development; or those that have proved largely unmanageable so far. The extent to which a problem creates stress within your family may also affect the level of priority you give it. Your child's teacher can be an especially valuable contributor to this discussion because he observes your child daily within the context of an average range of same-aged children and thus may have a good idea of how disabling a particular behavior is.

Finally, it is important to review your target goals to make sure they are realistic within your child's and family's abilities to achieve and will result in improvement that can be observed and measured. Your child's pediatrician or other medical professional will be able to advise you on which goals are realistic and what types of results you can reasonably expect from which types of treatments. Expecting all As on your child's next report card may not be a realistic expectation no matter what treatment is chosen, but changes from Ds to Bs in certain subjects may be realistic and possible. One of the greatest risks children with ADHD face is the loss of self-esteem as they experience academic failure, teasing from peers, and other demoralizing effects of their inability to manage their behavior. Setting the bar a bit lower than ideal as you create a first set of goals will make it easier for your child to succeed, may give her a boost in confidence at a critical moment, and will ensure greater success down the road.

Involving Your Child

Once your child's target outcomes have been identified, placed in order of priority, and screened for feasibility, take a moment to make sure that she understands them as fully as possible given her level of development. Treatment for ADHD should never be a process that is done to your child, but one that is as much as possible implemented by her with your support, guidance, and educated assistance as well as support from the rest of her treatment team. If any treatment plan is to succeed, your child needs to understand the nature of ADHD, think and talk about ways in which she would like to improve her functioning, and feel comfortable participating in the treatment process to the extent that she is able. Your child should be present whenever possible for at least part of meetings that concern her, and parts of the discussion should be addressed directly to her at her level of understanding. Adolescents may also benefit from time alone with their doctor without parents present. Your child's reports on her day-to-day experiences with issues related to ADHD should be heeded and carefully considered. Her prioritizing of ADHD-related problems should be taken seriously and addressed. In a sense, she is embarking on an apprenticeship in self-understanding and self-management. By teaching her to consider her obstacles and abilities to function in different situations and to monitor any changes, you are helping her prepare for the day when she will be in charge of her own care.

Becoming the Case Manager

Identifying target outcomes is only the first step, but an important one. Even though your child's pediatrician, teacher, and psychologist will take the primary responsibility for coordinating many aspects of his care from time to time, as your child's parent you should still expect to serve as the primary overall coordinator. As time goes on you will need to act as a kind of case manager—soliciting teachers' comments; providing your own observations and feedback; reviewing new evaluation results with medical personnel; staying informed on ADHD-

related research; and seeking out the emotional and behavioral support that you, your child, and other family members need. The more thorough you are in playing this role, the more organized your child's treatment is likely to be. Many of the details of this role will be discussed in Chapter 5.

What Works and What Does Not—What We Know About Treatment

Once you, your child, and the treatment team have identified the target outcomes you hope to achieve, it is time to create a treatment plan to address those goals. With the help of the professionals on your treatment team, you will need to educate yourself on the various treatments that are available and what effects and limitations each is likely to have. (Reliable information on these topics is available in these pages and from other sources recommended in the Resources section at the back of the book.) As you begin to make decisions regarding treatment, keep in mind a central fact about treatment for ADHD: nothing is written in stone. Because ADHD symptoms tend to change over time, your child may have different target outcomes at different stages of life and require different types of treatment. (What worked well during third grade may not work for fourth grade.) Because individual children respond to different therapies in a variety of ways, it may take several tries before you find a treatment program that works well. For all of these reasons, your child's treatment plan will consist of an ongoing process of treatment decisions, observation, review, and, in most cases, treatment revision.

Choosing One or More Types of Treatment

In the years since ADHD symptoms were first described, a variety of treatment approaches have been tried and tested for their effectiveness. Only 2 of these approaches—use of medication and behavior therapies (a set of systematic, consistent techniques that parents and teachers can use to help a child better manage his behavior)—have been shown to have consistent effects. Medical professionals and other experts have also studied traditional psychotherapy, cognitive-behavioral techniques, special diets, biofeedback, allergy treatments, vision training, sensory integration therapy, chiropracty, and many other methods. Most of these approaches have either not been studied adequately or have been shown to have minimal or no long-term effect. Some will be discussed in more detail in Chapter 9. The following table summarizes the most proven treatments for ADHD and accompanying problems.

▲   ▲   ▲   ▲

THE EVIDENCE SHOWS

Treatment For	Possible Treatments*
ADHD as a chronic condition	• Education for parents and treatment • A team approach • Empowerment of children and adolescents to "own" and help carry out their own treatment plan • Careful setting and monitoring of treatment targets, goals, and plans
Core symptoms of ADHD (inattention, impulsivity, hyperactivity)	• Stimulant medication (first-line treatment) • Proven behavior therapies • Atomoxetine, tricyclic antidepressants, or bupropion (second-line treatment) • Individualized Education Program (IEP) based on 504 or Individuals with Disabilities Education Act legislation

THE EVIDENCE SHOWS

Treatment For	Possible Treatments*

Oppositional and defiant behavior and serious conduct problems	• Behavior modification and management techniques
	  – Parent training
	  – School behavioral programs
	• Medication management if appropriate
	• IEP based on behavioral needs that cannot be met in the context of a regular classroom

Depression, anxiety, and problems with self-control and anger management	• Cognitive-behavioral therapy • Selective serotonin re-uptake inhibitor or other antidepressant medication management if appropriate
Significant difficulties in family functioning	• Family therapy

Underachievement and learning and language disorders	• IEP that includes
	  – Educational management
	  – Optimizing the classroom environment
	  – Addressing individual learning and language abilities and learning style

*These treatment options will be described in detail in chapters 4 through 8.

An Overview of Medication and Behavior Therapy for ADHD—The Mainstays of a Treatment Plan

The use of stimulant medication (methylphenidate, dextroamphetamine, etc; see Chapter 4) is a high-profile issue. This is mainly due to the enormous spectrum—from accurate to misinformation—that has been disseminated in the popular media. In fact, stimulants have been the widest and best studied of any group of medications for the behavioral and emotional problems faced by children. Taken as recommended, they are effective and safe for most children with ADHD. Side effects mostly occur early in treatment, tend to be mild and short-lived, and in most situations can be successfully managed through adjustments in the dose or schedule of medication.

Parents are often confused by the fact that *stimulants* are the most frequently prescribed medications for ADHD. Why use stimulants, they wonder, when their child is already overactive and overstimulated? The reason is that such medications are thought to work by "stimulating" the brain to make slightly more of the brain chemicals (neurotransmitters) that help all of us focus our attention, control our impulses, organize and plan, and stick to routines. With effective stimulant medication treatment, children with ADHD are better able to manage academic work and social interaction, attend to behavior modification techniques, and follow rules. Far from making a child someone he is not, as the word *drugs* implies, stimulants act as *medications* that can help many children with ADHD be who they are—with more appropriate attention, impulse control, and activity level.

The advantages and disadvantages of stimulant and non-stimulant medications will be discussed in greater detail in Chapter 4. For now it is important to consider that while many parents view placing their children on stimulant medication as a last resort—after all other measures have been tried—research has shown that such other treatments are more likely to work if the child is also taking stimulants. By helping the child focus, stimulants *lay the groundwork* for him to be able to respond better to behavior management techniques, academic instruction, and other demands on his attention.

Stimulant medication can be prescribed in a variety of doses and schedules. Because there has been so much controversy about ADHD in the media, many parents ask for and many physicians prescribe, the lowest dose of stimulant medication that leads to *any* improvement. It is now known that the best results from medication treatment are achieved by the dose that shows the *most* improvement with the least side effects.

Children with ADHD who have additional medical conditions or reasons why taking stimulant medication is not advisable may be prescribed non-stimulant medications, such as atomoxetine, tricyclic antidepressants, or bupropion (second-line treatments). Children who were originally prescribed stimulants but experienced excessive side effects improved for only very short periods or responded insufficiently may also switch to non-stimulants. These second-line medications have been shown to have positive effects on the core symptoms of ADHD. In general, non-stimulants have not been studied as extensively as stimulants. The strengths and weaknesses of this type of medication will be discussed more fully in Chapter 4.

Behavior therapy (see Chapter 6) is considered another proven first-line treatment for ADHD. Behavior therapy emphasizes ways in which adults can better manage and shape their child's behavior by using sound behavior management, including the principles of behavior modification and social learning theory, and includes techniques for giving instructions and commands in a way that builds children's self-control and self-esteem. Programs that teach behavior therapy focus on how to give clear commands, use time-outs effectively, create effective rewards systems, and otherwise structure a child's environment in ways that work. Parents and teachers can learn to use these techniques effectively. This approach, which focuses on how adults can help children develop more appropriate and positive behaviors, has been shown to be effective, while child-focused approaches (such as traditional psychotherapy) have not. You will learn more about the specifics of behavior therapy in chapters 6 and 7.

The largest study of long-term treatment for ADHD to date (known as the Multimodal Treatment Study of Children with Attention Deficit Hyperactivity Disorder [MTA], published in 1999) found that stimulants used as the sole form of treatment lead to significantly better results for the core symptoms of ADHD than behavior therapy used alone. A *combination* of the 2 approaches, however, has been shown to lead to the best overall improvement in the core symptoms of ADHD, especially when the areas of oppositional and aggressive behavior, social skills, parent-child relations, and some areas of academic achievement are considered along with these core symptoms. The use of behavior therapy can also lower the rate of medication required in some cases. Parents in the MTA study who used this combined approach were often significantly more satisfied with the treatment plan than those whose children received medication alone. In this study, medication management and behavior treatment guidelines were carefully developed and followed. When the study guidelines were followed in this way, about 60% of children treated with medication alone could not be distinguished from their peers (who did not have ADHD) at the end of the 14-month study. When children were treated with medication *and* the highly specific behavior treatments, this number increased to 70%. It is important to point out that all medication and behavior approaches are not the same—one size does not fit all. The most successful approaches, like those in the MTA study, are evidence-based (see Introduction)—they have been carefully researched and found to work. Evidence-based approaches for the treatment of ADHD will be reviewed in the chapters that follow. More untested treatment approaches are not as reliable. For example, in the MTA study, only about 25% of the children treated with less rigorous approaches than the study used, even if they include the use of medication and some form of behavior management, did as well as their peers.

Other Components of the Treatment Plan

Other treatments, including psychotherapy and family or marital therapy, may provide valuable assistance to families who have problems that are not directly caused by but are related to and affect ADHD. The stress that a child's behavior may place on the family can prevent them from carrying out a treatment plan unless such issues are addressed. When one parent or partner also has ADHD (a frequent occurrence because the condition runs in families), this can put even more stress on family functioning.

The fact that ADHD symptoms frequently manifest themselves in school settings, and children with ADHD may also have learning disabilities and other learning-related conditions, means that academic intervention can make a difference for your child even if it does not directly affect her ADHD symptoms. Children with clearly diagnosed learning disabilities (significant differences between their abilities and their achievement in subjects like reading and math) qualify for special education services in school. In this situation, schools are federally mandated to develop Individualized Education Programs (IEPs) that detail exactly what services will be offered and how they will be delivered. The same is true for children who have behavioral needs too severe to be handled in a regular classroom.

Fortunately, students who have learning or behavioral needs related to their ADHD but do not have diagnosed learning disabilities or such severe behavioral needs can also receive services. More information on school issues and laws related to academic and behavioral services for children with ADHD can be found in Chapter 7. While such programs, strategies, and considerations do not directly address the core symptoms of ADHD, they support the child with ADHD academically and behaviorally and, thus, help maintain their success and self-esteem.

Clearly, because each of the treatments discussed targets different results, it is most common to use several types of treatment at any given time. While most children's treatment plans may begin with medication and behavior therapy, additional approaches such as academic intervention, psychotherapy, and family therapy may provide added support. When choosing from the menu of treatment options, you will need to consider whether

- You have the time and energy necessary to adhere to them.
- They address one of your child's most important 3 to 6 target outcomes.
- Your family can realistically afford them.

Consider how good a match each of these approaches is for your child, and whether the results can be satisfactorily monitored. How smoothly can each treatment be combined with the others that you plan to implement? How available are these techniques or programs in your community? How long are the benefits likely to last after the treatment has ended? Are there any possible negatives or side effects? How well do the positive effects translate to your child's everyday life (are you still using the parenting techniques 3 days after the training session and are they helping with her behavior)? How well does the treatment method coincide with the values and goals of your family as a whole? Most importantly, how does your child feel about this type of treatment? Will she feel stigmatized by her friends or family because of it?

In the end, no matter how effective the other members of a treatment team believe a certain approach to be, it will most likely break down unless the child herself understands its purpose and is committed to making it work. For this reason, the litmus test for any mode of treatment should be whether it promotes your child's self-confidence, self-management, and higher self-esteem. It may take more than one try to create this type of treatment plan, and you should expect to be constantly reshaping it, but the potential benefits are worth the effort.

Following Up and Making Changes to the Plan

"At first I was surprised to hear from other families how often kids switched their medication or tried new doses or schedules," writes the father of a 9-year-old. "I guess my first reaction was, 'Don't the doctors know what they're doing? Why can't they get it right the first time?' After we started the treatment process, though, I found it very reassuring that Tina's pediatrician wanted our feedback on how the medication was working, and how we were doing with the behavior therapy. Tina experienced some irritability in between doses with her first prescription so we switched to a long-acting medication where she only had to take one dose per day. That worked a lot better, and then we figured out that working more in concert with her teacher on the behavior techniques improved the situation even more. As Tina started doing much better, she became more eager to participate in the plan. By the end of the first year I felt like we'd all worked as a team to put together the best program we could for her. It was great, knowing we had all these people's support and that as Tina's life changed her treatment could change along with her."

In this chapter, you have learned how important it is to monitor the effects of your child's treatment once a plan has

▲ ▲ ▲ ▲

AGENDA FOR YOUR CHILD'S FOLLOW-UP VISITS

The AAP recommends that physicians periodically provide systematic follow-up for your child. You can help structure each visit so that you and your physician can include as many of the following steps as possible.

1. Discuss and review your own observations of your child, his most recent teacher's reports, and the results of any rating scales completed since the last visit.
2. Share information about the target behaviors and how they might have changed since the last visit.
3. Review the plan agenda—the target behaviors and the current methods of treatment.
4. Screen for new coexisting conditions.
5. If your child is taking medication, review any possible side effects.
6. Review your child's functioning at home, including his behavior and his family relationships.
7. Review your child's functioning at school, especially relating to academics, behavior, and social interaction. Make sure that some information is obtained directly from your child's teacher (particularly important before changing any medication dose).
8. Discuss your child's self-esteem, and review his behavioral, social, and academic self-management issues.
9. Assess and supplement your child's understanding of ADHD, coexisting conditions, and treatment as appropriate for his age.
10. Discuss any current problems relating to organizational skills, study skills, homework management, self-management skills, anger management, etc.
11. Make sure that you get all the information you need to enable you and your child to make informed decisions that promote his long-term health and well-being.
12. Review and revise your child's treatment plan.
13. Make sure that there is a system in place for communication among you, your child, his teacher, and the clinician between visits.

been implemented. This may not be easy at first as you adjust to what may be a complex medication schedule, start learning new behavior therapy techniques, and meet with specialists regarding any coexisting conditions. As the weeks pass, however, you will grow more adept at integrating all the information you receive and keeping other members of the treatment team informed through phone conversations, behavior rating-scale checklists, written reports, and office visits. You will be better able to observe your child's progress and judge whether her treatment plan is effective. At each follow-up visit with your child's pediatrician or other medical professional, you will be able to share information, ask questions, and, if necessary, take steps to change your child's treatment.

Follow-up visits should cover all of the ground since your last visit. This includes sharing your own observations of your child's recent behaviors, ongoing problems, and new concerns and screening for any new coexisting conditions. You and your child should be given the opportunity to ask questions and should be informed about any major new research or other information pertaining to her condition or her treatment. The most recent rating scales, teachers' observations, and other progress reports should be reviewed. Finally, your child's target outcomes can be reviewed and, if your child is clearly not meeting the current goal for each one, her treatment can be reassessed.

If your child is not meeting her specific target outcomes, you, your child's pediatrician, and your child should consider the following issues:

- Were the target outcomes realistic?
- Is more information needed about your child's behavior?
- Is the diagnosis correct?
- Is another condition hindering treatment?
- Is the treatment plan being followed?
- Has the treatment failed?

- What coping strategies can you learn to deal with target
  behaviors that cannot be fully resolved through appropriate
  treatment?

No treatment for ADHD is likely to completely eliminate all
the symptoms of inattention, hyperactivity, and impulsivity and
associated problems and conditions. Children who are being
treated successfully may still have trouble with their friends or
schoolwork. Still, you should see signs of progress relating to
your child's specific target outcomes or general behavior. If not,
your child's diagnosis and/or treatment should be revised. A
revised diagnosis is not a sign of failure in you, your child, or
her pediatrician. It is merely a signal that your child's treatment
team has yet to create the optimal response to her symptoms.
Treatment of ADHD is in many cases largely a matter of continually monitoring and reshaping the plan, and you can expect
treatment to change as your child adjusts to treatment, grows,
and develops over time. As these changes are made, continue
to make sure that any and all treatments are aimed at fostering
good self-esteem and that your child understands them to the
extent possible given her developmental level. Follow-up visits
should be geared in large part toward educating your child
and empowering her to participate more and more in decision
making as she approaches adolescence. Adolescents who "own"
their problems and treatment plans are much more likely to
make progress. Those who feel that treatment changes are
being "shoved down their throats" will naturally resist or
abandon treatment and are at high risk for school failure,
poor peer relationships, low self-esteem, substance abuse,
and conduct problems.

Treatment for ADHD is generally considered to have failed
only in cases when a child shows no response to appropriate
trials and alterations in medication at maximum doses without
side effects, when she cannot learn to control her behavior in
spite of appropriate behavior therapy, or when a coexisting

condition persistently interferes with the meeting of target outcomes. In each of these cases, the diagnosis would need to be carefully reconsidered and additional consultations would be appropriately called for.

In treating, monitoring, and following up on treatment for your child with ADHD, communication is key. As treatment continues in one form or another throughout your child's early years, you will need to make sure that

- She understands and supports the goals and methods of her treatment.
- Other family members are equally informed and supportive.
- Teachers continue to work with her in effective ways and pass their observations on to her and you.
- Pediatricians and other medical personnel receive this feedback from you, her teachers, and others who spend time with your child.
- You and other members of the treatment team remain up-to-date on the legal, medical, educational, and psychological issues that affect your child.

A child who knows as much as possible about ADHD will be better prepared as she faces challenges at home and school. A sibling who understands the steps involved in the treatment process may be more patient when you need to take time out for a parent training course. A pediatrician who is informed of any new family problems or stressors can make better decisions regarding treatment. Finally, educators who know that you and your child understand the nature of ADHD are often more eager to work together to manage it.

Attention-deficit/hyperactivity disorder is not yet curable, but it is certainly treatable. With attention, dedication, and a long-term outlook, you and your family may be able to look forward to continuing progress in the target areas you have defined.

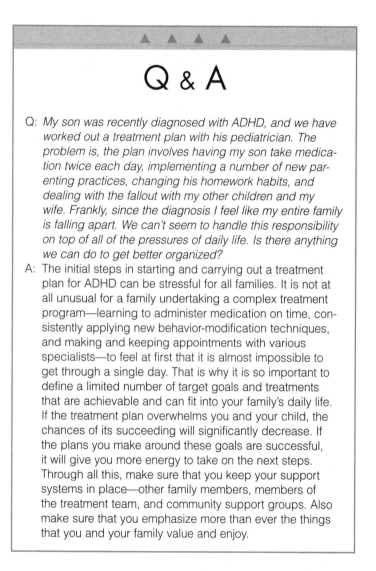

Q & A

Q: *My son was recently diagnosed with ADHD, and we have worked out a treatment plan with his pediatrician. The problem is, the plan involves having my son take medication twice each day, implementing a number of new parenting practices, changing his homework habits, and dealing with the fallout with my other children and my wife. Frankly, since the diagnosis I feel like my entire family is falling apart. We can't seem to handle this responsibility on top of all of the pressures of daily life. Is there anything we can do to get better organized?*

A: The initial steps in starting and carrying out a treatment plan for ADHD can be stressful for all families. It is not at all unusual for a family undertaking a complex treatment program—learning to administer medication on time, consistently applying new behavior-modification techniques, and making and keeping appointments with various specialists—to feel at first that it is almost impossible to get through a single day. That is why it is so important to define a limited number of target goals and treatments that are achievable and can fit into your family's daily life. If the treatment plan overwhelms you and your child, the chances of its succeeding will significantly decrease. If the plans you make around these goals are successful, it will give you more energy to take on the next steps. Through all this, make sure that you keep your support systems in place—other family members, members of the treatment team, and community support groups. Also make sure that you emphasize more than ever the things that you and your family value and enjoy.

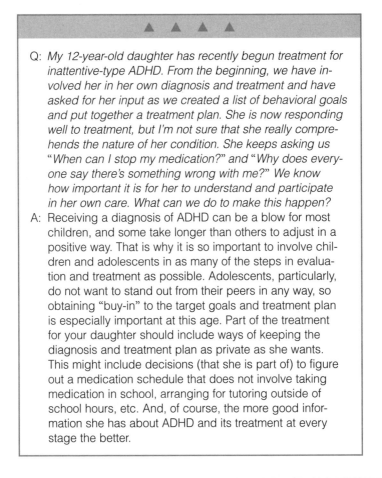

▲ ▲ ▲ ▲

Q: *My 12-year-old daughter has recently begun treatment for inattentive-type ADHD. From the beginning, we have involved her in her own diagnosis and treatment and have asked for her input as we created a list of behavioral goals and put together a treatment plan. She is now responding well to treatment, but I'm not sure that she really comprehends the nature of her condition. She keeps asking us "When can I stop my medication?" and "Why does everyone say there's something wrong with me?" We know how important it is for her to understand and participate in her own care. What can we do to make this happen?*

A: Receiving a diagnosis of ADHD can be a blow for most children, and some take longer than others to adjust in a positive way. That is why it is so important to involve children and adolescents in as many of the steps in evaluation and treatment as possible. Adolescents, particularly, do not want to stand out from their peers in any way, so obtaining "buy-in" to the target goals and treatment plan is especially important at this age. Part of the treatment for your daughter should include ways of keeping the diagnosis and treatment plan as private as she wants. This might include decisions (that she is part of) to figure out a medication schedule that does not involve taking medication in school, arranging for tutoring outside of school hours, etc. And, of course, the more good information she has about ADHD and its treatment at every stage the better.

CHAPTER FOUR

The Role of Medications

▲   ▲   ▲   ▲

If your child has been diagnosed with attention-deficit/ hyperactivity disorder (ADHD), you may be asked to consider using medication as part of his treatment plan. As we pointed out in Chapter 3, stimulant medications have been shown to provide a proven safe and effective way to manage the core symptoms of ADHD (hyperactivity, inattention, and impulsivity). Thus they are a first-line treatment recommendation for most children who have this condition—often in combination with behavior therapy and other forms of treatment. The use of stimulants can be compared to wearing glasses for a person with poor vision, because stimulants help "put things into focus" for a child when they are active in his system. As soon as the effects of the dose of stimulant wear off—or the glasses are taken off—things go just as out of focus again. Stimulants help children improve their functioning in measurable ways—just as glasses enable the child with poor vision to learn to read. But keep in mind that just as glasses can help focus but do not make a child a reader, so stimulants do not "make" a child perform better—he has to do that work himself.

It is one thing to understand how stimulants might help a child, but quite another to consider giving this medication. You have probably heard of Ritalin, a commonly known brand name for the medication methylphenidate—just one member of the class of medications known as *stimulants.* The sharp increase in recent years in the production and prescribed use of methylphenidate has led to a great deal of concern in the media and among parents that stimulants are being overprescribed for children with ADHD. In fact, methylphenidate production increased 5-fold between 1990 and 1995, but, even with that, the amount of medication presently produced does not seem to exceed the amount needed to treat legitimately diagnosed cases of ADHD in the United States. Most of this increase in stimulant medication use likely stems from better recognition and diagnosis of ADHD (including a greater awareness of ADHD in girls) and from the trend for children to be treated for longer periods, sometimes through adulthood. This is not to say that ADHD is not overdiagnosed or underdiagnosed, and that is why you need to be so careful about having an accurate diagnosis for your child before you even think about embarking on a course of medication management (see Chapter 2).

You learned in Chapter 3 that stimulants are presently considered effective and safe medications, and there are few situations in which they are medically inadvisable. However, they are not for everyone. A small number of children and their families will find that the side effects are too intrusive at the doses that are most effective for that individual child. Some parents may find that their own negative feelings about the medication, or some other issue within the family, prevents them from properly implementing this part of the treatment plan. Non-stimulant medications are also available for the treatment of ADHD and will be discussed in this chapter. Ultimately, you and your family must weigh the pros and cons of choosing medication as part of the treatment plan for ADHD. The more educated you are about the medication process, the better prepared you will be to make this decision. In this chapter, you will learn

- What types of medication are used to treat ADHD
- How your child's medication dose and schedule will be determined, monitored, and adjusted

- What other types of medication are available to children with ADHD
- How to talk with your child about the use of stimulants or other medications
- How to make the most of the benefits that medications provide

A PARENT'S STORY
Missed Clues and Lost Opportunities

"Like most parents, I didn't like the idea of my child using stimulant medication to manage his ADHD. But I was very concerned about his behavior and ability to learn, and I felt we needed to do whatever was necessary to help him in those areas. We tried stimulants, and within the first few days we began to see an amazing difference. His concentration improved. He stayed focused on his tasks. We still had to try several different types of stimulants during that early period and adjust the dose a few times, but eventually he was able to retain what he had learned much better than before. Where there was once frustration, I began instead to see a content little boy.

"Once I saw that medications could help him succeed, I felt we had made the right decision. When people ask me about stimulants now, I tell them they're a helpful treatment that gets a bad rap for reasons that now I don't entirely understand. Still, I think families rely too much on them sometimes. Parents still need to learn how to help their child improve his behavior, organizational skills, and school support to figure out the best approaches to learning. Medication can help but, as I see now, that's mostly because the child and his family have also put in a lot of hard work."

Margaret, Sacramento, CA

What You Need to Know About Stimulant Medications

In Chapter 3 we explained that stimulant medications are thought to work by stimulating the brain to make available slightly more of the brain chemicals (neurotransmitters) that help our brain cells communicate more efficiently. This increased efficiency allows us to better focus our attention, control impulses, organize, plan, and stick to routines—leading to a reduction in the core ADHD symptoms of hyperactivity, inattention, and impulsivity. Parents of a child with ADHD who is taking stimulants may notice a decrease in the number of accidental injuries their child experiences as her impulsivity declines. They may also observe that her social relationships may improve as her intensity decreases, her social judgment improves, she responds more positively to others, and she is able to communicate more effectively. The significant improvement in the child's school behavior—sometimes to the point at which it is indistinguishable from that of her classmates—is particularly satisfying to most families. Children treated with stimulants for ADHD can also enjoy a longer attention span, an increased ability to stay focused on a task, and more productivity and accuracy in schoolwork.

Once again, stimulants are generally considered effective and safe medications. They are, though, categorized by the Drug Enforcement Administration as Schedule II drugs—medications that have been approved for medical use but have a high potential for abuse in adults if they are not used properly. Because of this, the rules for prescribing stimulants may differ from those for other medications (such as antibiotics) from state to state. Although there is a lot of discussion in the media about the potential for the abuse of stimulant medications, used properly, there is no evidence that they produce "speedlike" or "euphoric" effects in children or adolescents when restricted to normal treatment doses. In addition, the use of stimulants by children with ADHD has not been found to lead to street drug use in teenagers. On the contrary, substance abuse of such drugs as alcohol and marijuana is more common in adolescents with ADHD who are not treated.

Stimulants work similarly in people who do and do not have ADHD—they can help most children and adults achieve better focus and concentration. Because of this, having a positive response to stimulants is not a test of whether a child has ADHD. Nor does needing a higher dose than another child mean that your child's symptoms are more severe. Doses vary with the individual regardless of the severity of symptoms. Some children with mild symptoms may need higher doses of medication while others with more severe symptoms require lower doses.

Medications can be described by their generic (chemical) names but are most often known to parents by their brand names. The 2 generic classes of stimulants proven to be effective for the treatment of ADHD are methylphenidate and amphetamines. The brand names of the methylphenidate preparations currently available to children with ADHD are Ritalin, Metadate, Methylin, Focalin, and Concerta. A number of different amphetamine medications are also available and include Dexedrine, Dextrostat, Dexedrine Spansules, and Adderall. Pemoline, a long-acting stimulant, is now rarely prescribed and should not be used routinely because of rare but potentially serious liver damage.

Different preparations have different durations of action, as described in the table on page 72. Comparing doses of different medications can be confusing to parents. The amount of each medication prescribed (in milligrams per dosage or per day) is unique to that particular medication—so, for example, 5 mg of methylphenidate (Ritalin) is only about half as strong as a dose of 5 mg of dextroamphetamine (Dexedrine).

Studies have shown that each of these stimulants (methyl-phenidate or amphetamines) is potentially equally effective in treating the symptoms of ADHD. However, individual children may respond better to one particular stimulant or be limited, due to side effects, from taking another. This is why it is neces-

MEDICATIONS USED IN THE TREATMENT OF ADHD			
Generic Class (and Brand Names)	Daily Dosage	Duration of Positive Behavioral Effects*	Prescribing Schedule
Stimulants (First-Line Treatment)			
METHYLPHENIDATE *Short-acting* (Ritalin, Methylin, Focalin)	Twice a day to 3 times a day	3–5 hr	2.5–20 mg twice a day to 3 times a day
Intermediate-acting (Ritalin SR, Metadate ER, Methylin ER)	Once a day to twice a day	3–8 hr	20–60 mg once a day or 40 mg in the morning and 20 mg in the early afternoon
Extended-release (Concerta, Metadate CD, Ritalin LA)	Once a day	8–12 hr	Concerta: 18–72 mg once a day; Metadate CD and Ritalin LA: 10–60 mg once a day

▲ ▲ ▲ ▲

MEDICATIONS USED IN THE TREATMENT OF ADHD

Generic Class (and Brand Names)	Daily Dosage	Duration of Positive Behavioral Effects*	Prescribing Schedule
Stimulants (First-Line Treatment)			
AMPHETAMINE *Short-acting* (Dexedrine, Dextrostat)	Twice a day to 3 times a day	4–6 hr	5–15 mg twice a day or 5–10 mg 3 times a day
Intermediate-acting (Adderall, Dexedrine Spansule)	Once a day to twice a day	6–8 hr	5–30 mg once a day or 5–15 mg twice a day
Extended-release (Adderall-XR)	Once a day	10 hr	10–30 mg once a day

*Some side effects (such as behavioral rebound as the medication wears off or difficulty falling asleep at night) can occur after the behavioral effects of the medication have worn off.

sary to begin with one stimulant, monitor the dosing and results, and perhaps alter the dose or switch stimulants until optimal results are achieved. No laboratory tests, electrocardiogram (EKG) monitoring, or psychological tests are routinely necessary for monitoring the use of these medications.

How Will My Child's Medication Treatment Be Determined?

You and your child's pediatrician will need to consider 3 elements when arriving at the best stimulant medication plan for your child: the type of stimulant medication, the dose, and the medication schedule. As we pointed out earlier, all of the commonly used stimulants can be equally successful at treating the symptoms of ADHD, though it is not possible to predict which one will work best for a particular child.

Dosage

You may already be aware that the dosage of many medications, including antibiotics, cold medications, and other over-the-counter drugs, is determined by a child's weight. This is not the case with stimulant medications. Just as individual children respond differently to different stimulants, so each child requires a different dosage that cannot be predicted in advance. The best dosage for a child with ADHD is the one that achieves the *best possible* results without troublesome side effects—*not* the minimum dose that leads to any level of positive response (even though in the past this has been a fairly common practice among physicians). Because the dosage is determined by its results, and because it varies so widely among children, your child's pediatrician may need to adjust the dosage a number of times before finding the best level.

Your child's pediatrician may choose to start with a low dose, and then review the results with you, your child, and his teacher. Remember that you have already targeted specific behaviors that you hope to see improve with medication management. Ideally, your child's pediatrician will review these with you, and will also ask for teacher input regarding these targets in the form of a phone call or written report, perhaps supplemented with standardized behavior checklists. A good way to organize these reports is to set up a daily "report card" that can track teachers' observations about each target. The more objective these reports can be—for example, how many times in a half-hour period a child blurts out answers without raising his hand, or how many math problems were completed correctly in a 15-minute period—the better. These report cards can then be brought into the doctor's office for review.

Once your child's doctor has reviewed any changes in your child's target behaviors, the medication dose can be gradually adjusted upward until the best results are achieved. Again, your doctor may not stop increasing the dose when you first notice a positive result, but will likely continue to increase it until there is no further improvement. If a higher dose produces side effects or no further improvement, she will reduce it. This gradual method of arriving at the proper dose can minimize some of the initial side effects that might have occurred if she had started with the higher dose from the beginning. In some cases a particular stimulant will have little effect. If this is the case with your child, a second stimulant can be tried. If 2 or more stimulants fail to be effective (an uncommon occurrence), a review of his diagnosis may be in order—or an alternative medication plan that includes one of the non-stimulant medications described on page 84.

Many parents become concerned that the frequent dosage and medication changes (particularly as the medication is being started) may mean that their child's pediatrician does not know what she is doing. On the contrary, the only way to know how effective stimulant medications will be is to try a given medication and review changes in an organized way over a period. So expect medication changes until you and your child's pediatrician arrive at the most effective medication and dosage for your child.

Medication Schedules

As is evident from the table, stimulants are available in short-acting (about 4-hour), intermediate-acting (about 8-hour), or extended-release (about 12-hour) forms, making the dosing schedule of your child's medication quite flexible. Your child need not be limited to only one form, and, for example, you may choose to combine short-acting forms with intermediate-acting or extended-release forms to create a schedule that best suits his needs. Many children prefer to take a longer-acting preparation (8–12 hours) before leaving for school in the morning because this makes it unnecessary to take any medication at school (so that their classmates will not even know they are taking it). If your child has after-school activities that cause her to put off doing homework until after the longer-acting medication has worn off, she may want to use an additional short-acting dose at that later time. In this case, she could take an 8-hour dose in the morning before school and another 4-hour dose half an hour before beginning her homework in the evening. Some college students prefer 4-hour medications because they can schedule these doses for the times during the day when they most need the medication. Again, think of stimulants as helpful tools, like glasses—children can use them at the times of day when they need to focus or achieve other target outcomes, and may prefer not to use them at other times. Just

as with glasses, continuous coverage throughout the entire day with minimal side effects would be ideal, and researchers are presently working toward this goal.

Some physicians and families extend the logic of this type of tailored use of stimulants even further, taking "medication holidays"—stopping medication on weekends, during summer vacation, or over other longer periods when they feel their child needs them less. These breaks may speak to a desire of parents or children to minimize the use of stimulants, but there is no reliable evidence indicating that they are helpful or necessary from a medical point of view. In many cases, families find that continuing the medication schedule outside of school hours and school days helps family relationships by supporting better listening skills and helps the more hyperactive and impulsive child better enjoy social experiences such as scout meetings, church activities, and sports.

Side Effects

As discussed previously, the dose of your child's medication should be increased until optimal results are achieved without serious side effects. Only a small number of children who are introduced to stimulant medication in the systematic way we have described—and who follow their medication schedule consistently—will find side effects too intrusive. Any side effects that do occur are likely to be mild and short-lived, and most can be relieved by adjusting the dose or schedule of medication or by switching to another stimulant. While each medication can potentially create side effects in some children, there is no way to predict which child will experience side effects with any one medication. One child may experience side effects on dextroamphetamine (Dexedrine) but not methylphenidate (Ritalin), for example, while another may report opposite results. Again, it is necessary to try a stimulant and monitor the results.

▲   ▲   ▲   ▲

CONTROVERSIES SURROUNDING SIDE EFFECTS OF STIMULANT MEDICATIONS

In recent decades, several controversies have arisen regarding the side effects of stimulant medications. One persistent belief was that stimulants reduce growth in children—a belief that led many families to take summer-long and other medication holidays in hopes of preventing this effect. Most reliable studies, however, demonstrate that while concerns about growth delays have been raised, taking stimulants has no long-term effect on a child's ultimate height.

About 15% to 30% of children may experience minor motor tics while taking stimulant medication. Most of these are temporary and go away with or without stopping the medication. However, because stimulant medications have also been suspected of increasing the severity of existing tics, parents of children with both ADHD and Tourette syndrome (about half of children with Tourette syndrome [or other chronic tic disorders] also have ADHD) or any other tic-related disorder often hesitate to use them. Recent studies have demonstrated that at moderate, carefully monitored doses, the frequency or severity of tics in these children is unlikely to be affected, while the ADHD behaviors are successfully addressed.

Some authorities have also warned that stimulants should not be used in children who have had seizures. Recent studies, however, have not shown an increase in the number or severity of seizures when stimulants are added to appropriate doses of seizure medications.

Side effects caused by stimulants tend to occur early in treatment and are generally mild. The most common side effects include decreased appetite, stomachaches, headaches, difficulty falling asleep, jitteriness, and social withdrawal. Rarely, children who are overly sensitive to stimulants or on too high a dose can become overly focused and seem dull. Other less common side effects include dizziness, rebound effect (increased activity, irritability, or sadness for a short time as the medication wears off), and transient tics (repetitive eye blinking, shoulder shrugging, etc) most common when a new stimulant is first taken.

Your child's pediatrician can manage most of these side effects through adjustments in dose amount or schedule, the use of alternative medication preparations, or, occasionally, by adding other medications. It is important to pay attention to the timing of side effects. For example, if your child seems irritable 4 hours after an intermediate-acting dose, this may suggest too high a dose of medication. If the irritability occurs 8 hours after an intermediate-acting medication it may indicate withdrawal or rebound effect.

Monitoring the Results

When stimulants are tried in the systematic way described in this chapter, at least 80% of children will respond well to one of them. The key word here is systematic. The medication must be initially prescribed according to a reliable plan. After the initial dose has been established, adjustments can be made in response to frequent, regular feedback provided by you, your child, *and his teachers.* To avoid the natural tendency to believe a method is working just because it is being used (according to studies, teachers initially rate up to 45% of children on placebos as having completely normalized their behavior), your child's pediatrician should

- Regularly see your child and ask him about his medication.
- Regularly ask you specific questions about changes in behavior or performance.
- Help you develop home and school "report cards" (see box on page 80) to measure progress relating to the target outcomes you have selected.

▲ ▲ ▲ ▲

DAILY SCHOOL-HOME REPORT CARDS

Daily report cards can help provide immediate feedback on your child's behavior. This feedback can be used to help you and your child's pediatrician decide if your target goals are being met and if medication adjustments might be helpful. Some typical target areas include

- Academic productivity
- Following classroom rules
- Peer relationships
- Teacher relationships
- Behavior outside the classroom
- Time-out behavior
- Responsibility for belongings
- Homework

After picking the most appropriate general target areas for your child, as you read in Chapter 2, you will need to describe representative behaviors in detail. For example, if "behavior outside the classroom" is a major problem, your target behavior list might include items like

- Follows the rules at lunch and in the hallway with 4 or fewer violations per day
- Walks in line appropriately (appropriate behavior needs to be defined and agreed on)
- Follows the rules on the bus with 2 or fewer violations
- Needs 2 or fewer warnings for exhibiting bad table manners in the lunchroom (eg, playing with food, throwing trash on the floor)
- Changes into gym clothes within 6 minutes

Note that these items are all carefully defined and countable. This makes it easier to track progress. The number of allowable violations listed should also be realistic enough that the goals can be achieved. You will read more about school-home report cards in Chapter 7.

Adapted with permission from William E. Pelham, Jr, PhD. School-Home Daily Report Card packet available for downloading at no cost at www.ctadd.com and http://wings.buffalo.edu/adhd.

- Ask your child's teacher structured questions or to complete structured behavioral and performance rating scales, rather than simply ask you if your child is "doing better." Teacher input is especially important when starting medication or changing the dose of any medication.

Structured questions, reports, charts, and rating scales from teachers can also measure (in numeric terms wherever possible) any improvement in your child's treatment targets such as classroom productivity, on-task behavior, and other function-related goals. Because many of the better rating scales your child's pediatrician will be familiar with have been used on a broad sample of hundreds of children the same age as yours, they will place your child's performance in the context of his peers and classmates. By continuing to assess and measure selected targets in a consistent way, you can also compare your child's performance with how he was doing 2, 6, or 12 months ago.

As you begin to review your child's progress, keep in mind that children respond at different rates in different target areas, and that not all of the goals that you set for your child can be turned into targets that are medication-sensitive. Almost everyone who is hyperactive improves rapidly on some dose of stimulant medication. But, for example, if inattention has led to falling behind in reading, it may take several weeks or months to see improvement. However, if the reading lag is due to a learning disability (see Chapter 7) rather than poor attention while learning, it will not be expected to respond to medication management. As always, your focus should remain much more on improvements in your child's ability to function in the previously identified target areas—whenever possible, assessing behaviors that can be counted and measured—rather than on general impressions about improvement in "his ADHD."

When attending follow-up visits with your child's doctor, come prepared with specific (and, if possible, countable) examples of changes in the target areas you are measuring. If you have been using school-home report cards you should chart them. You should also ask your child's teachers to prepare a narrative report of your child's progress since your last visit, or fill out any specific rating scales suggested by your child's pediatrician that could be used for making decisions about the medication management plan. During your visit, these materials should be reviewed before determining whether any changes need to be made in the dose, scheduling, or type of stimulant medication. The more systematically and frequently feedback from home and school is obtained at follow-up visits, the greater improvement your child is likely to experience.

A major reason for frequent follow-up visits is to make certain that your child's medication dose is optimal. In the large ADHD treatment study (the Multimodal Treatment Study of Children with Attention Deficit Hyperactivity Disorder [MTA]) described in Chapter 3, special care was taken to find an optimal dose of medication according to preset guidelines during the first few weeks of treatment. These optimal doses were higher on average than among children who were not on the study medication management guidelines but being treated by the individual plans of their own physicians. In addition, the dosage in the study guidelines spanned the school day as well as the early evening, as opposed to the common practice of prescribing just enough medication to cover the school day. Once treatment began, children and families in the study met with their physician for half an hour each month to discuss concerns and review the teacher's monthly report. During these sessions a great deal of parent and child education was carried out. Changes in the child's treatment were then made, if necessary, in response to feedback from parents and schoolteachers. If the child experienced difficulties, the physician adjusted the medication, and these adjustments occurred frequently. In contrast,

the children with ADHD being treated by their own physicians
generally met with them only once or twice a year, had shorter
and less comprehensive visits, were on lower doses of stimulant medication, and had teachers who were not as consistently
involved in the treatment process.

As was pointed out in Chapter 3, about 60% of children
with ADHD who received this optimal dose of medication with
frequent and regular doctors' visits and careful monitoring by
parents and teachers were rated by teachers as indistinguishable
in many areas from their peers without ADHD. This was even
more enhanced with a combined medication and behavior
approach. However, only about 25% of children being treated
for ADHD by their own physicians (and most of the time the
treatments included medication) were so rated. Experts feel
that this may be due, to a large extent, to not following the
kind of careful and organized approaches discussed previously.
Of course you live in the real world, not under the ideal conditions of a study. Monthly visits may be impractical. But by using
the principles used in the MTA study—using a medication dose
that causes the most improvement (rather than the lowest

possible dose), making sure that homework time is also covered by medication, setting up reasonably frequent and highly structured follow-up visits, etc—you can achieve the best evidence-based medication regulation possible for your child.

If your child has tried 2 or 3 stimulants and none have helped, or if your child had side effects that could not be controlled, another type of medication may be an option. Stimulants also may not be an option for children who are taking certain other medications or who have certain medical conditions. In these situations, ask your child's pediatrician for advice and refer to the information on non-stimulants below.

What Other Types of Medications Are Available?

Proven alternate choices to stimulant medications include atomoxetine, the tricyclic antidepressants (TCAs), and bupropion. Because they have not been studied as rigorously or used as much as stimulants, these medications are considered second-line (second-choice) treatments. Some non-stimulants may be appropriate for children who have been diagnosed with ADHD and certain coexisting conditions—such as ADHD with accompanying tic disorders (such as Tourette syndrome)—because they can in some cases treat both conditions simultaneously.

Atomoxetine

Atomoxetine (Strattera) is a recently released medication for ADHD. It is in the class of medications known as selective norepinephrine reuptake inhibitors. Because atomoxetine does not seem to have a potential for abuse, it is not classified as a controlled substance. Side effects are generally mild but can include decreased appetite, upset stomach, nausea or vomiting, tiredness, problems sleeping, and dizziness. It is safer than the TCAs, and seems to be more effective than bupropion.

Tricyclic Antidepressants

Tricyclic antidepressants have also been shown to have a positive effect on children's inattention, impulsivity, and hyperactivity. Your child's pediatrician may also consider them as an option if your child has problems with insomnia or tics when her ADHD symptoms are treated with stimulants. Tricyclic antidepressants have a longer effect than stimulants, and have no behavioral rebound effects and no risk for substance abuse. However, they can cause side effects, especially in the higher doses generally needed for the greatest and longest-lasting improvements. Side effects may include dry mouth, constipation, vivid dreams, headaches, insomnia, drowsiness, or upset stomach. Because minor effects on EKGs (heart tracings) can be seen (including speeding up of the heart and a slowing of electrical conduction), your child's pediatrician may obtain EKGs as a routine part of monitoring these medications. Regular blood tests are also routine because children show a great deal of variability in how quickly they eliminate these medications from their systems. A few reports of sudden and unexplained deaths in children treated with desipramine have raised some questions about its safety—though the findings were imprecise and uncertain, and thus there is no proof that this medication actually caused the deaths. Even so, TCA use should be carefully monitored. The need for such careful monitoring is another reason why TCAs are considered second-line medications for ADHD.

Bupropion

Bupropion is a unique type of antidepressant that has been even less frequently studied as a treatment for ADHD, but studies that have been done indicate that bupropion is effective in reducing ADHD symptoms at the same dose level used for treating children who are depressed. The side effects, though usually minimal, can include irritability, decreased appetite, insomnia, and a worsening of existing tics. It is important to note that at higher doses these antidepressants may make some individuals more prone to seizures, so bupropion should be used cautiously in children who have seizure disorders. No laboratory tests or EKG monitoring are necessary when using bupropion.

Clonidine and Guanfacine

Clonidine and guanfacine, similar antihypertensive drugs, have been occasionally used for the treatment of ADHD. Limited studies suggest that they can be useful for children who are very hyperactive and impulsive, oppositional or defiant, or who also have sleep disturbances or accompanying tics or Tourette syndrome.

	▲ ▲ ▲ ▲	
SECOND-LINE MEDICATIONS		
Generic Class (Brand Name)	**Daily Dosage**	**Prescribing Schedule**
ATOMOXETINE Strattera	Once a day to twice a day	1.2 mg/kg per day– 1.4 mg/kg per day
TRICYCLICS Imipramine, Desipramine, Nortripyline	Twice a day to 3 times a day	2–5 mg/kg per day
BUPROPION Wellbutrin	Once a day to 3 times a day	50–100 mg 3 times a day
Wellbutrin SR	Twice a day	100–150 mg twice a day

How Can I Talk to My Child About Medication?

If medication issues seem complex and sometimes confusing to parents of children with ADHD, they can be even more so to the children themselves. Your child may strongly resist the idea of sticking to a regular schedule of medication—because he fears that this will remind him on a daily basis that he is not "normal" or that other children will tease him, because he resents the intrusion in his everyday routine, because he is afraid of the consequences of taking any medication, or because he strongly wishes to control his behavior.

The more information you can give your child about medications, the more actively and productively he can participate in his own treatment decisions. In fact, while on a medication he should be better able to accurately evaluate his own behavior and performance. Parents sometimes worry that their child will begin to attribute his successes to the medication rather than to himself, but, in fact, children on medication most often cite their own efforts or abilities (not the medication) as the explanation for their success. All of this is important because children's active participation in their own treatment plans leads to better treatment results. Sometimes he may not notice any changes in himself, but will notice that he gets into less trouble or completes more of his work.

To some degree (depending on his age and level of comprehension) your child will need to know what stimulants are, what effects they are likely to have, how long most children continue to take them, how doses and schedules can vary, and how the treatment process is likely to proceed. Medications should be discussed as tools that can be used effectively *or ineffectively* to achieve behavior or learning goals. As you and your child's doctors explain these issues, encourage your child to ask questions, voice his fears and concerns, and incorporate his ideas into the medication treatment plan. Your child's desire to address his problems "on his own" may not be an option, but respecting his choice of how and when he takes the medication may be.

If your child is upset or worried about other children making fun of him, remind him that long-lasting stimulants can make it unnecessary for him to take the medication at school. (Your own efforts to educate him about medication will help bolster his confidence as well, making him less vulnerable to this type of teasing.) Especially if he complains about having to take pills every day, give him choices about his dosage regimen. By high school, depending on study habits and extracurricular activities, his medication plan may need to change again. For example, the 12-hour dose from 7:00 am to 7:00 pm that worked well in junior high school may need to be reconsidered if homework now usually gets done between 7:00 and 11:00 pm.

As your child begins the process of taking medication, first and foremost, listen carefully to him. If he reports that he "feels different," consider whether he is reporting side effects or just describing the hoped-for positive effects of the medication. Remind him (and yourself) that the goal is to preserve all of his positive personality traits and help him focus and allow him mental time to think before doing—so that he can think about his choices and pick the best one.

In general, helping your child become as knowledgeable as possible about the effects and side effects of medications should lead to greater engagement in his own treatment. One of the ways in which he can maximize the potential of his prescribed medication is to monitor his own responses to it and report them to the other members of his treatment team. He should be sufficiently aware of possible side effects so he can report them to the treatment team if and when they occur. He should also report any positive effects and actively participate in at least part of all meetings where his treatment is discussed. Your child's pediatrician should take the time to explain to him how any changes in his functioning have come about—particularly what is the result of the medication versus what is caused by his own efforts.

Your child should also understand the limitations of medication—that while medication can help with the core symptoms of ADHD, he will need to use this advantage to actively improve his functioning in his target areas. With consistent effort and education he can learn to use his medication to help him overcome social, academic, and behavioral challenges. But if he leaves all the work to the medication, he will see fewer positive results.

Many new issues can arise during the teenage years. As your child approaches adolescence, it will be appropriate to transfer to him as much of the responsibility for his medication regimen as he is able to responsibly handle. For example, a teenager may actually begin to dislike the feelings that a particular medication creates so a reconsideration of the dose or specific medication may be a reasonable solution. A teenager who takes an active part in his treatment plan is likely to consider these options, whereas an adolescent who is not involved with the treatment plan may decide to just stop taking the medication. The more empowered a teenager feels in his own treatment process, the more likely he is to live up to his responsibilities. Adolescents may have a particularly hard time accepting the idea of taking medications due to their age-appropriate desire for independence, resistance to adult direction, and need to conform to their peers. The best way to deal with your teenager's new attitudes toward medications is to listen even more openly to his opinions and feelings on the issue and to allow him as much control of his treatment as possible. Because this is a time developmentally when youths may begin to experiment with drugs (including stimulants), medications can now have street value. This issue warrants a serious discussion. Adolescents do not want to stand out or be different, and they may begin to question whether they still need to take medications. Teenagers who "own" their own problems, successes, and treatment plan by this age will do much better with continuing their treatment. At times it may be helpful to have a period off of medication with structured teacher feedback to demonstrate to your adolescent the significant differences that medications can make.

Teenagers need to be involved in all areas of decision making related to their medication management. As an adult, he will need to be able to routinely manage his own medication and other issues related to ADHD. His desire to begin practicing self-management now is a healthy sign of growth, and should be encouraged with your careful attention and guidance. The bottom line here is that the more empowered your child feels in his own treatment process at all stages of development, the more likely he is to live up to his responsibilities—and the more effective his treatment plan will be.

Making the Most of Medication

It is important to remember that medication is only one component of your child's treatment, but can provide a powerful springboard from which your child can begin to master the challenges of ADHD. While it can be difficult at first to understand and properly use any type of medication, you and your child will soon grow comfortable with the routines and considerations that can maximize its benefits. You, your child, and her teachers must actively monitor its effects and discuss them with her pediatrician. To enjoy maximum success, effective parenting techniques and teaching and self-management tools (see chapters 5–7) will also need to be used where appropriate. Treatment plans that include medication and effective behavior therapy may even be achieved with lower medication doses than when medication alone is used.

Over time, you will find that active monitoring of and participating in your child's treatment can be extremely rewarding for you and your child as you watch her day-to-day functioning, performance, and self-esteem improve. In the meantime, as you become acquainted with the process of using medications, consider sharing your new experiences with other families in your situation. Your local support group for children with ADHD and their parents can provide you with validation and practical advice during this challenging time. As you will discover, many families have been where you find yourselves today—and most will tell you how glad they are that they informed themselves about this type of treatment as they took action regarding their child's future.

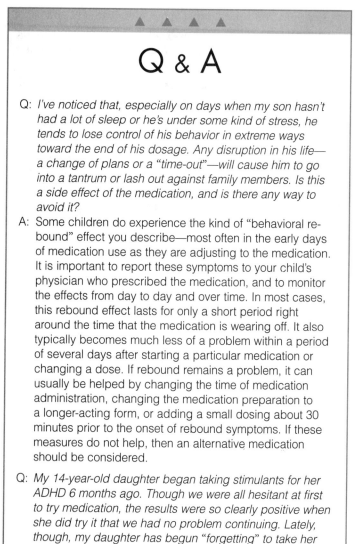

Q & A

Q: *I've noticed that, especially on days when my son hasn't had a lot of sleep or he's under some kind of stress, he tends to lose control of his behavior in extreme ways toward the end of his dosage. Any disruption in his life— a change of plans or a "time-out"—will cause him to go into a tantrum or lash out against family members. Is this a side effect of the medication, and is there any way to avoid it?*

A: Some children do experience the kind of "behavioral rebound" effect you describe—most often in the early days of medication use as they are adjusting to the medication. It is important to report these symptoms to your child's physician who prescribed the medication, and to monitor the effects from day to day and over time. In most cases, this rebound effect lasts for only a short period right around the time that the medication is wearing off. It also typically becomes much less of a problem within a period of several days after starting a particular medication or changing a dose. If rebound remains a problem, it can usually be helped by changing the time of medication administration, changing the medication preparation to a longer-acting form, or adding a small dosing about 30 minutes prior to the onset of rebound symptoms. If these measures do not help, then an alternative medication should be considered.

Q: *My 14-year-old daughter began taking stimulants for her ADHD 6 months ago. Though we were all hesitant at first to try medication, the results were so clearly positive when she did try it that we had no problem continuing. Lately, though, my daughter has begun "forgetting" to take her pill in the morning. The more we remind her, the more resistant she gets. Her typical response is, "OK, Mom,*

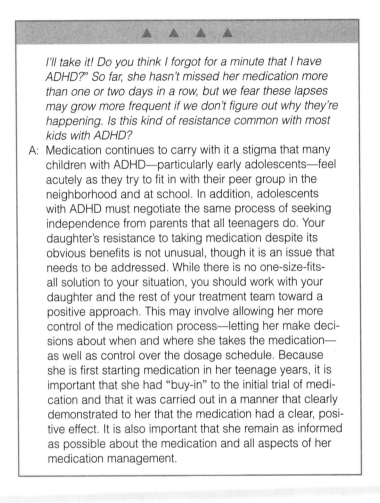

I'll take it! Do you think I forgot for a minute that I have ADHD?" So far, she hasn't missed her medication more than one or two days in a row, but we fear these lapses may grow more frequent if we don't figure out why they're happening. Is this kind of resistance common with most kids with ADHD?

A: Medication continues to carry with it a stigma that many children with ADHD—particularly early adolescents—feel acutely as they try to fit in with their peer group in the neighborhood and at school. In addition, adolescents with ADHD must negotiate the same process of seeking independence from parents that all teenagers do. Your daughter's resistance to taking medication despite its obvious benefits is not unusual, though it is an issue that needs to be addressed. While there is no one-size-fits-all solution to your situation, you should work with your daughter and the rest of your treatment team toward a positive approach. This may involve allowing her more control of the medication process—letting her make decisions about when and where she takes the medication—as well as control over the dosage schedule. Because she is first starting medication in her teenage years, it is important that she had "buy-in" to the initial trial of medication and that it was carried out in a manner that clearly demonstrated to her that the medication had a clear, positive effect. It is also important that she remain as informed as possible about the medication and all aspects of her medication management.

CHAPTER FIVE

ADHD at Home: General Measures

▲   ▲   ▲   ▲

Caring for a child with attention-deficit/hyperactivity disorder (ADHD) takes a great deal of patience and commitment. For many parents, the daily struggles with uncontrolled behavior, inattention, distractibility, and even defiance or depression can prove overwhelming at times. The challenge becomes even greater when others who do not understand ADHD mistakenly imply that your child's difficulties are a result of poor discipline, poor diet, or other factors within your or your child's control. Of course you know that his tendency to interrupt conversations, knock the silverware off the table, make an inappropriate amount of noise, or ignore adults' questions are typical examples of ADHD-related behaviors, not a poorly structured home environment or poor parenting. Still, it is only human to feel embarrassed and even self-doubting when others question your competency.

The good news is that while poor parenting does not cause ADHD, a number of specific home measures and parenting techniques have been shown to significantly improve the functioning of many children with ADHD. When properly implemented and consistently applied, these approaches may not only help reshape your child's behavior at home and in public, but also decrease tension, strengthen family relationships, improve academic performance, and lead to an increase in your child's self-esteem. Introducing and maintaining new routines and styles of interaction is never easy, but it is worth the effort to observe for yourself that children with ADHD *can and do* learn, adapt, and succeed.

As you have already learned, medication management and behavior therapy are the most proven, evidence-based mainstays of treatments for ADHD. They can measurably improve the lives of many children with ADHD. However, there are also many other helpful general approaches to parenting and to your child's everyday life at home that can increase the positive effects achieved through these forms of treatment, create a supportive and structured home environment, foster positive family relationships, and bolster your child's self-esteem. This chapter will review these measures. The following chapter (Chapter 6) will then focus specifically on parent training—the parent version of behavior therapy.

In this chapter, you will learn how to

- Help your child focus on his strengths rather than his disabilities.
- Simplify, organize, and structure his home environment to help him succeed.
- Monitor your child's daily routines and rhythms and use this knowledge to help him become better regulated.
- Facilitate better communication with your child and within the family.
- Organize your own life in ways that will allow you to manage your family's challenges and have time for yourself.
- Help your child establish and maintain new, rewarding relationships.

Focusing on Strengths

You have already learned that it is always better to look at your whole child—her special interests and unique personality—

rather than constantly focusing on "her ADHD" and coexisting conditions. All children, whether they have ADHD, do best when their parents build on their strengths. As was pointed out in Chapter 1, many highly successful and creative people—including photojournalists, entrepreneurs, and artists—have been able to use aspects of their ADHD symptoms to great advantage. Any competent photojournalist can capture the image of the main speaker at a large event, for example—but a photographer with ADHD, whose attention is less narrowly focused, may be more likely to notice and photograph a parent and child in the audience whose poignant pose stands as a powerful metaphor for the event and thus makes an outstanding front-page photograph. By identifying and nurturing your own child's special abilities and talents as they manifest themselves, you can encourage the self-esteem, confidence, and competence necessary for her to succeed in life despite many of the obstacles that may stand in her way.

One of the best ways to help your child focus on what she can do, rather than what she cannot, is to help her experience as many concrete successes as possible. The more she sees what she can accomplish in her world, the more optimistic and confident she is likely to feel. Instruction in any of your child's evolving interests—sports, art, computers, woodworking, music, martial arts, or any other area—can lay the groundwork for such achievement, especially when augmented by your praise for her efforts as well as her successes. If your child's interests are not clear, help her discover some by actively finding areas where she can succeed. Talking with your child and supporting what she most enjoys and is best at may help her start to think about who she is and what she can do instead of who or what she is not.

Simplifying, Organizing, and Structuring the Home Environment

We all experience more success when our lives are well organized, and your child with ADHD is no exception. You will find that her ability to progress in nearly all areas of self-management and social interaction increases when her environment is structured to meet her unique needs. If your child is physically impulsive or accident-prone, she will get through life with fewer negative experiences if you take the time to unclutter and safety-proof your home. Some children with ADHD may benefit from an orderly physical environment with a place for each object, while keeping the environment (eg, your child's room) organized may be a hopeless task for others. Try helping your child organize her room at a level she can manage. However, if even modest attempts at organization are still overwhelming, do not make a big deal of how messy her room is—you and she have other, more important issues to tackle. However, predictable daily routines are an absolute necessity for many chil-

dren with ADHD. Consistent limit-setting with predictable consequences, along with limited choices (not "What do you want to eat?" but "Do you want an apple or a boiled egg?"), also make your child's world more manageable and help her meet her goals. Written lists of chores or other daily tasks are especially useful in helping your child keep track of what she needs to do, and keeping lists is an excellent habit for her to carry into adolescence and adulthood.

When considering how to structure your child's day-to-day experiences in ways that will help her function, it may help to picture your growing child as a building in progress. The limits, lists, routines, and other measures you are putting in place today are like scaffolding that will provide the necessary support as she develops fully. As she turns these routines into daily habits and becomes more self-directed, some of these supports can be gradually removed while her underlying functioning remains well in place. (You may no longer have to create homework checklists with her, for example, because she has learned to make them herself.) Far from "babying" your child, helping to structure and organize her world allows her to add to her competencies and experience many more small triumphs, increasing her self-esteem.

Following are a number of general tips that parents of children with ADHD have found helpful for simplifying their children's lives. At the same time, it is always important to consider your own child's specific needs when structuring her environment. If one of her goals, for example, is to complete more of her homework assignments, you will want to provide her with a consistent, organized workspace. You may also need to make sure the space is free of sibling interruptions and other possible distractions, such as the television, to allow her to focus and concentrate. If, however, too much silence just prompts her to seek attention and stimulation—you may find she does better working at the kitchen table where a modest amount of activity is taking place (a radio or music playing softly in the background would be an example). Likewise, a child entering middle school may benefit not only from a weekly organizer with daily lists of homework assignments, but also a list of each day's class schedule, with room locations and teachers' names, to help her adjust to a more complex routine.

TIPS FOR STRUCTURING YOUR CHILD'S HOME ENVIRONMENT

- *Keep your child on a daily schedule.* Try to keep the time that your child wakes up, eats, bathes, leaves for school, and goes to sleep about the same each day.
- *Cut down on distractions.* Identify the things that distract your child the most at important times (like during homework), but do not jump to conclusions—the distractions for each child are different. As you identify them, eliminate them one by one.
- *Organize your house.* If your child has specific and logical places to keep his schoolwork, toys, and clothes, he is less likely to lose them. Save a spot near the door for his school backpack so he can grab it on the way out the door.
- *Use charts and checklists.* These written reminders can help your child track his progress with chores or homework. Keep instructions brief. Offer frequent, friendly reminders to check his list and make sure each task has been completed.
- *Limit choices.* Help your child learn to make good decisions by giving him only 2 or 3 options at a time.
- *Set small, reachable goals.* Aim for slow progress rather than instant results. Be sure that your child understands that he can succeed best by taking small steps and slowly building on those successes.

Just as you have observed that your child may feel less over-whelmed when her home life is well-organized, so you may find that organizing your own family life as thoroughly as possible will help you, too, feel calmer and more in control. (This is even more likely to be the case, of course, if you have ADHD.) With the number of medical visits, teachers' conferences, and treatment reviews necessary to maintain your child's well-being and continued progress, a family calendar including all scheduled activities can be an essential for many families. Daily lists of tasks to perform and errands to run will help you stay organized just as they help your child. Many parents find it worthwhile to devote a private 10 minutes to half an hour before the kids get up in the morning to "regroup"—thinking about everything that must be accomplished that day and arranging tasks in order of priority.

Daily Routines and Rhythms

As the parent of a child with ADHD, you may already be aware of certain times of day that are more difficult than others. If your child has begun taking a stimulant medication, you may notice fluctuations in her attention and behavioral control throughout the day as each dose of medication begins to take effect, works well, and then wears off. With stimulant medications, effects such as behavioral rebound (a short period of irritability or moodiness as the medication is wearing off in about 4, 8, or 12 hours [see Chapter 4]) may lead to difficulties at around dinnertime or bedtime that had not generally occurred before. You can help your child adjust to these changes by observing how and when her emotions and behavior tend to fluctuate each day and arranging her schedule as much as possible to accommodate these ups and downs. If you know, for example, that she is usually somewhat unsettled and irritable for a half hour after her arrival home from school, schedule her homework for after that time. If her medication suppresses her appetite at certain times during the day, schedule meals to avoid these periods. Take special care to prepare her for transitions between activities because these are likely to be especially difficult times for her.

Another issue to consider is the way a specific length of time can sometimes feel to your child with ADHD. For a child who struggles with managing her behavior or retaining focus for more than a few minutes at a time, tedious, repetitive, or boring activities can seem exceedingly long and soon become absolutely unbearable. Forcing your child to participate in such an activity (requiring her to sit still for long periods while you chat with a friend, introducing her to clubs or groups that involve little physical action and too much down time, expecting her to pick up all the toys at once in a disorderly room) will probably only lead to failure and the probability of subsequent punishment. Even fun activities can be strenuous in the same way. For example, baseball, which includes long periods of inactivity while on the field, may not be as good an activity for children with ADHD as soccer, which has a much faster and continuous pace. By avoiding such situations or breaking up activities (including homework) into short chunks of time, you can help your child experience success as she struggles to manage her responses. It may also help to let your child know ahead of time how long a particular activity will last, and even to place a timer in view to help her awareness of how much time has passed. If she knows she has already been working on her homework or practicing the piano for more than half the allotted time, she may be able (with your support and coaching) to continue to the end.

Optimizing and Facilitating Communication

Children with ADHD frequently experience difficulty participating in elements of sustained and focused day-to-day conversation. Adapting your style of communication to your child's needs can help him maintain a connection. As you learn the principles of behavior therapy (see Chapter 6), you will learn how to pause, get your child's attention (call his name before giving a command), maintain eye contact, and perhaps have him repeat back or explain what you have told him to be sure he has heard and understands. This approach works well not only when issuing commands but also when beginning any sort of conversation with your child. If he tends to interrupt, help him out by keeping your sentences brief and focusing only on what needs to be said. It is best to avoid interrupting him frequently yourself because he may not be able to stay engaged in this type of interaction. If you sense that his attention is wandering, touch his arm, take his hand, or otherwise make physical contact. Some parents find that conversation flows more smoothly if they are also involved in a physical activity with their child such as washing dishes or making dinner. Finally, if you are telling your child something that you want him to remember, write it down in simple terms or encourage him to write it down himself. Helping your child learn to make lists and keep track of them in an organized way can be a progressively important tool as the complexity of home and school demands increases with age.

Your behavior therapy training (see Chapter 6) may introduce you to some new terms as well as techniques that will improve communication with your child. Introducing concepts such as "consequences," "rewards," and "positive and negative behavior" into the family vocabulary can go a long way toward clarifying communications. Where you might have previously ordered your child to "Go to your room!" for example, you can now inform him that his behavior has led to a "time-out"—and by the time you give this command, he will know the exact rules that apply to this term. Specific behavior therapy language strategies, such as when/then statements ("When you finish your homework, then you can go play baseball"), may also prove useful when interacting with all of your children and can improve communication and morale in the family as a whole.

Educating, Reframing, and Demystifying

Children with ADHD face a daily struggle with adult disapproval and other negative interactions that result from their behavioral and social difficulties. Such frequent negativity can easily lead to a loss of confidence and low self-esteem that, if left unaddressed, can result in even more self-defeating behavior. Designing an effective treatment plan is one way to prevent this negative cycle from occurring with your child because it is likely to lead to more positive feedback and better self-control. You can further increase your child's chances for improvement by taking the following steps:

- **Educating** your child about ADHD and how to manage it
- **Reframing** any negative attitudes or assumptions and reshaping the responses that have developed as a result of these attitudes and assumptions
- **Demystifying** the treatment process and clearing up any misunderstandings

The more fully a child with ADHD can begin to understand and "take ownership" of her own challenges, the more committed she is likely to be to treatment, the more successful she may become at self-management, and the higher her self-esteem is likely to be. Thus, *educating* your child about the nature of ADHD is a critical part of successful treatment at every stage of development. From very early on, you and your child's pediatrician can begin talking with your child about the nature of ADHD, what it is and what it is not, and how she can learn to manage it. As she grows older, her pediatrician or other clinician can meet with her alone so that she can feel free to seek any information she needs to become the most active participant in her own care plan. She may also benefit a great deal from your efforts to provide her with age-appropriate and developmentally appropriate books about ADHD and responsible Web sites (see Resources) that provide updated information on ADHD and related disorders. Support groups for children and families with ADHD are another source of valuable information as well as an emotional resource. By her teenage years, your child should have had the opportunity to build up an informed knowledge base on which to rely when making decisions about treatment, social and academic pursuits, plans for the future, and so on. Taking control of her own life in this way can be enormously empowering for a child who has struggled with ADHD and can make all the difference in how she views her life and academic, professional, and personal potential.

It is important to keep in mind as your child grows that she is a child and may therefore forget or misinterpret some of what she is told about the nature of ADHD. To minimize her confusion, make sure that you and her pediatrician talk with her regularly and repeatedly about ADHD (not just at the first meeting) and ask her to repeat back to you what she understands, listening carefully to her interpretations of what she has learned. Always keep these discussions simple and brief enough for her to participate fully. Keep an ear out for misperceptions at home as well, and work to clarify issues such as how much of her behavior is "the ADHD" and how much she can control, whether ADHD is related to intelligence, what her responsibilities are in improving her own behavior while on medication, and so on. The clearer she is on who she is and where she stands in relation to ADHD, the more competence and confidence she will have in managing it.

Because discouragement is a constant danger for children who face such frequent obstacles, be prepared to confront your child's negative ideas and help her *reframe* them in positive ways. If your child starts to develop the attitude that, "I'm different from 'normal' kids, and ADHD limits what I should expect of myself," help her to reformulate it as, "Everyone has attention problems from time to time. I just have them so often that they interfere with my best functioning—but I have learned that there are plenty of things I can do about this." If she begins echoing the feedback she gets at school ("I'm different. I can't do anything right."), get out any supportive evidence you have—her report cards, test scores, artwork, or other concrete forms of achievement—to show her in objective ways how she is making progress.

In some cases, it may also help to focus on your child's effort (how persistent she was or how much thought she gave to the organization) rather than the outcome (what grade she got)—particularly because it is so common for ADHD to involve work production problems. "I'm so proud of you for working so hard on that report" is as powerful a comment, coming from you, as "I'm so proud of you for getting an A." You may also find that it helps to put your child's struggles in context for her. Point out that nearly every child has some type of challenge to overcome—whether it is a learning disability, coordination problems in sports, difficulties with friendships, or a complex home situation.

Reframing negative attitudes goes a long way in helping a child focus on her strengths rather than her disabilities. Your child will also feel much more empowered if you help her develop tools to actively improve the negative situations that disturb her most. Many of the tools for this are similar to those you, your spouse, and your other children have developed yourselves, and sharing your experiences and the responses you have developed will help her feel supported and understood. Your child's pediatrician or counselor can also help her practice specific techniques. For example, many children are advised to deal with teasing by ignoring it, yet ignoring or displaying a sense of anger rarely works, and often even escalates the teasing. Reframing the teasing by turning it into a joke or putting a humorous spin on it can be much more effective. (If teasing becomes a major problem, it needs to be dealt with at school. See Chapter 7.)

Demystifying the nature and treatment of ADHD can be very helpful because children often see their diagnosis as a stigma and their treatment plan as something "done to me" by pediatricians, teachers, and parents instead of seeing themselves as active participants and acknowledging their own successes. Her pediatrician's explanations about the nature of ADHD— that it has no relation to intelligence, that it is a disorder that can be managed, that many successful adults have this condition—will also help reduce some of her major concerns. Often the issue of taking medication is especially sensitive. Your child may initially feel devastated by the prospect of taking medication for a "brain problem." She may worry a great deal about other kids' or adults' reactions should they learn she is taking stimulants. She may even assume that this treatment decision means there is "something wrong" with her, that she is "stupid," "weird," or "different" from everyone else. Educating your child about how stimulants work—in any brain, not just those with ADHD—can demystify some of her fears and help her feel more positive about treatment. Beyond these steps, however, you can emphasize to your child that medication is a *tool* that she can use—like glasses for a person with poor vision who is learning to read, or a hammer for a carpenter building a house. Instead of thinking of herself as a passive object being "fixed" or "cured" with stimulants, your child needs to understand the active role she must take in improving her functioning while using medication as a tool that allows her to focus better than before. The more you can encourage her to learn how to use and to take advantage of medication, rather than relying on it to "take care of her," the more progress she is likely to make— and the better she is likely to feel about herself as she learns just how well she can do.

Integrating ADHD Management Into Your Family's Life

Successfully managing ADHD takes a great deal of time and effort on your part as well as your child's. If you, your partner, or any of your other children also have ADHD (not unlikely because the condition can run in families), the amount of time and effort spent is further compounded. Family members without ADHD may resent the time and attention that they feel are taken from them to meet the needs and address the issues of those who have it. It is no surprise, then, that the pressure to satisfy everyone's demands sometimes becomes overwhelming. One way around this is to formally schedule regular personal time with each child and with your spouse as well. These periods do not have to be lengthy—half an hour at a time may do—but they should be frequent and as predictable (daily, for example) as possible, and you should make sure they actually happen. When you are spending time with one of your children or your spouse, make it a policy not to bring up divisive issues. Try to keep your time positive and focused on the present relationship so that both of you will have more emotional energy for the rest of the family later on. If you are the parent taking most of the responsibility for dealing with issues related to ADHD, it is also a good idea to try to delegate other daily chores as much as possible. Allow your partner, older children, or other relatives to take over duties that free up your time, and, when possible, take advantage of time-saving services such as online banking, drive-through services, and so on. Every minute you save from these uninspiring yet necessary errands is a valuable minute you can give to your child with ADHD, other family members, and, just as important, yourself.

Becoming Your Child's Case Manager

Becoming your child's case manager means serving as the vital link connecting all aspects of his treatment plan at home, at school, and in the community. This requires a great deal of thought and organization, and can make an enormous contribution to your child's progress and your family's welfare. Organization needs to extend beyond some of the aspects already discussed, such as calendars and time management. A child with ADHD accumulates a lot of records—from teachers, physicians, mental health professionals, medical insurance companies, and so on. Keep these papers neatly filed and available for when you need them. By organizing reports and treatment decisions chronologically, you can create an excellent database for future discussions with treatment providers and school personnel about how your child is progressing. Always keep a pen and pad of paper or your personal organizer on hand as well to record any information you feel might be useful at the next treatment review meeting with your child's pediatrician. Because concrete, quantitative information is so valuable in evaluating his progress, you will want specific notes on your child's behavior rather than general, half-remembered impressions. Once you have instituted these organizing principles, you will likely find that you have more complete records than any of your child's physicians, psychologists, or teachers, and that you have indeed become the true case manager.

Educating Family Members

While you, your child with ADHD, and other adults involved in her care have probably focused a great deal of attention on learning about the nature of her condition, it is important to keep in mind that your other children and relatives are likely to understand much less. They will need your help in learning

how to respond to your child's behavior and to support her efforts to function successfully. If a family member seems to resent or blame your child for her ADHD-related actions, take the time to talk privately with them about the challenges she faces. Discuss treatment decisions with everyone in your family, explaining the reasons for your choices. If you are implementing behavior therapy techniques in your home, other family caregivers will need to learn to implement them as well. (Fortunately, all the tools and techniques you will learn through parent training apply equally well to other children in the family and can be equally helpful.) Teach other family members to frame ADHD-related challenges positively and to work with your child to solve problems. You might ask them to write down any issues they have (such as, "Frances interrupts me all the time!") and then think about how to rephrase them in ways that will help solve the problem ("I need for Frances to wait until I'm finished talking before she talks."). Once this is done, family members can discuss possible solutions, try one out and evaluate it, and move on to another solution if that one does not work (see Chapter 6).

Sometimes family members refuse to cooperate, express chronic resentment, or seem unable to act in positive ways. These are common issues; you might consider locating an ADHD support group in your area and/or seeking family therapy to help everyone adjust. In the meantime, let your child communicate directly to her other family members whenever possible instead of always "defending her" yourself. Such conversations can be quite effective in smoothing relationships and helping your child become a respected part of the family.

Taking Care of Yourself

As difficult as it can be at times, it is vital to do whatever you can to avoid letting all the issues you are dealing with interfere significantly with your own sense of competency and well-being. Temporary resentment and stress are inevitable in any challenging family situation, but it is best to just let these moments "roll over" you while doing what you can to address the underlying issues. If you are criticized for poor parenting or your child with ADHD fails to meet his behavior goals, try not to take it personally. Giving both of you credit for trying—and maintaining a sense of humor—can get you through many a difficult day. If you are feeling chronically anxious or depressed, be sure to talk with a psychologist or other mental health counselor. You may benefit from stress management techniques and "reframing" approaches similar to those you used to improve your child's understanding of his ADHD. For example, by re-framing the thought, "I handled that situation so poorly. It just goes to show what a terrible parent I am," to "I'm glad I reviewed the way I handled that. I can definitely find a better solution," you can transform thoughts that interfere with your functioning to thoughts that facilitate it.

You may also find it stressful at first to carry out some of the behavior management techniques that you will learn in Chapter 6—such as actively ignoring your child's undesirable behavior. Mental and physical relaxation or other techniques can help you learn to detach yourself emotionally in healthy ways during these times. For example, if you are about to react to a situation that you know you should really ignore, you can run through a "mental tape," telling yourself, "OK, stop....Relax....What are my choices?...What is my best response?" Reminding yourself to stop and relax, and to think about whether a particular response is the best way to accomplish your goal, can put some time and space between your impulse to react and your understanding of why you should ignore that particular behavior. This type of technique allows you to make better choices and set an example of sound behavior management for your child.

If you find that the stress of parenting a child with ADHD has caused problems in your relationship with your spouse or partner, do not hesitate to seek marital counseling to address any ongoing problems. Keep in mind that ignoring problematic issues rarely makes them go away. Your, and your partner's, physical and emotional health must remain top priority—not only for your child's sake, but also for your own.

Peer Relationships: Getting Along With Other Children

It can be painful to observe the insensitive ways in which children with ADHD are sometimes treated by their peers. Your child may long to be one of the popular kids and, while this may not be a fully realistic option, you can do a lot to help her make friends and work cooperatively with others. Social relationships are critical to address and important to long-term adjustment, but difficult to change. Social skills counseling or formal group instruction can often be ineffective because children with ADHD can find it difficult to transfer a skill that they have learned in therapy or in a class to their everyday school environment, unless they are given all the tools and ample opportunity to practice how to use them. Social skills programs offered at schools or in settings like intensive summer camp programs may be more effective because the child interacts in class with other children in the actual setting similar to those she encounters every day. The training is most successful if it allows the child to practice new skills first in the social skills class and then prompts her to use them in supervised natural settings, such as the playground—and also provides rewards for their appropriate use. Programs such as special therapeutic summer camps (see Chapter 7) for children with ADHD are particularly effective for teaching social skills and sports competencies that can improve peer relationships.

Your guidance within the context of your child's daily life will be an important tool in helping her improve social relationships. Many of the techniques that parents use with any child can be used in a more focused, deliberate way to help your child with ADHD. While all parents teach acceptable social behavior by modeling it themselves, you may want to be especially sure you are demonstrating certain skills, including using appropriate body language that you hope your child will learn everytime you interact with her. Narrating your behavior as you interact with your child can also set a good example ("Here, Joanie, I'll let you have a turn now. We get along better when we take turns.") and help your child focus on the issue at hand. Meanwhile, keep an eye out for—and strictly limit or eliminate—such negative social interactions as seen on violent television shows or computer or video games, violent behavior in other family members, and overaggressive playmates.

Older children can benefit from conversations about particular issues and from your interpreting social interactions as they happen. ("It makes me angry when you take food from my plate without asking. I feel like you don't respect my rights as a person. Now I'm going to ask you to put it back.") Many parents also find it helpful to reward their child's progress in targeted social interactions with stickers or other small rewards. Small fines or loss of privileges for violating important social rules may prove effective too.

Finally, one of the best ways to boost your child's self-esteem is to encourage her to participate in extracurricular social activities that are set up to foster positive peer relationships (such as Scouts, sports teams, and church youth groups). The key to your child's success in these extracurricular activities is to have them supervised by adults who are familiar with ADHD and know how to apply the principles of behavior therapy (see Chapter 6). Parents can be better and more effective soccer coaches for your child and all team members if they use effective behavior management techniques. Becoming part of a small group or team under these conditions can be a great morale booster as your child experiments with making friends in a safe, limited, supervised setting. Such groups can be especially effective if they involve an activity your child especially enjoys or is good at because she can then rely on her skill to help make up for any social weaknesses. Again, summer programs that focus on peer relationships and on sports skills can be particularly helpful in this regard. If your child is taking stimulant medication, she may find that the medication helps her considerably in controlling her impulsivity in these types of social situations and allows her to participate more fully. If her daily long-acting medication has worn off by the time her group activity begins, an extra short-term dose half an hour before the meeting begins may help her participate more fully.

Seeking Out Other Positive Relationships

Many children with ADHD have difficulty making friends among children their age. If you sense that your child feels lonely and isolated, even after trying some of the social skills techniques outlined previously, consider also the people in your community who might serve as positive role models, supportive mentors, or friends. An older teenager or adult who shares one or more of your child's interests and understands how his over-activity or impulsivity interfere with his social relationships can make a huge difference in his self-esteem by just listening care-fully and offering empathy and advice. Even if your child has a positive, supportive relationship with you, having another adult or older teenager in more of a mentor role can be quite beneficial, because this is a different kind of a relationship with a unique payoff. Search among your relatives and friends for a responsible person who might be willing to provide this sup-port for your child. If none are available, ask your local ADHD support group for leads or advice. Your religious institution, local social service agency, or mentoring organization (such as Big Brothers Big Sisters) may be another source of help.

Finally, keep in mind that your own presence means a great deal to your child—not just when engaged in practical activities but when both of you are free to just play or hang out together. Your supportive presence, sharing an activity or just talking, lets your child know that you love and like him and can help to balance social disappointment that he may have experienced elsewhere. Sometimes children with ADHD view their parents as the only people consistently in their corner. In addition to providing your child with social and emotional benefits, a close, positive relationship can make you a more effective reinforcer, leading to a decrease in disciplinary problems.

Being Your Child's Best Advocate

As you discover new ways to facilitate positive behaviors, learning, and self-esteem in your child, be sure to pass these techniques on to the other people in her life—adults in your household, other caregivers, relatives, teachers, and, when appropriate, even empathetic peers or siblings—so that they can help maintain the consistency, structure, and clarity your

child needs. If necessary, remind them that ADHD is a neu-
robehavioral disorder, not the result of poor discipline, and
that specific, consistent, positive techniques and attitudes can
help to improve a child's ability to manage her behavior. Show
caregivers and close relatives how to implement the techniques
you have learned and talk with them periodically about how
your child is responding and what if any changes they
have observed.

"One of the worst aspects of having ADHD for my daughter
was the fact that it seemed like no one else in our area had it,"
writes one mother living in a rural town in the Midwest. "The
other kids at school called her 'crazy' all the time, and I think
she really believed she would never be OK. Then, when she was
about nine, we got her a computer and linked her up to a cou-
ple of ADHD Web sites. She started reading some of the bul-
letin boards and 'personal stories' and also using some of the
'ask the experts' options. We made sure that the sites she visited
were responsible. After a while we saw her attitude really start to
change. Not only had she learned a lot of really valuable information about ADHD on the Internet, she also began to feel less
isolated and more supported. I don't know how she would have
gotten through junior high and high school without that computer. Those resources gave her the confidence she needed to
get through school."

The symptoms of ADHD can seem so overwhelming at first
that many parents fear there is nothing they can do to provide
substantial help for their child. Yet while it is true that treating
ADHD and managing its symptoms requires time, patience, and
a great deal of attention, the benefits can be enormous to family
functioning and family relations. Attending treatment review
meetings with your child's pediatrician, implementing behavior
therapy techniques, talking with your child about the challenges
she experiences, and providing her with resources may seem like

tiny steps on the road to better functioning, but together they really do have a positive impact. Children, who naturally want most of all to be like every other child, often tend to resist thinking about or wanting to address the issues that ADHD symptoms impose. Therefore it is up to you to provide your child with the services she needs, the extras that can so greatly improve her daily life, and the support and education she needs to see them as useful tools for her. For your entire family's sake as well as your child's, keep yourself aware of the latest research on ADHD, engage your child's teachers in her evaluation and treatment plan, and do what you can to help your child learn to recognize her own strengths and manage her own targeted problems. With the help and guidance of physicians, a therapist, counselors, teachers, and other professional advisors, you can make an enormous difference in your child's life. Adults with ADHD successfully attend college, marry, have families, and enjoy fulfilling careers—thanks in large part to the parents who took the time and made the effort to help them navigate their journey.

Q & A

Q: *My nine-year-old son was recently diagnosed with ADHD. He seems to be responding well to treatment and discussions of what ADHD is and how he can work to manage his problems. However, his older sister, who is thirteen, has responded to the news much more negatively. She resists going anywhere with the family where she might be seen by classmates in the company of her brother. At home, she calls him "weird" and yells at him to stay away from her and her friends. I understand that it can be difficult for an adolescent to deal with anything "different" about her family, but her behavior is rude and is damaging to my son's self-esteem, hard as we are working to build it up. What can we do to persuade our daughter to be more supportive of her brother?*

A: It may help to look at a situation like this as a kind of blessing in disguise because it gives you an opportunity to work with your daughter on general issues relating to sensitivity to others, respect for family members' rights and feelings, and acceptance of the challenges that each person must face, as well as issues directly related to ADHD. As you are already doing with your son, your daughter needs to be educated regarding what ADHD is and is not, which of your son's behaviors are typical of children with ADHD and which are just part of normal sibling conflicts, and how her responses can help him achieve better self-control and improve general family functioning. If you have not already spoken directly with your daughter about these issues, be sure to do so—you might do some of this in the context of a "family meeting." Your family may also benefit from one or more sessions with a family therapist, or from a support group for families of children with ADHD that may help your daughter understand that the problems that she faces with her brother are common and provide her with positive approaches for interacting with her brother.

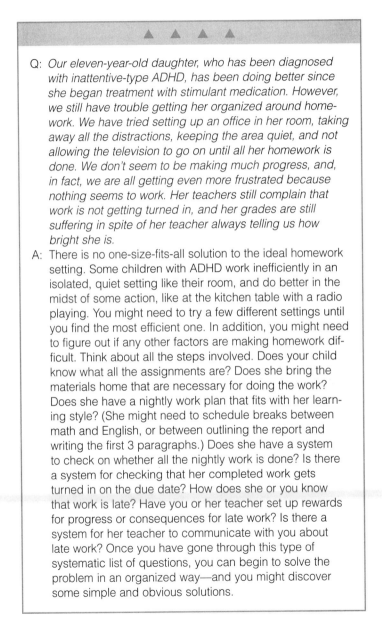

Q: *Our eleven-year-old daughter, who has been diagnosed with inattentive-type ADHD, has been doing better since she began treatment with stimulant medication. However, we still have trouble getting her organized around home-work. We have tried setting up an office in her room, taking away all the distractions, keeping the area quiet, and not allowing the television to go on until all her homework is done. We don't seem to be making much progress, and, in fact, we are all getting even more frustrated because nothing seems to work. Her teachers still complain that work is not getting turned in, and her grades are still suffering in spite of her teacher always telling us how bright she is.*

A: There is no one-size-fits-all solution to the ideal homework setting. Some children with ADHD work inefficiently in an isolated, quiet setting like their room, and do better in the midst of some action, like at the kitchen table with a radio playing. You might need to try a few different settings until you find the most efficient one. In addition, you might need to figure out if any other factors are making homework dif-ficult. Think about all the steps involved. Does your child know what all the assignments are? Does she bring the materials home that are necessary for doing the work? Does she have a nightly work plan that fits with her learn-ing style? (She might need to schedule breaks between math and English, or between outlining the report and writing the first 3 paragraphs.) Does she have a system to check on whether all the nightly work is done? Is there a system for checking that her completed work gets turned in on the due date? How does she or you know that work is late? Have you or her teacher set up rewards for progress or consequences for late work? Is there a system for her teacher to communicate with you about late work? Once you have gone through this type of systematic list of questions, you can begin to solve the problem in an organized way—and you might discover some simple and obvious solutions.

CHAPTER SIX

Behavior Therapy:
Parenting Techniques That Work

▲　▲　▲　▲

"It was difficult to understand at first why my parenting approach had so little effect with my youngest, Suzanne, who has ADHD," a mother writes. "I treated her the same way I treated all my other kids, but it seemed like every time I figured out how to help her change her behavior in a positive direction she'd fall back into her old habits before the week was up. She was also a lot angrier and more defiant than her older sisters. By the time she was diagnosed with ADHD, I was at my wits' end. Nothing I tried with her—talking, rewarding, punishing— seemed to work. It was only after I took the parent training course recommended by her pediatrician that I started to understand why my approaches were not effective and how she and I could work together to shape her behavior."

Many parents share this mother's dismay on discovering that their child with attention-deficit/hyperactivity disorder (ADHD) does not respond to parenting techniques they used successfully with their other children. The failure to comply with family rules or expectations can be especially upsetting because it leads others to assume that a child's behavior is due to faulty parenting rather than a diagnosed condition. Your negative experiences with your child may convince you that she is unable to understand or to remember your instructions and therefore can never improve her behavior.

In fact, your child with ADHD is able to comprehend and retain what you tell her, just as her siblings are. But because she has difficulties with the ability to control her actions, organize her thoughts, think before she acts, or create a plan of action and follow through, she may not be able to *perform* in a way she knows is correct. She may understand, for example, that it is not right to interrupt you repeatedly while you are talking on the phone, or to wander away when you are talking to her, but be unable to stop herself. The way she operates may seem more like, "ready...fire...aim!"—she thinks about the rules after she has already broken them instead of before. This is why the parenting approaches that worked with your other children are often ineffective. Again, it is not that your child does not know what the appropriate behaviors are, it is just hard for her to carry them out.

At present, behavior therapy, a form of therapy taught to parents as *behavioral parent training,* has been proven to be reliably effective in moving children with ADHD from understanding appropriate behavior to actually functioning in more positive ways. This form of therapy focuses on teaching parents and other caregivers *specific behavior management techniques* based on

- Concentrating on your child's behaviors instead of her feelings or emotions
- Changing her behavior through providing her with new learning experiences and giving her a chance to watch you model appropriate behavior
- Emphasizing how to evaluate problem behaviors
- Having the plan carried out at home and school by you and other people in your child's everyday life instead of in an office with a therapist

Parent training's emphasis on ways in which adults can better manage and shape their child's behavior differs from other approaches that focus directly on the child and are designed to change her emotional status (such as traditional psychotherapy) or patterns of thinking (such as cognitive-behavioral therapy). These latter approaches have not been found consistently helpful in the treatment of ADHD. In this chapter, you will be introduced to the principles underlying behavior therapy for families of children with ADHD. You will learn

- What behavior therapy consists of, who it is for, and where it is available
- Which specific parenting techniques have been found to be effective in improving children's functioning and how they must be implemented
- How the gains achieved through behavior therapy techniques can be preserved

As you will learn, behavior therapy techniques are often taught in highly structured 8- to 12-week individual or group parent training sessions by therapists or specially trained teachers, usually consisting of one session per week. Such courses have been shown to be effective for families with ADHD because they allow for weekly feedback—letting parents ask questions and receive helpful advice from the instructor as they are learning to implement the techniques—and may offer parents the chance to share their experiences with others in similar situations. Unfortunately, while parent training is now available in many communities, it may not be in yours, or may be available but not be covered by your insurance plan. Even if this is the case, by reading the material in this chapter you should be able to apply many of these principles in your daily interactions with your child. You may find it even more useful to work with a child therapist or your child's pediatrician to adapt these techniques to your own unique situation even if it is not in the exact systematic approach described here.

This chapter will provide you with a description of the basic behavior management techniques common to nearly all behavior therapy parent training programs—materials that you can use for reference and reassurance as you introduce these behavior therapy principles into your family's life.

What Is Behavior Therapy, Who Is It For, and Where Is It Available?

Simply put, behavior therapy parent training consists of a set of practical, tested procedures designed to provide you with the strategies you need to improve family interactions and your child's ability to manage his behavior. Parent training is just that—a program aimed at training you, the parents, to success-fully manage and shape your child's behavior. By focusing less on the child's emotional state and more on his actual behaviors, it attempts to turn parents into their child's "therapist" by teach-ing them how to encourage positive behaviors, determine which behaviors can be actively ignored, and know when and how to set and enforce rules. All forms of behavior therapy, including parent training, share a common set of principles and offer an array of techniques that can be combined in different ways to help increase a child's abilities for self-regulation. A sound parent training program should help you to

- Gain a better understanding of what behaviors are normal for your child.
- Learn to achieve consistent and positive interactions.
- Cut down on negative interactions such as arguing or constantly having to repeat instructions.
- Provide appropriate consequences for your child's behavior.
- Become more empathic of your child's viewpoint.
- Help your child improve his abilities to manage his own behaviors.

Who Benefits Most From Behavior Therapy?

In most cases, the younger your child is, the more successful a behavior therapy program is likely to be because it is easier to change negative behaviors that have not been in place for very long. (Still, even teenagers can benefit from a sound and consistent behavioral approach. See Chapter 10.) Because behavioral parent training requires sufficient verbal skills for your child to understand what you are telling her, and to discuss her present behavior patterns and the plan for behavior change, it usually is not recommended for families until the child is at least preschool-aged. Children who have more serious conduct problems may need additional professional help, or a different type of help, to improve their functioning.

As was pointed out in Chapter 3, behavior therapy may be most effective in some situations when it is used along with stimulant medication that allows the child to fully attend to the techniques being introduced. Combining medication management with behavior therapy can, in many cases, modestly but significantly increase the chances that parents and teachers will regard a child's behavior as comparable to that of children who do not have ADHD. While your own child's behavior may not necessarily fall within the "totally average" range for her age group as a result of parent training, even small improvements can make a big difference. Whether your child is taking medication, behavior therapy may help improve your relationship with her. Parents and children report greater satisfaction when behavior therapy is included in their overall treatment plan, and in some cases the benefits of parent training include being able to reduce the dose of stimulant medication needed to achieve targeted behavioral goals. An additional benefit to parent training is that the principles work well for all children in the family, not just for children with ADHD, and adopting a parenting approach that uses these techniques can lead to better overall family relationships.

Coexisting Conditions and Family Issues

If your child has been diagnosed with ADHD and other co-existing conditions, his pediatrician will help you determine the behavioral treatment priorities for your child based on his individual needs. For example, if your child has been diagnosed with ADHD and also has anxiety, either behavior therapy or medication management may lead to similar gains. However, children with ADHD, anxiety, and oppositional and defiant or conduct disorder (see Chapter 8) may benefit more from combined treatment that includes both medication and behavior therapy than medication alone. Children with coexisting pervasive developmental disorders (including autism) or severe depression may require different medication management and a different type of behavioral treatment plan. The kind of parent training described in this chapter may not be appropriate in these situations.

Ideally, at the time that your child was diagnosed with ADHD, any coexisting disorders were also identified. Keep in mind, though, that certain conditions may escape notice early on or only surface at a later time. If your child exhibits symptoms that make you suspect he has a disruptive behavior disorder, depression, or anxiety—if he loses his temper frequently; is deliberately destructive; responds violently when disciplined; or frequently lies, steals, or otherwise violates societal norms, or seems excessively sad or anxious—discuss your concerns with his pediatrician. It may be necessary to reconsider his diagnosis and to change his treatment plan accordingly.

Family circumstances may also affect your ability to make gains using behavior therapy techniques. If communication among members of your family is extremely difficult, you are experiencing serious marital problems, or family members are struggling with multiple, major issues including any form of family violence, parent training may not work for you. In these circumstances, meeting with a psychotherapist for family therapy may be a more helpful strategy.

Where Can I Find a Parent Training Program?

If behavioral parent training programs exist in your community and are covered by your health insurance, your child's pediatrician can point you toward an appropriate resource. Check to be sure that the therapist or training leader is a qualified mental health or other medical professional and that the program follows a systematic format adapted specifically for parents of children with ADHD. The best programs are evidence-based—they have already been found effective through carefully conducted research. While less standardized parent training programs may be available, they are not as likely to be as helpful for families dealing with ADHD.

As you will learn in Chapter 7, some schools have been able to fund and train their teachers in the use of behavior therapy techniques. If your child's teacher is able to participate in such courses, she and your child would probably benefit enormously. By participating in parent training with your partner and sharing behavior therapy strategies with your child's other caregivers (including her teacher), you can help others support your child's efforts to meet the target outcomes that you and her treatment team have identified.

If no formal parent training programs are presently available in your community, you can still apply these principles to the specifics of your own situation, and may be able to use the information in this chapter to advocate for the development of these services through your child's pediatrician, your school system, or other local agencies or support groups. Take the time to review the information that follows in this chapter, and think about the ways in which you may be able to incorporate these practices into your daily life with your child.

Behavior Therapy: The Specifics of Parent Training

Research confirms that behavioral parent training programs are valuable tools to help parents guide, support, and live more comfortably with their children with ADHD. They are considered by the American Academy of Pediatrics to be a first-line treatment approach for children with ADHD. Following are brief descriptions of some of the topics and techniques that parent training programs introduce through direct instruction, demonstrations, role playing, readings, discussions, and "homework assignments" that parents can use with their own child.

Setting the Stage for Positive Learning: Learning How to Play or "Hang Out" With Your Child

Behavior therapy is not just about a child's behavior, but about improving the relationships between a child and his parents (as well as others) and the interactions within the family. As a parent, you can take the first step toward improved relationships by understanding how discouraging your child's daily experiences can be to him and by countering that negativity with positive messages and support. Your child needs to know that you are not only interested in helping him adjust his behavior, but that you also appreciate him as a person and enjoy just being with him. Feeling that you are there for him, ready to listen, empathize, and help him recover from the many setbacks he encounters will set the stage for the most effective implementation of parent training principles. So before beginning "training" techniques, you must make an effort to befriend your child and show him that you are members of the same team.

Many experts in behavior therapy, including Dr Russell Barkley (see Resources), suggest that a good way to do this is to make a point of regularly and frequently spending time playing with your younger child, or hanging out with your older one, with no one else present. During this time, your goal is not to teach your child anything or to shape his behavior. It is to let him know that you are interested in him and want to spend time getting to know him better. This can be accomplished by announcing that from now on you will reserve time during several days each week to be with your child (his other parent should do the same) and, during this time, allow him to decide on the activity (any activity that allows the 2 of you to interact is fine—playing with board games or dolls for example, but not watching television or playing organized sports). While you are involved in the activity, allow your child to take the lead. Comment occasionally to show you are paying attention and are involved, and provide positive feedback now and then, but do not try to take over the activity or conversation. The point is to simply be with your child—to let him be the center of your attention and to show you his world. By regularly participating in these activities with your child you are learning to *listen* and *observe* while avoiding constantly giving commands or instructions—the first skills necessary to begin reshaping his behavior and changing his relationships within the family. You are also demonstrating in the most effective way possible that your child does not need to engage in negative behaviors to win your attention. Once he learns he has his parents' interest, he can rely on this in trusting them to help him figure out how to get along better and develop more positive relationships with others.

Responding Effectively to Your Child's Behavior

Once you and your child have begun to establish a basis of trust and positive support, it is time to look at the ways you hope to improve your interactions with him at home. Parent interactions can be improved, and improved interactions can set the stage for the successful use of parent training tools and techniques. One of the first principles of parent training is to expand the notion of the word *discipline.* Many parents assume that the term refers to ways to carry out effective punishment.

However, teaching discipline to a child really means teaching self-control—and that is the broad goal of parent training. Fortunately, behavior therapy programs take a more positive approach than just constantly devising punishments for breaking rules. As your child's "teacher-coach-therapist," you will learn how to choose the most effective response to any given situation. In most cases, you will find that you have 3 choices when confronted with a particular behavior in your child: you can *praise* the behavior, deliberately *ignore* it, or *punish* your child for it. Behavior therapy is about deciding correctly which response to choose, following up on that decision, and being consistent about your choices from one event, and one day, to the next.

Of course, it is not always easy to decide whether a behavior deserves to be ignored or punished, and it is not always obvious when and how to provide praise. These and other topics will be discussed in this chapter. In the meantime, though, it is important to consider how much more powerful and, in most cases, preferable positive reinforcement and ignoring are to punishment, even though in the heat of the moment this may

▲ ▲ ▲ ▲

THREE BASIC RULES
WHEN RESPONDING TO YOUR CHILD'S BEHAVIOR

Many parents making use of behavior therapy techniques find it helpful to rely on the following simple rules when interacting with their child:

- If you want to see a behavior continue, praise it.
- If you do not like a behavior but it is not dangerous or intolerable, ignore it.
- If you have to stop a behavior that is dangerous or intolerable (for instance, your child's hitting a sibling to hurt her, not just to get your attention), punish it.

go against your instincts or intuition. It may help to think about how much more likely you are to work hard when your boss recognizes and praises your efforts, and how poorly motivated and resentful you may feel if he frequently criticizes you. In the same way, your child is more likely to respond positively to your actions if you react positively to his, while a negative comment or response on your part is likely to lead to more negative behavior. This is why in behavioral parent training, parents are encouraged to praise their child's behavior whenever possible, and ignore it when necessary, as a strong way of shaping behavior while minimizing the need for punishment.

Giving Clear Commands

The first step in helping your child learn to follow rules, obey your commands, and otherwise manage her own behavior is to make sure that the commands you are giving her are clear. Adults are often accustomed to couching their commands in a variety of "softening" or ambiguous gestures and phrases. Many of us also tend to react too strongly or impulsively to behavior we consider unacceptable. But children with ADHD need to be told what to do in a clear, straightforward, and nonemotional way if they are to learn to control their actions. You can give effective commands by

- **Minimizing distractions.** Turn off the television or computer game before you address your child, or ask her to turn it off. If you are in a noisy setting, try to move to a quieter place before speaking to her. Most children with ADHD find it difficult to pay attention when surrounded by a lot of competing noise or activity.

- **Establishing good eye contact.** You must fully engage your child's attention by making good eye contact if she is going to hear and follow what you say. At first, you may find it helpful to touch a younger child's arm or hold her hand before addressing her.

- **Clearly stating the command.** You can make commands
  clear to your child by first stating what therapists call a
  terminating command—a simple, nonemotional statement
  of what you want your child to do ("You need to stop
  pushing your brother."). If the behavior does not stop
  immediately, you can then follow up with a *warning* that
  includes the exact limit and the consequences ("If you push
  your brother one more time, you'll be in time-out. If you
  stop immediately the two of you can go on playing."). When
  stating a command, keep your tone of voice firm and neutral. Refrain from yelling, or looking or sounding angry. It
  is especially important to monitor your body language
  because these nonverbal messages are so easy to overlook.
  State the command as an instruction, not as a question
  (Not, "Would you please stop teasing your brother?" or
  "Stop teasing him, OK?" but "You need to stop teasing
  your brother.").

If you are not sure your child heard the terminating command or warning, ask her to repeat it back to you. Then pay
attention to how well she carries out your instructions and
respond immediately to her behavior. If she responds as you
have asked, follow this up with a positive—praise, thanks, a
thumbs-up, or other acknowledgment that she has done well.
If her response is not exactly what you had hoped for but is in
the right direction, offer her immediate praise for the part of
your command that she did carry out. If your child does not
start to cooperate according to the limits you have set ("one
more time" or "within the next two minutes") invoke the consequences, calmly narrating what is happening as you do so.
("You did not stop pushing your brother, so you are having
the five-minute time-out that we just talked about.") Keep in
mind that because you have given a warning and a terminating

command and spelled out the consequences of disobeying, you have not "put her in" the time-out—she has "chosen" the time-out for herself as an alternative to following your command.

If you make a point of following through on the positive or negative consequences of *each* command, every time, you should soon find that you will not have to repeat your instructions over and over as you probably did before. Your ultimate goal will be to give a command only once for it to be obeyed. The elimination of constant pleading, nagging, or threatening is a great relief to most parents and goes a long way toward improving your interaction with your child. If you are tempted to "let it slide" when she ignores a command (telling yourself, perhaps, that she *does* have ADHD, after all), consider how hard it will be to make up for this inconsistency in the future and carry out the promised consequences. If you are going to try to follow up on every command you give, you will need to consider beforehand how important the command you are about to give is. Limiting the number of commands you give will make it easier for you to follow up on each and every one, thus increasing your chances of success.

At first, as you practice giving commands according to these guidelines, you will need to keep things simple. Make sure that all your commands are achievable by your child, and wait until your child has completed one step of your instructions before giving another. If necessary, break a complex command down into smaller steps ("Take off your shoes. Good job! Now take off your socks."). While your child is carrying out your instructions, avoid distracting her. Be sure to follow up on each command, avoid giving commands unless you mean for her to follow them (do not tell her to go to bed until it is really time), and stick to commands that you know can be carried out successfully by your child. It is usually best to give a time limit ("by the third time," "by three minutes") for each command as well, to help her focus on accomplishing it and to help you both define when it has or has not been accomplished. Keep in mind, however, that children with ADHD often have particular problems with time awareness and time limits. You will need to keep such limits simple, and consider using egg timers or other devices to make these time limits more concrete. By doing so, you can turn commands that have previously ended in failure and frustration ("Go upstairs and clean your room.") to commands that end in success and build on your child's self-esteem ("Put your video game player away by the time this bell goes off in three minutes.").

Shaping Behaviors Gradually: Small Steps in the Right Direction Add Up

Children with ADHD, like all of us, will probably have particular difficulty changing a complex or long-standing set of behaviors. Expecting your child to make a major behavioral change all at once will most likely result in frustration and failure for you both. As mentioned previously, you can support your child's efforts to change a complex set of behaviors by breaking the plan down into smaller, achievable steps, and tackling one at a time. This is called "shaping" your child's behavior. The idea is to break down tasks to the point at which each step is achievable and ends in success and praise for your child instead of failure and frustration. Parent training will help you learn to do this by having you review the targeted outcomes for your child and ways you can help him achieve them. You as parents (or other primary caregivers) can start by writing down what you see as each step toward completing a task or correcting a complex behavior and follow up by creating a plan for working on each step, one at a time. You can incorporate your child in the development of each plan at the level that he can appropriately participate. Even minor goals can be broken down in this way—

writing down the steps involved in completing a chore, for example, you might list the steps that your child needs to take in cleaning up his room as

- Puts dirty clothes in a hamper
- Puts books away
- Puts toys in the drawers under his bed
- Pulls up the covers

Then you can start with a single command—"You need to start cleaning up your room by putting the dirty clothes in the hamper." When this is done successfully, you can praise him— "Good job!" If you had just said, "You need to clean your room," and he *had* put his clothes in the hamper, but not put his books and toys away and pulled up the covers, he would not have been successful and you would have ended up making a negative remark or giving a consequence. At the point that putting his clothes in the hamper when you ask becomes automatic, then, after a few days, you can add the next step—putting the clothes in the hamper *and* putting his books away, praising him for the successful completion. When this is successful you can add the next task, and so on, until the list is complete. In this way you can "shape his behavior" and at the same time turn what used to be negative interactions into positive ones that build on his self-esteem and competence. You can help your child learn to focus better and accomplish tasks more quickly by timing certain tasks as well and encouraging him to try to break his own speed record again and again. Such small triumphs can mean a great deal to children who have experienced repeated failure or frustration at home or at school. Behavior shaping techniques also heighten your child's awareness of each successful step, helping him to "own" his behavioral successes.

Choosing What to Praise, Ignore, or Punish

The next step in parent training is learning to recognize behaviors that require positive, ignoring, or punishment-type responses. You will be encouraged to do your best to "catch your child being good" and praise her for it whenever possible because this allows for positive interaction and enhances her relationship with you as it strengthens her positive behaviors. Praise should be simple and straightforward ("I like the way you did that."), and not spoiled by negative references ("Great job—why can't you always do it like that?"). In many cases a simple smile, hug, or an arm around your child's shoulders is even more effective than words. Such immediate positive reinforcement is actually a much stronger (and less risky) way to change behavior than larger, long-term rewards, such as the offer of a video game system for maintaining all Bs or staying on the honor roll all semester. However, you may still decide to offer your child stickers, points in a token reward system, or other prizes for putting in the effort to help change behaviors you are working on.

"Active ignoring" is one of the most powerful behavioral tools available to parents, but one of the hardest to carry out. Once you give a command, you must follow it through to the end if it is going to be effective and meaningful to your child. Many parents are in the habit of giving frequent corrections all through the day, and then either do not follow through on many of them or dole out so many punishments that they become ineffective and set up a negative relationship with their child. Learning how to actively ignore certain situations can lead to many fewer commands and significantly improve this situation.

In fact, you may be surprised at how effective ignoring a negative behavior can be. This is especially true once your child has grown accustomed to the positive attention she enjoys in your special times together and no longer needs to demand your attention in negative ways. A child who interrupts your phone conversations over and over is, in most cases, only doing it to get your attention. If you respond by saying something like, "Sarah, I'm on the phone—wait until I get off!" you may think you are giving a command to stop the behavior but you are actually rewarding her by giving her the attention she wanted in the first place. If, instead, you ignore her behavior (by not looking at her or responding in words), her attempts to distract you while you are on the phone may escalate at first, while she tries even harder to get the attention that she is used to. This is what behavior therapists call an "extinction burst"—the behavior gets worse before it gets better. However, if you consistently ignore her, she will gradually learn more functional ways to have her needs met. In this way, ignoring works as a powerful tool for behavior change. A good proportion of behavior problems can be addressed with a combination of praising and ignoring techniques.

As part of a typical parent training program, you will identify the few behaviors that you consider so dangerous (running into the street without looking, for example) or intolerable (hitting other children to hurt them) that they must meet with immediate punishment. Your therapist will teach you how to discuss these behaviors with your child, figure out the punishments that will follow, and figure out possible ways to avoid the same situation in the future. He will help you understand how much more effective punishment can be if it is limited to only your child's most dangerous or intolerable behaviors. When punishment occurs too frequently (as it often does for children with ADHD), its effects are diminished and the child may no longer consistently respond to it. In addition, most parents do not realize that *negative attention can be reinforcing,* and, because of this, negative consequences should be reserved for those few instances when parents feel they must do something immediately (and not just ignore). Any punishment should be preceded, whenever possible, by a terminating and a warning signal. That way your child will always have the opportunity to exert self-control and avoid the punishment.

No matter what your response to your child's behavior, it will be most effective if it takes place immediately. Putting off a discussion until later, or offering a reward at the end of the week for general good behavior, will greatly diminish its effect on a child with ADHD. The response you have chosen to a particular behavior should be as consistent as possible as well. If you responded appropriately to your child's pushing her brother down with punishment yesterday, respond in the same way today. Your parent training therapist will help you decide in advance on the best responses to your child's most frequent behavior issues so you can carry out these actions with confidence.

Using Rewards to Motivate Positive Behavior

Praise is a powerful motivator for all children, but many also especially enjoy and respond to additional, tangible motivators such as reward charts and token economies. Reward charts usually consist of daily calendar sheets listing 4 or 5 achievable chores, behaviors, or other goals on which you and your child have agreed. Before instituting the reward chart with your child, you will have observed your child enough to know that he can successfully complete most of the behaviors listed. The description of each behavior needs to be clear, countable, and unambiguous (for example, "is upstairs brushing his teeth within 5 minutes after being told" or "gets out of bed by the third time he's asked"). You might have 5 items on a chart—4 of which are easily achievable by your child with an additional 1 that you are presently working on. Charts can be reviewed daily, and this becomes a time to let your child know how proud of him you are for working on his chores or behavior. If too many of the items are not achievable and do not end up with stars or stickers, your child will get easily frustrated and negative about participating. Each time your child accomplishes the goal he receives a sticker, a star, or other mark of achievement on the chart. Many younger children are happy enough just to receive the stickers or stars themselves, but some older children may want to accumulate numbers of stars or stickers and redeem them for privileges—such as a trip to a baseball game or to the beach, or modest, prearranged material rewards. These rewards do not need to be new privileges. What you are really doing is putting some of his everyday privileges under his behavioral control, knowing in advance that he will experience success.

The table on page 140 summarizes some of the key concepts described in this section.

▲ ▲ ▲ ▲

EFFECTIVE BEHAVIORAL TECHNIQUES FOR CHILDREN WITH ATTENTION-DEFICIT/HYPERACTIVITY DISORDER

Technique	Description	Example
Positive reinforcement	Providing rewards or privileges dependent on the child's performance.	Child completes an assignment and is permitted to play on the computer.
Time-out	Removing access to positive reinforcement contingent on performance of unwanted or problem behavior.	Child hits sibling impulsively and is required to sit for 5 minutes in the corner of the room.
Response cost	Withdrawing rewards or privileges contingent on the performance of unwanted or problem behavior.	Child loses free-time privileges for not completing homework.
Token economy	The child earns rewards and privileges contingent on performing desired behaviors. This type of positive reinforcement can be combined with response cost, where a child can also lose the rewards and privileges based on undesirable behavior.	Child earns stars for completing assignments and loses stars for getting out of seat. The child cashes in the sum of stars at the end of the week for a prize.

Another type of reward system, called a token economy, also involves receiving tokens, stars, stickers, or points for behaving appropriately or complying with commands. Token economies are similar to reward charts in that they can often be helpful when praise alone is not enough to motivate a child to complete tasks or stick to routines. The gains from using a token economy approach can often be seen quickly, but can also fade unless this kind of system is kept up for some time. Each targeted behavior is given a value (3 stickers, 4 points) depending on how difficult a challenge it is for your child. You and your child can then create a list of fun activities or treats that he can "buy" with a prearranged number of stickers or points. Response cost—the withdrawing of rewards or privileges in response to unwanted or problem behavior—can be eventually added onto this system if necessary. In that case, your child's failure to accomplish a targeted behavior on his own or after an agreed-on limit results in the same number of stickers or points being deducted from his total. Before response cost is introduced, you need to make sure your child is earning tokens and has "bought into" the token economy plan. Make sure that you see it as motivating and that your child sees it as fun. Otherwise, it will become a frustrating exercise to your child and therefore useless as a strategy.

Reward charts and token economies are good ways to help motivate children to take responsibility for their own behavioral improvement when praise alone has not been effective enough. They also help parents facilitate these gains in structured, positive, consistent, and objective ways. These techniques work especially well when the rewards for compliance are immediate (getting the tokens as soon as possible after complying, and going on the earned and agreed-on trip to the beach within a week). Their effectiveness is also enhanced when your child gets the opportunity to help create the list of goals, assigned value of each behavior, and rewards that follow satisfactory compliance. It is also best to do what you can to keep point deductions to a minimum (by breaking tasks up into reasonable steps and not expecting too much too soon) so that your child does not become too discouraged and give up. Some children do not start to warm up to token economies until they have experienced one or more of the promised "big rewards," so be sure to continue the technique for 1 or more months—as long as your child does not become too frustrated or resistant—before deciding whether it is useful for him. Keeping his goals achievable and the program positive will go a long way toward making this approach successful.

Using Punishment Effectively

No one likes to invoke negative consequences for unacceptable behavior, but doing so calmly and consistently is a necessary part of helping your child learn new ways of functioning. At first it can be difficult to decide when punishment is appropriate because it is easy to attribute much of your child's failure to manage some of her behaviors appropriately to "her ADHD." Refusal to obey, when it does occur along with ADHD, *can* be greatly reduced with effective parenting techniques.

When parents think about "discipline" and punishment, they often think about spanking (without causing physical injury) as a way to reduce or stop undesirable behavior. Many studies have shown that spanking is, however, a less effective strategy than time-out or removal of privileges for achieving these goals. In addition, spanking models aggressive behavior as a solution to conflict, and can lead to agitated or aggressive behavior, physical injury, or resentment toward parents and deterioration of parent-child relationships. The use of spanking as a strategy for punishment is discouraged by most experts and organizations, including the American Academy of Pediatrics.

Time-outs and loss of privileges are the 2 forms of punishment that have been proven most effective for children with ADHD. They are appropriate tools for responding to the few behaviors you have identified as intolerable. Time-outs, most often used with younger children, involve sending your child to a specified room (with no entertaining distractions and a door that can be closed) or chair (where you can see her) until the end of a preset time—usually about 1 minute per year of the child's age (usually 5–10 minutes). Before instituting time-outs, you must discuss your intention with your child, explaining that they will be the consequence of violating the family's most important rules. Explain that you will always give a terminating command ("Give your brother's toy back.") and a warning ("If you don't give it back within one minute you'll be in time-out.") before you impose a time-out, so that your child will always be able to choose to avoid it by changing her behavior on the spot. Keeping in mind the difficulty with time perception that some children experience, tell your child that you will use a timer to measure the length of the time-out, and demonstrate to her how the timer works.

Once your child understands how time-outs will work, you can begin to implement them when appropriate. When your child displays an unacceptable behavior

- Warn her that a time-out will occur if she does not respond to your warning in a specific amount of time ("Anna, stop pushing your sister. If you haven't stopped by the time I count to three, you will have a time-out.").
- If she does not comply in the specified time, firmly but calmly send her to the time-out setting. Do not give her more time to comply or let her engage you in any distracting interaction.
- Tell her how many minutes the time-out will last, set a timer, and leave her alone—do not start negotiating whether she can get out earlier, or avoid going in. Some experts suggest adding another minute to the time-out each time your child leaves the time-out space or is disruptive, then allowing her out at the end of that time if she is quiet and cooperative.
- When she has completed the time-out process, make a point of praising her next positive behavior so that the negative "punishment" experience is fully ended.

Be prepared for a great deal of resistance the first few times when time-outs occur. Soon, however, your child will learn that you are remaining consistent; that resisting, arguing, or negotiating no longer work; and that it is better to change the original behavior and avoid the time-out altogether. Meanwhile, remember that the goal is for your child to focus on *staying out* of time-outs rather than *getting out* of them once she has "chosen" to take the time-out rather than complying with your request to stop an unacceptable behavior. Remember also that "time-out" is time out from "time in"—meaning that the only reason your child will care if she gets a time-out is if she is used to loving, positive, and fun family interactions that will be missed during the time-out period. By supporting your child

in these positive ways while sticking to the rules you have created, you can help your child learn to control her behavior and
respect your fair and consistent authority.

Loss of privileges, a more appropriate negative consequence
for older children and teenagers, consists of invoking a "cost"
for intolerable behavior. If your child breaks a family rule or
ignores a command after a pre–agreed-on number of warnings,
privileges are removed for a time appropriate to the seriousness
of the transgression. This technique works best if your child has
participated in decisions about exactly which behaviors will
merit a loss of privileges and agrees in advance to some prenegotiated penalties. It is also a good idea to try to relate the
penalty as closely as possible to the transgression. Your child's
failure to complete her homework, for example, may cost her
television privileges the next day, while a teenager's failure to
return home after curfew may cause her to lose car privileges
for the weekend.

If you find that your child continues to strongly resist
time-outs or loss of privileges while continuing the negative
behaviors, consider the way in which you are implementing
these techniques. If you have been giving in to her resistance—
allowing her out of the time-out area if she yells and kicks long
enough, or letting her negotiate you out of a loss-of-privilege
punishment—she will have learned that resistance allows her to
have her way. If you have been enforcing the rules sometimes,
but not every time, she may not be able to resist testing your
responses on every occasion to learn what you will do this time.
If you have successfully carried out an effective punishment
procedure but neglected to add praise afterward and at other
times during the day, your child may have decided she will
never be able to succeed and give up trying. These are the reasons why it is so important to remain calm, firm, and consistent while invoking a punishment and to follow up as soon as

possible with reassuring praise.

Managing Your Child's Behavior in Public

With proper training and practice, behavior therapy techniques can become relatively simple to implement at home, where a time-out area is clearly identified and it is possible to respond immediately to unacceptable behavior. Parents are often most disturbed by intolerable behavior when it occurs in public, however, because they feel that other adults—who do not know that their child has ADHD and have no idea how much progress he has already made—are negatively judging their child and their parenting skills. In any case, children with ADHD need to learn to manage their behavior wherever they are, so it is important to establish methods for implementing disciplinary techniques outside the home.

The most effective behavior management methods for use in public are the same ones you have developed with your child at home. If he is already familiar with the standard costs for certain types of behavior, you may need only remind him privately before you enter the new environment which 2 or 3 behavior rules he most needs to keep in mind, what rewards will result from his following them, and what the cost will be for breaking these rules. To help him maintain his efforts to comply, praise his positive behaviors occasionally during the outing and let him know you appreciate how hard he is trying to follow the rules—"catch him being good." If he manages to control his behavior throughout the entire period, acknowledge the difficulty of this feat and give him special praise. If you have also offered a reward, then provide it as soon as possible.

If your child refuses or fails to behave acceptably, even after a final warning, you will need to invoke the appropriate negative consequence. Do not delay just because you are among other people—delay will probably just lead to increased misbehavior. You can enforce token economy "fines" or removal of privileges

practically anywhere (as long as you keep your conversation private), but you may need to talk with your therapist ahead of time about how you might implement them discreetly yet effectively at the supermarket, your friend's house, church, or wherever you expect to be.

Your child needs your competent handling of rewards and limits as he practices new behavioral rules in public, but he also needs your thoughtful planning if he is to successfully maintain his best self-control in these situations. Planning in advance can make all the difference in his ability to control his restlessness and stay focused. Whenever you take him along on errands, to a restaurant or friend's house, or for a trip—even across town— be sure to pack some activities to keep him happily occupied (activity books, handheld computer games, paper and pen). Once you are in public together, involve him in your activity if possible (helping choose items at the store, helping to make a snack at your friend's house).

Maintaining the Gains From Parent Training After the Sessions Are Finished

Before your behavioral parent training program is complete, you should discuss ways in which you can continue to help your child work toward his targeted outcomes in the months and years to come. You will have learned how to recognize when a desired goal has been reasonably achieved and when and how to formulate new targets with your child, his teacher, and the rest of his treatment team. You should also discuss the ways in which you will need to adapt your parenting techniques to your growing child's new stages of development. While behavioral parent training programs do focus in large part on younger children, you will learn how to move from time-outs to response-cost–type techniques as your child grows and to include him more and more in discussions about behavioral goals, rewards and punishments, and treatment decisions.

Making the Most Out of Parenting Techniques

Clearly, parent training and techniques take a great deal of effort on your part. It is always difficult to change old habits, and altering your parenting approach can be especially challenging because it often springs from family tradition and deep-seated childhood experiences. As you read at the beginning of this chapter, being able to participate in a formal parent training program is an optimal way to learn, practice, and get feedback on the techniques discussed in this chapter, but, if this is not possible for any number of reasons, you can also work on these principles with your child's pediatrician or psychologist in a less formal way. While reading this material can give you a general idea of how behavior therapy works, actually participating in parent training or working with professionals in other ways allows you to tailor its methods to your own unique situation, try out some of the techniques under expert guidance, and get regular feedback on what is and is not working and on how to adjust your approach. Without this focused support, you might find success more limited.

Keep in mind, too, that behavior therapies, including parent training, have been shown to be effective only while they are being implemented and maintained. (Your child is not likely to keep up his improved behavior if you drop the effective techniques you have learned.) Even during periods when you see little progress, it is important to remain consistent. During those times when you feel exhausted and discouraged, and wonder what the point is of trying (and most parents of children with ADHD do get to that point once in a while), consider how hard your child must also work to continue trying to maintain his best self-control. By focusing as much as possible on the positive, thinking creatively, and asking for expert help when needed, you can maintain the supportive structure you have created for your child and eventually see measurable improvement.

Additional Treatment Approaches

As noted previously, a variety of factors may limit the effectiveness of parent training in some circumstances. When ADHD is accompanied by oppositional defiant disorder, conduct disorder, and mood and anxiety disorders, these coexisting conditions can compound the behavioral challenges presented by children and adolescents with ADHD and can contribute to aggressive behavior, poor tolerance for frustration, inflexibility, poor problem-solving skills, heightened difficulty in complying with parents' instructions, and significant family conflict. When such conditions are present, additional treatment approaches may be useful.

One such model, developed by Dr Ross Greene and colleagues (see Resources), is called the Collaborative Problem-Solving (CPS) approach. This cognitive-behavioral approach arises from the same underpinnings of parent training, but focuses more on helping adults and children become proficient at resolving problems collaboratively as a means of defusing conflict.

According to this model, an adult's parenting style is a major factor influencing the frequency and intensity of oppositional outbursts. The CPS approach describes 3 basic strategies for handling situations where children do not meet their parents' expectations, including (a) a parent imposing their own will, (b) collaborative problem-solving, and (c) removing the expectation. Imposing a parent's will is the most common cause of oppositional outbursts. Removing the expectation is effective at reducing tension between the child and parent and decreasing explosive outbursts, but not effective in helping children learn to meet their parent's expectations. The CPS approach is an effective way to pursue expectations without increasing the likelihood of oppositional outbursts. It also gives parents and children training and practice in regulating their emotions, dealing with frustration tolerance, problem-solving, and adaptability. Treatment sessions focus on helping children and adults successfully master the CPS approach.

Adults are viewed as the "facilitators" of collaborative problem-solving. In fact, adults are often told that their role is to (a) help their child reduce the likelihood of oppositional outbursts in the moment and (b) help their child develop skills to handle frustration and resolve problems over the longer term. Adults are trained to proactively focus on the events that precipitate the oppositional outbursts rather than just reacting to the outbursts by imposing consequences. In other words, adults are strongly encouraged to adopt a "crisis prevention" mentality instead of a "crisis management" mentality. As part of this mentality, adults are also helped to concentrate on the situations that may be associated with oppositional outbursts, and are taught that most of these outbursts are, in fact, quite predictable.

The CPS approach differs from other anger management and problem-solving training programs in its emphasis on helping adults and children develop the skills to resolve disagreements collaboratively. These techniques are particularly effective because they can be used right at the moment that the oppositional behavior is about to occur, but are even more effective when problems likely to precipitate oppositional episodes are resolved proactively, well in advance, and when all of the adults at home, and even teachers, are involved and trained.

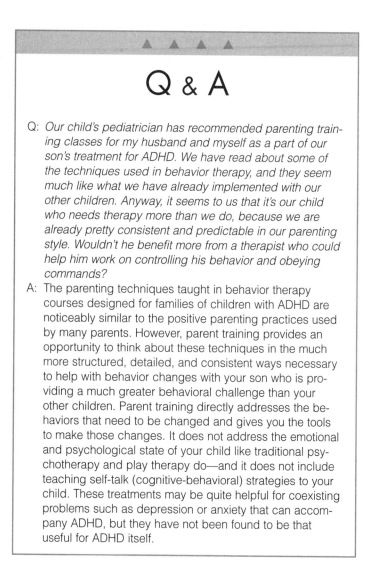

Q & A

Q: *Our child's pediatrician has recommended parenting train-ing classes for my husband and myself as a part of our son's treatment for ADHD. We have read about some of the techniques used in behavior therapy, and they seem much like what we have already implemented with our other children. Anyway, it seems to us that it's our child who needs therapy more than we do, because we are already pretty consistent and predictable in our parenting style. Wouldn't he benefit more from a therapist who could help him work on controlling his behavior and obeying commands?*

A: The parenting techniques taught in behavior therapy courses designed for families of children with ADHD are noticeably similar to the positive parenting practices used by many parents. However, parent training provides an opportunity to think about these techniques in the much more structured, detailed, and consistent ways necessary to help with behavior changes with your son who is pro-viding a much greater behavioral challenge than your other children. Parent training directly addresses the be-haviors that need to be changed and gives you the tools to make those changes. It does not address the emotional and psychological state of your child like traditional psy-chotherapy and play therapy do—and it does not include teaching self-talk (cognitive-behavioral) strategies to your child. These treatments may be quite helpful for coexisting problems such as depression or anxiety that can accom-pany ADHD, but they have not been found to be that useful for ADHD itself.

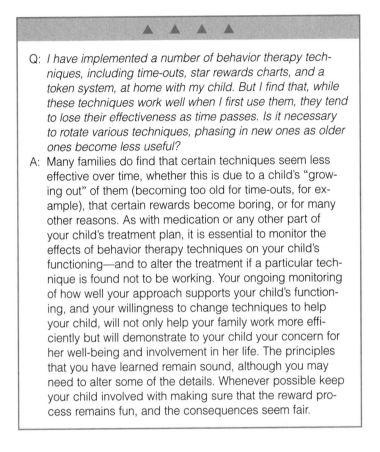

Q: *I have implemented a number of behavior therapy techniques, including time-outs, star rewards charts, and a token system, at home with my child. But I find that, while these techniques work well when I first use them, they tend to lose their effectiveness as time passes. Is it necessary to rotate various techniques, phasing in new ones as older ones become less useful?*

A: Many families do find that certain techniques seem less effective over time, whether this is due to a child's "growing out" of them (becoming too old for time-outs, for example), that certain rewards become boring, or for many other reasons. As with medication or any other part of your child's treatment plan, it is essential to monitor the effects of behavior therapy techniques on your child's functioning—and to alter the treatment if a particular technique is found not to be working. Your ongoing monitoring of how well your approach supports your child's functioning, and your willingness to change techniques to help your child, will not only help your family work more efficiently but will demonstrate to your child your concern for her well-being and involvement in her life. The principles that you have learned remain sound, although you may need to alter some of the details. Whenever possible keep your child involved with making sure that the reward process remains fun, and the consequences seem fair.

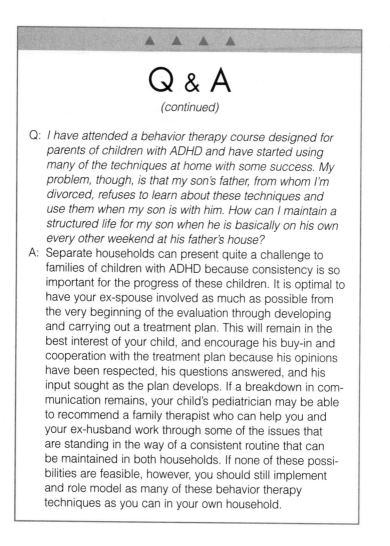

Q & A

(continued)

Q: *I have attended a behavior therapy course designed for parents of children with ADHD and have started using many of the techniques at home with some success. My problem, though, is that my son's father, from whom I'm divorced, refuses to learn about these techniques and use them when my son is with him. How can I maintain a structured life for my son when he is basically on his own every other weekend at his father's house?*

A: Separate households can present quite a challenge to families of children with ADHD because consistency is so important for the progress of these children. It is optimal to have your ex-spouse involved as much as possible from the very beginning of the evaluation through developing and carrying out a treatment plan. This will remain in the best interest of your child, and encourage his buy-in and cooperation with the treatment plan because his opinions have been respected, his questions answered, and his input sought as the plan develops. If a breakdown in communication remains, your child's pediatrician may be able to recommend a family therapist who can help you and your ex-husband work through some of the issues that are standing in the way of a consistent routine that can be maintained in both households. If none of these possibilities are feasible, however, you should still implement and role model as many of these behavior therapy techniques as you can in your own household.

CHAPTER SEVEN

Your Child at School

▲　▲　▲　▲

School can be particularly challenging for children with attention-deficit/hyperactivity disorder (ADHD), who often experience poor academic performance, behavior problems, and difficulties with social interaction. Coexisting conditions such as a learning disability, an anxiety disorder, or disruptive behavior problems can make it even more difficult for a child to succeed. The situation can be further complicated by the fact that there is no typical, predictable classroom style common to all children with ADHD—some parents of children with ADHD may receive reports that their child is "not trying hard enough" academically, while others may be told that their child turns in acceptable work but frequently violates classroom rules. It can be hard for you as a parent to tell how much of any problem identified by a teacher falls into the normal range of child development, how much is due to ADHD, and how much is due to a coexisting problem (see Chapter 3). Add to this the fact that the focus of your child's problems may change from year to year—from largely behavioral to academic, from academic to social, and so on. It is small wonder that children with ADHD and their families often find school issues so central to their overall concerns.

The better informed you are as a family about the many ways in which ADHD may affect your child's school experience, the better prepared you will be to anticipate and deal with problems before they become insurmountable. You can use

the information provided in this chapter to help foster your
child's academic and social success in school. In the following
pages, you will learn:

- What types of school-related challenges children with
  ADHD face most often
- How to identify your own child's particular areas of concern
- Which classroom structures, school policies, teaching styles,
  and accommodations can best support your child's learning
- What an Individualized Education Program (IEP) is
  and how to work with your child, his teachers, and his
  pediatrician to create one
- How to promote school success at home and elsewhere

What Types of Challenges Do Children With ADHD Typically Face at School?

Because ADHD can limit a child's ability to pay attention and
control impulses and behavior, it is easy to imagine how problems in these areas can affect many aspects of school life, and
how such problems can increase if not addressed effectively
early on. In general, children with ADHD experience their
greatest challenges in the areas of *behavior management, academic progress,* and *social interaction.* Due to changing school
demands and changes in your child's symptoms, she may face
greater problems in one area at a particular age, and in another
as she grows older. It is important to continue observing your
child's functioning in each of these areas, and to encourage her
to gain skills in monitoring her own functioning, to address
any emerging problems as soon as possible.

Behavior Issues

Disruptive behavior is a common expression of hyperactive/
impulsive- and combined-type ADHD, and can begin to create
real problems as a child enters kindergarten or elementary

school. Because so many of the demands in the early school years involve following rules and settling down, the inability to meet these demands is what frequently leads to questions about whether a child might have ADHD. A teacher may report that such a child "talks too much," "acts out constantly," or "doesn't seem to recognize limits." Teachers may suggest that the child's impulsive behavior is alienating the other children or making it difficult to maintain order in the classroom and on the playground. As a child with hyperactive/impulsive- or combined-type ADHD grows, the ADHD symptoms may begin to be expressed less in physical terms and more verbally. The child may interrupt frequently or speak out of turn, and perhaps even "mouth off" to authority figures or his classmates.

Other factors not directly attributable to ADHD may increase your child's behavior problems at school. Parents' or teachers' lack of knowledge about how to support or work with a child with ADHD, or a child's past negative preschool or child care experiences, can damage his self-esteem or attitude. This can cause him to give up trying to follow rules or please authority figures, at least temporarily. Coexisting conditions such as depression can also intensify a child's difficulties.

Even the normal developmental stages of childhood, such as a sixth-grader's testing of boundaries (refusing to do homework) or an adolescent's desire not to seem different from his classmates (avoiding taking medication), can have a negative effect on his functioning. Problems in the home environment—marital conflict, financial difficulties, discipline problems, or other issues—can also affect your child's behavior at school. Finally, it is important to remember the role that general health plays in your child's behavior. Every child, including children with ADHD, should receive routine checkups and have his vision and hearing tested.

Academic Concerns

While behavior management issues are often the first school-related problems that children with ADHD experience, academic progress often becomes an area of increasing concern. Regardless of your child's intellectual abilities, she may find it hard to meet academic expectations as her symptoms interfere with her ability to learn, she fails to receive some of the academic supports that she needs, or she experiences a decrease in self-esteem. Because it is difficult for many children with ADHD to stay on task and work independently for long periods, they often complete less work and thus have fewer chances to respond appropriately during the teacher's instruction. Problems with work production (incomplete work, sloppiness, failure to follow instructions) and inconsistency (satisfactory work one day and poor output the next) can become major barriers to school success. This may partially account for the estimates that 60% to 80% of children with ADHD underachieve academically and are identified by their teachers with some performance problems. About 20% of children with ADHD have specific learning disabilities such as a reading disorder, mathematics disorder, or expressive language disorder that are separate from their ADHD symptoms (see Chapter 8).

It is easy to see how many ADHD-type behaviors can interfere with successful learning in a typical classroom. Your child's distractibility and lack of persistence may prevent her from retaining material taught in class. Her impulsivity may cause her to rush through schoolwork and respond spontaneously to questions instead of thinking ideas through. A poor sense of time, characteristic of many children with ADHD, can make long homework assignments, time-limited tasks, and test-taking extremely difficult. Organizing, planning, and sequencing problems lead to incomplete work, poor note-taking skills, or an inability to follow a work schedule or finish a long assignment.

Poor fine motor planning can make the actual writing process difficult—limiting your child's ability to take notes, complete tests, and write effortlessly. Short-term memory problems can make it difficult to memorize facts. Inconsistencies and fluctuations in performance are common. Children with ADHD can also do well in any of these areas one day and poorly the next.

Around the fourth grade, as more academic focus and work production is required (as students move from "learning to read" to "reading to learn"), children with inattentive- or combined-type ADHD often begin to fall behind academically. Failure to pay attention to classroom lectures or turn in homework are typical symptoms that alert teachers to a child's difficulties.

As children with ADHD enter middle school and high school, they may encounter new challenges due to poor organizational skills, incomplete work, or a failure to turn work in. Because many of these behaviors are also experienced by children who do not have ADHD, your child's teacher may suggest that these problems are due to lack of motivation, low self-esteem, or other psychological causes. However, as you will read, when children with ADHD have these problems, they may qualify for extra support in school to help with overcoming or bypassing these obstacles. By middle school academic performance can also decline if medication schedules are not adjusted to cover lengthening homework time (in situations where medication is indicated and has been helpful), or if a child's treatment plan fails to meet her changing needs in other ways.

When a child is far behind in learning, a learning disability should be suspected. Children with coexisting learning disabilities may experience more long-lasting and serious academic difficulties than those struggling academically on the basis of ADHD alone. Learning disabilities are diagnosed when a child

has not developed specific academic skills at the expected level
in spite of adequate intelligence and education. The diagnosis is
based on significant discrepancies between a child's abilities (as
measured by a standard, individually administered IQ test) and
her achievement in school subjects (as measured by standard,
individually administered achievement tests). Learning disabilities are recognized in reading, mathematics, and written
expression, and will be discussed in more detail in Chapter 8.

A student with a learning disability in one area may excel
in others. Some children with learning disabilities may have excellent verbal and reading skills, for example, but do poorly in
math, while others may have the opposite profile. Learning disorders will be discussed in detail in Chapter 8. Keep in mind,
however, that ADHD is not itself a learning disorder, that it
does not *necessarily* lead to academic difficulties at school, and
that neither ADHD nor learning disabilities are signs of low
intelligence. In fact, children with ADHD display the same
range of intelligence as their classmates.

Social Concerns

For many children with ADHD, interactions with classmates
tend to become difficult at one time or another. Children with
ADHD can be disliked, ignored, or rejected by their peers. Some
children with ADHD can be impulsive and intrusive in social
relationships, physically or verbally overwhelming others.
Others may not initiate interactions with their classmates, or
miss the social cues necessary to establish positive relationships,
and thus become socially isolated. Inattentiveness or impulsivity
may decrease a child's success in games, sports, or other group
activities that would otherwise enhance popularity. Younger
children with hyperactive/impulsive- or combined-type ADHD
may frequently experience physical conflicts with their peers,
pushing their way into lines, or being "in their face." By middle childhood, a child's hyperactive-type impulsive behavior,

discipline problems, perceived "spaciness," or social awkwardness may lead to social rejection. Some adolescents with ADHD may be 1 to 2 years less mature than their classmates, further complicating their social relationships at a time when they are taking on great importance.

Later in this chapter, you will find suggested ways for you and your child's teacher to provide opportunities for your child to improve her social standing and interact more successfully with her peers. Meanwhile, social concerns should be discussed at any meeting aimed at evaluating your child's progress and needs.

Beginning to Identify the Key Areas of Concern

Helping a child with ADHD to better manage his school life is best done in the same way you began to address his functioning in other areas, by

1. Identifying the greatest obstacles to his best functioning
2. Creating a treatment plan to address these concerns
3. Establishing a system of review aimed at measuring the treatment's success and failure and adjusting the plan appropriately

Because problems differ from one child with ADHD to the next, and even from one year to the next in a single child, academic, behavioral, and social functioning should all be reviewed carefully. Your greatest ally in arriving at an accurate assessment is your child's teacher because she observes your child in the classroom each day and can compare his functioning to that of his peers. A teacher's willingness to work with you, your child, and your child's pediatrician to meet your child's needs—and your own efforts to show an equal willingness to work through any differences of opinion to come up with an effective education program—can be an important factor in the extent of your child's success and failure in any given year.

The first step in improving your child's experience at school is to arrange to meet with his teacher to discuss his functioning and to listen carefully to the teacher's description of your child's school problems. If at all possible, bring your child with you for at least parts of this and any other parent-teacher meetings so that he can help clarify some of the observations and participate in generating ideas for resolving problems. His participation may add important insights about his functioning, and his "buy-in" to the education program is necessary for success. If you suspect that you may miss or misunderstand important information conveyed by the teacher because of an emotional response to what you are hearing, take a notebook to your meetings to write down what she says for later review.

The emphasis at these initial meetings should be on describing problem behaviors that are specific and that can be measured, not on generalities about your child's symptoms, feelings, or intent. If the teacher suggests, for example, that your child does not seem to be trying to succeed academically, ask for specific examples, as in, "Is some of his homework turned in, or none of it?" "Is schoolwork complete one day and incomplete the next, or is it always incomplete?" "Does my child ignore deskwork, or try but fail to finish it?" "Does my child seem to deliberately try to disrupt the class while others are working?" If the teacher is concerned that your child is having problems getting along with others, ask whether this is due to a tendency to physically overwhelm them; intrude verbally on their conversations; seem isolated or unengaged; or have trouble participating in games due to a lack of coordination, lack of focus, or inability to wait his turn. Ask how frequently each type of conflict happens. These types of specific, quantifiable observations are also necessary for a good baseline for monitoring changes over time, and can help in identifying necessary modifications in your child's treatment plan. Do not become concerned if your observations of your child differ from his teacher's. This is common and can lead to some good discussions about why behaviors may be seen as differing between home and school.

At these first meetings, you and his teacher may not be able to precisely define the problems or agree on solutions. What is more important at this early stage is to *establish a cooperative relationship* and a plan for systematically gathering and analyzing observations in the future. This will be easier if you can set aside any past negative relations with school personnel and start fresh with this new person. Because more and more educators are learning about ADHD and the best ways to manage it at school, this year's teacher may show more insight into what is causing your child's problem or suggest some practical responses that have not been tried before. The more clearly you demonstrate your willingness to cooperate and be a member of the "treatment team," the more positive and effective your partnership with the school may become. Problems in the home environment—marital conflict, financial difficulties, discipline problems, or other issues—can affect your child's functioning at school and should be mentioned in your meetings with his teacher so that you can together arrive at an accurate picture of the challenges that your child faces.

Choosing the Most Appropriate Classroom Setting

Because most children with ADHD experience difficulties meeting some of the academic, social, and behavioral expectations of schools, schools need to play a critical role in providing behavioral and academic support for them. Unless your child has especially severe disruptive behaviors accompanying her ADHD or is diagnosed with certain coexisting conditions or disabilities, her needs can probably best be met in a regular classroom with proper treatment and appropriate support from you and the teacher. In fact, federal law mandates that children with disabilities, including those with ADHD, must be educated alongside children without disabilities as long as the regular classroom meets their needs and allows them to make educational progress. Still, a number of factors within your child's regular classroom environment—its physical setup, the sense of community that the students feel, the special resources provided, the educational approach used, the compatibility of your child's and his teacher's personal styles, and, most crucially, the experience and commitment of the teacher and other school personnel—can have a profound effect on your child's progress. If you are in a position to choose the school your child will attend, or at least have input into her teacher for the coming school year, thorough research and a well-informed choice can make all the difference for you both.

Your Child's Classroom

"My son's first-grade teacher has had a lot of problems with his behavior," writes one parent of a child with ADHD. "He has a

hard time sitting still and focusing on deskwork. The teacher has been talking with me about ways to help him get better at this skill. But I wonder if my son might be better off in a less-structured classroom where he does not have to sit still as much." Many parents of children with ADHD believe that a more free-flowing classroom environment may allow them to learn more effectively, in their own way. In some ways, it makes intuitive sense that a child who is not fettered by the need to remain still will be able to make use of his own unique learning strengths and style at his own pace. In fact, studies have shown that the opposite is usually true: children with ADHD make significantly better progress when the classroom is thoughtfully structured, that is, in an organized setting with clear rules and limits; immediate, appropriate enforcement; and a predictable routine. Traditional classroom seating arrangements (desks facing forward) often work better than open-plan designs (students seated around tables or desks arranged in a circle). This type of classroom environment can help to cut down on distractions, thus making it easier for a child to focus and receive and retain information. Like training wheels on a young child's bicycle, they provide the balance and reliable correcting mechanism that a child with ADHD may not be able to create on his own. Smaller class size can be another important element that can help prevent sensory overload and allow the teacher to provide the individual support your child needs. The smaller the class the better, in most cases, with no more than a few students who need special educational or behavioral services.

The structure in a classroom can affect your child's day-to-day academic and social success. If frequent social conflicts are a problem during instruction time, it is easy to see how these may be avoided if students are seated facing the teacher instead of one another. If your child has trouble staying seated or remaining quiet when this is required, then clear limits and rules can be set with immediate positive feedback for following the rules and some consequences for noncompliance. If your child has difficulty sticking to one task, frequent praise and encouragement when he is persistent may help extend his focus. Of course, just as with the behavior therapy parenting techniques you read about in Chapter 6, a structured environment works well only when it is designed to guide and support a child in positive ways rather than focusing on punishment and over-restriction. The thoughtfully structured routines of the ideal classroom environment should be balanced with a certain amount of variety, flexibility, and humor.

Your Child's Teacher
The most important member of your child's educational team is, of course, the teacher—particularly if your child will spend most or all of his time in a single classroom. The most effective teachers for children with ADHD are those who are generally informed and updated about it and the best ways to manage its related behavioral symptoms. If no such teacher is available, focus on choosing one with whom you feel comfortable and believe will be receptive to learning about ADHD from you, your

child's pediatrician, and others. Training in and comfort using behavior management techniques should be a primary consideration. A natural, structured, and consistent teaching style is also a plus. Finally, teachers who speak expressively and who use a variety of different approaches (lectures, class discussion, audiovisual aids, computers) tend to engage the attention of a child with ADHD most successfully. A teacher who is structured and disciplined, but also dynamic, fun, and engaging, is the best choice for any student, particularly students with ADHD.

If you have a chance to choose a teacher for your child, it can help to ask older students and their parents for advice based on their experience. It can also help to make appointments to speak to prospective teachers about your child and your concerns, and to get a feel for their general teaching style and their working knowledge about students with ADHD. It is essential that you and the teacher feel comfortable exchanging ideas and planning strategies. You will spend a substantial amount of time together over the course of the school year. If possible, choose a teacher who is not only capable and knowledgeable, but with whom you feel you can connect.

As you think about an ideal school environment outlined in this section, it may occur to you that, in many ways, your thoughts are similar to what every parent wants for his or her child

- Small class size
- Regular routines
- A teacher who is engaging, interesting, fun, and exciting: who provides a great deal of structure but can also be flexible; and who is able and willing to use multiple approaches to teaching

It may help to remind yourself as you visit schools and talk with teachers that you are looking for what would be best for any student—but that this environment will be especially important for your child with ADHD.

Special Educational Services—Federal Laws

For most children with ADHD, staying in a regular classroom with an excellent teacher, trained in and adept at behavior management, is the preferred situation. This is especially true if any necessary accommodations for your child can be put into place in that setting. Children with ADHD whose behavior cannot be managed in a regular classroom, or whose educational needs cannot be met through this format, may require special educational services or placement in a separate class. Two federal laws guarantee your child's right to receive such services, if deemed necessary, free of charge: Section 504 of the 1973 Vocational Rehabilitation Act, and a 1991 addendum to the 1990 Individuals with Disabilities Education Act (IDEA).

The IDEA

The IDEA was designed to guarantee the provision of special services for children whose disabilities severely affect their educational performance. A child can receive services under IDEA if she is learning disabled, emotionally disturbed, or "other health impaired." Your child may qualify for IDEA coverage if she has been diagnosed with ADHD and her condition has been shown to severely and adversely affect school performance. Note that both conditions must be met: an ADHD diagnosis alone does not guarantee coverage for your child unless it or another disorder is preventing her from progressing academically. In most cases, it is a child's coexisting learning, disruptive behavior, anxiety, or other functional problem—not the ADHD itself—that qualifies her for IDEA coverage.

The IDEA is based on providing services for categories of disability. It includes 13 categories that require coverage "without undue delay." Under this law, schools are responsible for identifying and evaluating children who are suspected of having disabilities and who may need special education services. Depending on her diagnoses and assessment, your child's disability may be categorized as "specific learning disability," "serious emotional disturbance," or "other health impairment." After these needs are documented, an IEP can be created to detail the special education services that are necessary.

Specific Learning Disabilities

The IDEA criteria for specific learning disabilities can vary from state to state. Children qualify for learning disabilities under this law if they have a processing disorder and a significant discrepancy between their ability and achievement in one or more of the following areas:

- Oral expression
- Listening comprehension
- Written expression
- Basic reading skills
- Reading comprehension
- Mathematics calculation
- Mathematics reasoning

Testing for learning disabilities is generally completed by the school psychologist.

Serious Emotional Disturbance

Children with ADHD and significant emotional problems can also receive services through IDEA. To receive these services, a child's *educational performance* needs to be impaired to a marked degree by

- An inability to learn that can be best explained on a behavioral basis
- An inability to maintain relationships with peers and teachers
- Inappropriate types of behavior or feelings
- A persistent mood of unhappiness or depression

- A tendency to develop physical symptoms or fears associated with personal or school problems

A comprehensive evaluation that meets federal and state guidelines needs to be completed before children can qualify for services as emotionally disturbed. A note from your child's pediatrician that your child is depressed or anxious will not be enough to qualify her for services.

"*Other Health Impaired*"

To qualify for services under "other health impaired," a child with ADHD needs to be documented as showing "limited alertness" that impairs her school functioning.

▲   ▲   ▲   ▲

"OTHER HEALTH IMPAIRED": CRITERIA FOR IDEA ELIGIBILITY

In 1999, the US Department of Education ruled that ADHD meets the eligibility requirement under the Individuals with Disabilities Education Act category of "other health impaired" when

- The student has been diagnosed with ADHD by the school district, or the school has accepted such a diagnosis by another qualified professional.
- The ADHD has led to limited alertness to academic tasks, due to heightened alertness to environmental stimuli.
- The effects of the ADHD are long lasting or acute.
- The effects of the ADHD have an adverse effect on educational performance, including grades and achievement test scores, behavior problems, impaired or inappropriate social relations, or impaired work skills.
- The student requires special education services to address the ADHD and its effects.

IEP Assessments

You as a parent can initiate a referral process if your child is doing poorly in academic, behavioral, or social functioning. The best way to make a referral is to write a letter to the principal outlining your concerns and requesting an evaluation. Send copies to your child's pediatrician as well as the school system's director of special education. The school principal will assign a committee and then hold a meeting to consider your request. The committee may suggest some modifications that teachers or other school personnel can try before recommending a more comprehensive evaluation. If your child's problems persist even with these measures, then a comprehensive evaluation should be completed at school expense. The law states that a group of professionals from different disciplines must take part in the evaluation, and that it needs to be comprehensive and objective. Typical evaluations include

- Assessing your child using reliable, valid, individually administered tests
- Reviewing teachers' and parents' written observations
- Comparing your child's progress to that of others her age
- Interviewing you, the child, her teacher, and others who know or have worked with her

As a parent, you need to give informed consent before any evaluation is done. Keep in mind that the team is not required to accept a diagnosis that is made by an outside pediatrician or psychologist, and they can refuse to provide services. If they refuse services for your child, however, their decision must be justified by an evaluation, and you have the right to appeal their decision.

An IEP That Meets Your Child's Unique Needs

After the assessment has been completed, you must receive a written copy of the results, and you should meet with the evaluation team to discuss the results in detail. If the team determines that your child is eligible for special services under IDEA, then the team will develop an IEP. The IEP needs to meet her unique educational needs in the academic, behavioral, or social areas, and will go into effect once you sign it and agree to the program. The IEP will

- Address your child's present educational performance and how her disability affects her progress.
- Outline all the supports to be provided including special education, related services, and any modifications.
- Set yearly goals and measurable, short-term targets and objectives.
- State any exceptions to a child participating with children in her regular class and in other school activities.
- Describe any necessary test-taking modifications.
- Describe in detail when, where, and how often services will be provided; who will provide them; and dates and places where they will be provided.

Your child is entitled to an IEP that meets her unique educational needs. Her IEP may call for adjustments within the regular classroom, such as a structured learning environment, individualized test-taking conditions; the use of a tape recorder or computer; modified textbooks; individualized homework assignments; modifications during nonacademic times, such as lunchtime or recess; or other accommodations. It may call for the use of a classroom aide or note taker, a trained tutor, or psychological or speech and language services. If your child's educational needs cannot be met through a regular classroom with these special supports, a self-contained special education classroom may be proposed.

After an IEP is written, then the special education team will meet at least once a year to see if the IEP needs to be modified for as long as your child is eligible for special education services. They can meet more often if necessary, if the program requires changes based on how well or poorly certain approaches work for her. If the school no longer feels that she needs these services, they need to reevaluate her to see if she still meets the IDEA eligibility guidelines. If her IEP is still in place during her high school years, then the team will also create a transition program to help with college or career planning.

If you and the school district disagree at any point in the process about the request for an evaluation, the evaluation itself, or the resulting determination of the services needed, a due process hearing can be called at your or the school district's request.

Section 504

If your child does not qualify for services under IDEA, he may still qualify for services under Section 504 of the Rehabilitation Act, which prohibits discrimination against any person with a disability. Section 504, a civil rights law, applies to all public and private schools that receive federal financial assistance, and is aimed at preventing discrimination against students with disabilities.

An important aspect of Section 504 is its emphasis on teaching students with disabilities *in the regular classroom* whenever possible, rather than placing them in a special education class or private school. This is done to help ensure that students with disabilities receive the same education as those without disabilities, while benefiting from whatever in-class accommodations are deemed necessary. Even if your child does not have a learning disability, he may still have difficulty in academic areas such as reading comprehension, written language, note taking, rote memory (such as memorizing math facts), variability in the quality of his work from day to day, study skills, completing assignments, and organization. Under Section 504 students can receive services such as

- Reduced class size
- Preferential seating
- Tutoring
- Modifications in homework and classroom assignments
- Extended time for testing
- Written instructions to supplement teachers' verbal instructions
- Behavior management strategies
- Help with organizing
- Note takers

▲ ▲ ▲ ▲

CHILDREN WITH DISABILITIES: CRITERIA FOR SECTION 504 ELIGIBILITY

Students with disabilities are defined in Section 504 as those who

- *Have a physical or mental impairment that substantially limits one or more "major life activities."* Because learning is considered a "major life activity," children who have been diagnosed with ADHD and who have significant difficulty learning in school are considered disabled under this law.
- *Have a history of such an impairment.*
- *Are regarded as having such an impairment.*

Students who fit into the first category are entitled to special educational services or other accommodations. Those in the second or third category who do not have documentation about how their life activities are limited by ADHD at the time of the request for these services are not entitled to such special arrangements, although they are still protected against discrimination.

▲ ▲ ▲ ▲

IDEA OR SECTION 504:
WHICH IS BEST FOR YOUR CHILD?

The laws and regulations relating to ADHD can be confusing, and parents are often unsure whether their child will benefit more by applying for coverage under IDEA or Section 504. When making this decision for your child, keep in mind that IDEA generally provides for *more special services* for qualified children, but *more children* with ADHD qualify for Section 504 benefits.

For this reason, if your child qualifies, it is usually best to take advantage of IDEA's provisions if your child with ADHD has more significant school difficulties because

- It provides for a more extensive evaluation.
- It sets out specific goals and short-term objectives that are regularly monitored for progress.
- It provides funding for programs and services (Section 504 does not).
- It provides more protections with regard to the evaluation, how often reviews are done, parent participation, disciplinary actions, etc.

A 504 plan is a faster and easier procedure for obtaining accommodations and supports. It may be more appropriate for

- Students with milder impairments who do not need special education
- Students whose educational needs can be addressed through adjustments, modifications, and accommodations in the general curriculum and classroom

Modified from American Academy of Pediatrics, National Initiative for Healthcare Quality. *Caring for Children With ADHD: A Resource Toolkit for Clinicians.* Elk Grove Village, IL: American Academy of Pediatrics; 2003.

Originally appeared in Reif S. *ADHD Book of Lists.* San Francisco, CA: Jossey-Bass Publishers; 2003. This material is used by permission of John Wiley & Sons, Inc.

In most cases, you will find that as a parent you are the driving force behind the evaluation process, and you may need to actively advocate for your child if he is to receive the services he needs. Parent support associations have made a great deal of progress in persuading states to follow federal guidelines, but cost considerations and lack of understanding of ADHD can limit a district's response. To learn about the federal, state, and local district guidelines regarding the services available to your child, contact your school district and your local chapter of Children and Adults With Attention-Deficit/Hyperactivity Disorder (CHADD), and consult the CHADD Web site (see Resources) and other sources of ADHD-linked support.

What Can Schools Do?

General Classroom Supports

Earlier in this chapter, you learned that certain aspects of your child's school environment, such as a structured routine and a

traditional seating arrangement, can affect her ability to function. Other environment-related strategies shown to help children with ADHD include seating the child near the teacher and away from distractions, such as the windows, hallway, or pencil sharpener, and surrounding her with students who focus well on their own work. The teacher may even decide to create a "buddy system" for your child or for the class as a whole, in which children remind one another of academic, behavioral,

---

HELPFUL TEACHER SUPPORTS FOR STUDENTS WITH ADHD

Keeping Things Simple and Doable

- Break down complicated instructions into doable steps.
- Adjust the length of assignments to fit a student's attention span.
- Keep the more academic subjects in the morning, when children are fresher and more alert.

Keeping Things Interesting

- Teach with enthusiasm and invite class participation.
- Vary lectures with hands-on experiences and physical activities.
- Supplement lectures with drills and computer games that teach the same materials to keep things novel, engaging, and motivating.

Keeping Things Organized

- Clearly state, repeat, and post the classroom rules.
- Preview the school day with a morning class meeting.
- Write things down for students who may miss verbal instructions or have trouble copying from the chalkboard.
- Encourage the use of simple daily planners that do not overwhelm students.

or social goals and where the class as a whole earns points or tokens that can be traded in for privileges like a class party. The less distracting your child's teacher can make your child's environment, the more likely it is that she will focus better on the task at hand. This way of preventing negative behavior from occurring in the first place is far preferable to trying to "fix" it later.

Your teacher will benefit from keeping the following mantra in mind as she works with your child in the classroom: *Keep things simple and doable, keep them interesting, and keep them well structured and organized.*

As you have seen, most methods your teacher can implement are likely to benefit all of her students, not just your child. Nearly all children, by nature, are distractible and have problems with organization and staying focused at one time or another, and your child's peers will profit from the teacher's efforts to overcome this.

Schools and Behavior

Teachers, who must constantly deal with behavior problems in their classrooms, are generally encouraged to try prevention first, rewards for positive behavior second, and discipline measures only as a final resort when managing problem behaviors in any student. When teachers take this approach there is usually a dramatic improvement in how well the classroom functions and a noticeable reduction in how much classroom time is taken up with disciplinary measures. For children with ADHD, IDEA actually mandates that the IEP team includes positive behavior approaches in the child's educational program.

Functional Behavior Assessments and Individual Behavior Plans

If the positive behavioral approaches described previously have proven unsuccessful, then a "functional behavior assessment" should be done. Functional assessments include a description

▲ ▲ ▲ ▲

WHEN DISCIPLINE IS AN ISSUE

Many parents of children with ADHD feel that disciplinary actions tend to target their children due to a lack of understanding of ADHD-type behavior and reluctance to make appropriate accommodations and allowances. Children with serious behavior problems, such as extreme impulsiveness or a conduct disorder, may find themselves suspended from school over and over while their behavior goes untreated.

Children covered under IDEA are protected to a large degree from such nonproductive disciplinary actions. Under the IDEA provisions, any child who has been identified as having a disability, who has demonstrated a need for services, or whose parents or teacher have expressed concern in writing or requested an evaluation may not be suspended or expelled for more than 10 consecutive days for behavior that is related to his disability. To determine whether the disability is a factor, the student's assessment team, which includes his parents, must determine whether the IEP and special education services were appropriate in relation to the behavior, the child was able to understand the effects and consequences of behavior, and the child was able to control the problem behavior. If the student's disability is determined to have been a factor, or IEP or special services are deemed inadequate, the child cannot be held to the same standards and arbitrarily suspended or reassigned to another program. Instead, changes must be made in the school's approach to the specified disability to prevent similar behavior problems in the future, and beyond the first 10 days of suspension in any school year educational services must be reinstated.

Children covered under Section 504 are not as well protected. Section 504 does not require the school to keep the child in school or in ongoing programs while a reassessment takes place. In general, schools are held less accountable for disciplinary procedures involving these children.

of the behavior problems, direct observations of your child in different settings, and positive strategies to gradually decrease the specified behavior and increase other behaviors that are appropriate. Functional assessments are generally done by the school behavior specialist, who analyzes the triggers for specific problem behaviors, the behaviors that arise, and the consequences that are in place when those behaviors occur. The information is then used to try to understand the function of the behavior. For example, if a student gets out of his seat frequently and this disrupts the class, a functional analysis can help to pinpoint the reason—is it to get attention?...to get something that he needs?...to avoid finishing an assignment?... to create some self-stimulation in a quiet classroom? Each of these reasons may have different solutions, and a one-size-fits-all approach is inappropriate. The value of a functional analysis is that it can lead to a specific plan for your child's individual needs. Once this analysis is done, then this type of positive individualized plan can be created. A typical plan may include instituting preventive measures, teaching the child new behavior strategies, and using behavior therapy techniques to help him improve his functioning.

Preventive measures include changes that the teacher can make in the classroom environment to help students with ADHD avoid targeted behaviors. These include measures such as changing the seating arrangement in the classroom, altering classroom routines, posting the 5 most important classroom behavior rules on the chalkboard, or allowing frequent breaks during long assignments.

Students with ADHD can also be taught new strategies to replace their problem behaviors. For example, if your child gets up from his seat and disrupts the class during long assignments, a teacher might arrange a "secret signal" that he can use to let her know that he needs a break. When the teacher sees the signal she can respond by asking him to do a task that involves getting up and walking around.

The plan can also include teachers using the same behavior therapy principles that are taught in parent training. Techniques that have been found to be most successful in the classroom include

- Clearly conveying and consistently enforcing class rules
- Giving clear, doable commands
- Establishing daily goals for the child, and for the class as a whole
- Praising students for positive behaviors and ignoring negative behaviors that are not intolerable
- Using rewards to encourage appropriate behavior, which includes using token economies (point, sticker, and poker chip reward systems) and cost-response systems (losing tokens for inappropriate behaviors)
- Using appropriate nonphysical punishments to cut back on unacceptable behaviors
- Using behavior report cards to motivate children and enhance parent-teacher communication

The use of these techniques can not only help your child, but all the other children in the classroom as well. Regular communication between parents and teachers is essential to make some of these measures as effective as possible. A good working relationship with your child's teacher and the development of mutual respect will set a good tone for a team approach. For example, tokens earned in the classroom can be converted into rewards at home if there is good communication between parents and teachers.

Ideally, your child's teacher has received training in classroom behavior therapy techniques. In some, but not all, areas of the country, more teachers are trained in behavior therapy now than ever before. If your child's teacher has not received training, you may be able to advocate for teacher training funds, especially if you have requested services for your child under IDEA or Section 504 legislation. However, limited funding and support for such training means that your child's teacher may have to seek some of this information on her own. If you have participated in parent training, you and your trainer may be valuable resources. You may want to share any teaching materials and workbooks you used. The CHADD Web site and books that specifically address classroom intervention and school behavior therapy training programs (see Resources) are other good sources of information for teachers. Local ADHD support groups and other community resources may be helpful as well.

ADHD and Academics

Even if your child does not have a learning disability, the academic side of school can be difficult for students with ADHD. Some common concerns and practical suggestions are listed in the table on page 183.

Additional ideas for promoting academic success are available through some of the references in the Resources section in the back of this book.

The Social Side of School

Social difficulties are an aspect of school life that can become especially painful for a child with ADHD. Your child may have difficulty forming friendships due to a tendency to act before thinking, disruptiveness, failure to make plans, or acting inappropriately in spite of knowing what she is supposed to do. Children with inattentive-type ADHD often tend to be socially isolated or withdrawn. If you are concerned about your child's social experiences at school, talk with her teacher about ways to bolster her social confidence, increase her status, and help her improve her skills. If improvement in specific social skills is already part of her IEP or other education program, you and

▲ ▲ ▲ ▲

ADHD AND ACADEMICS

Area of Academic Difficulty	Suggestions
Written Expression *Difficulty with* • Fine motor skills • Attending to all aspects of written language at the same time • Following multiple or sequential steps (as in spelling) • Writing (considers it boring)	• Stimulant medications can sometimes markedly help fine motor paper and pencil skills. • Students with ADHD can start instruction in word processing by third grade and be permitted to complete assignments by computer.
Note-Taking *Difficulty with* • Listening and taking notes at the same time	• Teachers can provide students with lecture outlines or notes. • Students can listen to lectures and borrow a classmate's notes to study. • Students can tape-record lectures, but this can become tedious and time-consuming.
Rote Memorization Tasks • Requires sustained attention to tasks that are frequently boring	• Computer software can be a helpful and motivating way to memorize material like math facts.
Variations in Performance • Can occur from day-to-day or one grading period to the next	• Token economies and reward systems can help with motivation.

▲ ▲ ▲ ▲

ADHD AND ACADEMICS
(continued)

Area of Academic Difficulty	Suggestions
Incomplete Assignments *Can occur from* • Problems in following multiple directions • Becoming bored with an assignment	• The use of study cubicles has not been found to be helpful in increasing attention or concentration. • Classroom seating next to a positive peer model can lead to fewer off-task behaviors and greater work productivity. • In-school solutions should be found for incomplete classroom work and teachers should avoid sending it home.
Organizational and Study Skills • Lost books • Assignments not turned in even if they have been completed • Messy and illegible papers	• Step-by-step tutoring on how to complete daily assignments and long-term projects. • Extra set of books at home. • Setting of homework time limits. • Modifications in homework assignments.

the teacher may already have brainstormed about behavior therapy techniques to reinforce and build on her skills in this area.

Sound behavior management and medication approaches can go a long way toward improving the social functioning of

ADHD AND ACADEMICS	
Area of Academic Difficulty	**Suggestions**
Reading Comprehension • Tuning out or getting distracted while reading	• Brief exercise breaks. • Parent reads part of the material while the child listens. • Parent and child discuss the material before, during, and after the material is read. • Older students preview the questions at the end of the chapter before reading the chapter so that they can focus on the most important points.

Modified from Hannah JN. The role of schools in attention deficit/hyperactivity disorder. *Pediatr Ann.* 2002;31:507–513. Table p 510.

Originally printed in Hannah JN. *Parenting a Child With Attention Deficit Hyperactivity Disorder.* Austin, TX: Pro-ed; 1999. Used with permission.

children with ADHD. You might also suggest to the teacher such actions as casually but publicly praising your child for her talents or choosing her for classroom duties in front of other children. This allows other children to see her in a positive light and can enhance her self-esteem and sense of acceptance. You can also ask her teacher to intervene in tactful ways when she begins to fall into social difficulty and to find ways to set social skills goals, monitor her progress, and set up a system of rewards and privileges to recognize her for meeting her goals. Your child and her classmates might also benefit from class discussions about how we all manage our feelings, the value of diversity, and the importance of respect. It is surprising how effective a well-timed word or action can be.

If your school offers social-skills training groups, consider enrolling your child. Although effective social-skills treatments have been difficult to develop, programs in school with the classmates that your child interacts with every day are more likely to be successful than those run in clinics or other settings outside of school. Some of the most effective programs incorporate parents and teachers, help children to be aware of and understand verbal and nonverbal social cues, and use the same types of well thought out reward and cost-response systems that you read about in Chapter 6. They teach socially significant skills like good sportsmanship, problem-solving, accepting consequences, being assertive without being aggressive, ignoring classmates when they are provocative, and recognizing and dealing with feelings. In the better programs children are coached and receive feedback, and techniques are taught by role-playing real-life situations and modeling by coaches and teachers. These types of programs can be incorporated into IEPs and behavior plans.

Closing the Gap Between Home and School

Daily Report Cards

Constant feedback for your child and frequent communication between you and her teacher are necessary components in keeping your child on track, and can make an enormous difference in how quickly positive results are seen. Both of these aims can be accomplished through daily report cards filled out by teachers and/or a journal for teachers' and parents' comments that your child keeps in her school backpack. A daily report card is especially effective because it identifies daily goals for your child, lets her see almost immediately how effectively she has met them, and motivates her to try harder to meet her goals as she receives agreed-on rewards for good reports. You and your child's teacher may find that it is best for you to provide some of these rewards at home because providing them in class takes up valuable class time, and some of the most effective rewards (such as telephone or television time) or negative consequences (such as restriction of privileges) may not be possible at school. Your willingness to respond appropriately at home can ease the teacher's workload and increase his willingness to work more closely with your child. Home-based reinforcements also highlight for your child the link between behavior at school and at home.

To develop this type of report card, you and your child's teachers first need to select the areas for improvement. A limited number of targeted behavioral or academic goals should be described as specifically as possible—in ways that are countable or measurable ("completes at least 80 percent of her worksheet during third period," not "stays on task"). These goals can then be translated into items to be checked off on the daily report that your child brings home from school. Before using the report card system, arrange for a meeting including you, your child, and her teacher at which the process will be explained to your child, with a home-based reward system also set up to motivate her. At regular parent-teacher meetings throughout the school year, you can use the accumulated report cards to monitor your child's progress in accomplishing each task and modify items on the card when necessary. For more information about setting up a daily school-home report card, check the Comprehensive Treatment for Attention Deficit Disorder (CTADD) Web site (see Resources).

A sample daily report card is provided on page 188. You can adapt this form to suit your child's targeted behaviors and the number of teachers she has. Again, the more precise and quantitative teachers can be when giving feedback, the more effectively these daily reports can be used to improve your child's education program.

SAMPLE DAILY REPORT CARD

Child's name _____ Date: _____

	Special	Language Arts	Math	Reading	SS/Science
Follows class rules with no more than 3 rule violations per period.	Y N	Y N	Y N	Y N	Y N
Completes assignments within the designated time.	Y N	Y N	Y N	Y N	Y N
Completes assignments at 80% accuracy.	Y N	Y N	Y N	Y N	Y N
Complies with teacher requests (no more than 3 instances of noncompliance per period).	Y N	Y N	Y N	Y N	Y N
No more than 3 instances of teasing per period.	Y N	Y N	Y N	Y N	Y N

Other

Follows lunch rules.   Y N
Follows recess rules.   Y N

Total Number of Yeses _____ Total Number of Noes _____ Percentage _____ Teacher's Initials _____

Comments

Adapted with permission from William E. Pelham, Jr, PhD. School-Home Daily Report Card packet available for downloading at no cost at www.CTADD.com and http://wings.buffalo.edu/adhd.

Your child's teachers can record more detailed observations or requests in a journal that your child carries with her between home and school. You can also use the journal to inform a teacher of the behavior modification reward or cost your child received for her school performance. (For more information on reward-cost systems, see Chapter 6.) Daily report cards and a shared journal are efficient ways to keep in touch without having to constantly schedule meetings. They can also help your child keep her goals in mind and include her more in her own education program.

Ideally, this system of constant communication will foster a positive working relationship between you and the teacher that can help your child achieve her goals. You may find, however, that you disagree with the teacher's approach or feel in conflict in some other way. If you have tried and failed to work productively as a team, consider asking your partner, the school principal or counselor, or even your child's pediatrician or therapist to mediate. Some local parent advocacy groups provide staff members to accompany parents to the school and help advocate for services. Your child's pediatrician or therapist may be able to help you locate this type of support. However, you will need to weigh the potential benefits of these types of actions against the possibility that the teacher may begin to see you as an adversary rather than a teammate—a position that will diminish your ability to advocate for your child. To help avoid such conflicts before they happen, be sure to express support for the teacher and help him in any way you can. If you are pleased with some aspects of his work, tell him and his principal. Your positive attention to the teacher will usually translate into positive attention to your child.

Homework

"I can't wait for summer to come!" writes the mother of a seventh-grader. "Suddenly the gloom lifts, the arguing stops, we relax, and we remember how much fun our family can have together." Dealing with issues around homework can be one of the most stressful and time-consuming elements of parenting in the family of a child with ADHD. Successfully dealing with homework production involves developing skills in time management, organization, and study habits; using behavior management techniques; and understanding your child's limits and frustration tolerance. Some hints are included in the Homework Tips for Parents box, and additional ideas are available through the Resources section at the back of this book.

▲ ▲ ▲ ▲

HOMEWORK TIPS FOR PARENTS

- Establish a routine and schedule for homework (a specific time and place), and adhere to the schedule as closely as possible. Do not allow your child to wait until the evening to get started.
- Limit distractions in the home during homework hours (eg, reduce unnecessary noise, activity, and phone calls; turn off the television).
- Assist your child in dividing assignments into smaller parts or segments that are more manageable and less overwhelming.
- Assist your child in getting started on assignments (eg, read the directions together, do the first items together, observe as your child does the next problem/item on his or her own). Then get up and leave.
- Monitor and give feedback without doing all the work together. You want your child to attempt as much as possible independently.

▲ ▲ ▲ ▲

HOMEWORK TIPS FOR PARENTS

- Praise and compliment your child when he or she puts forth good effort and completes tasks. In a supportive, noncritical manner it is appropriate and helpful to assist in pointing out and making some corrections of errors on the homework.
- It is not your responsibility to correct all of your child's errors on homework or make him or her complete and turn in a perfect paper.
- Remind your child to do homework and offer incentives: "When you finish your homework, you can...."
- A contract for a larger incentive/reinforcer may be worked out as part of a plan to motivate your child to persist and follow through with homework. ("If you have no missing or late homework assignments this next week, you will earn...").
- Let the teacher know your child's frustration and tolerance level in the evening. The teacher needs to be aware of the amount of time it takes your child to complete tasks and what efforts you are making to help at home.
- Help your child study for tests. Study together. Quiz your child in a variety of formats.
- If your child struggles with reading, help by reading the material together or reading it to your son or daughter.
- Work a certain amount of time and then stop working on homework. Do not force your child to spend an excessive and inappropriate amount of time on homework. If you feel your child worked enough for one night, write a note to the teacher attached to the homework.
- It is very common for students with ADHD to fail to turn in their finished work. It is very frustrating to know your child struggled to do the work, but then never gets credit for having done it. Papers seem to mysteriously vanish off the face of the earth! Supervise to make sure that completed work leaves the home and is in the notebook/backpack. You may want to arrange with the teacher a system for collecting the work immediately on arrival at school.

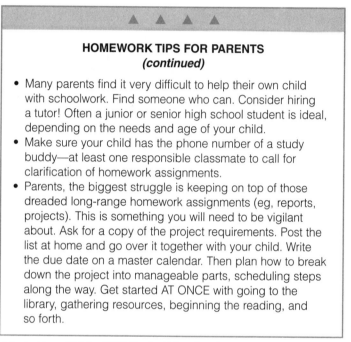

HOMEWORK TIPS FOR PARENTS
(continued)

- Many parents find it very difficult to help their own child with schoolwork. Find someone who can. Consider hiring a tutor! Often a junior or senior high school student is ideal, depending on the needs and age of your child.
- Make sure your child has the phone number of a study buddy—at least one responsible classmate to call for clarification of homework assignments.
- Parents, the biggest struggle is keeping on top of those dreaded long-range homework assignments (eg, reports, projects). This is something you will need to be vigilant about. Ask for a copy of the project requirements. Post the list at home and go over it together with your child. Write the due date on a master calendar. Then plan how to break down the project into manageable parts, scheduling steps along the way. Get started AT ONCE with going to the library, gathering resources, beginning the reading, and so forth.

Adapted from Rief S. *ADHD Book of Lists.* San Francisco, CA: Jossey-Bass Publishers; 2003. This material is used by permission of John Wiley & Sons, Inc.

Summer Camps and Programs

▲ ▲ ▲ ▲

SUMMER SCHOOLS AND CAMPS

Many families have found it useful to supplement home- and school-based behavioral training techniques with a specially designed summer school or camp program for children with ADHD and their parents. The best of these programs focus on improving learning and academic achievement—developing children's abilities to follow through with instructions, complete tasks that they commonly fail to finish, and comply with adults' requests. They also help children develop problem-solving skills, social skills, and the social awareness needed to get along better with other children. Parents, meanwhile, are taught how to develop, reinforce, and maintain these positive changes. Summer programs also provide an excellent environment in which to carefully monitor and adjust doses of stimulant medication. However, these programs are typically expensive and the generalization and maintenance of benefits into the regular school setting may be limited.

Detailed descriptions of summer school and camp programs are available on the Web site of Comprehensive Treatment for Attention Deficit Disorder, and a list of summer programs in the United States and Canada can be found on the Web site of the Center for Children and Families Summer Treatment Program (see Resources). If no program exists in your area, the information on these sites may help you advocate for one.

Medication Management

In addition to implementing behavioral training techniques that can help your child function successfully at school, your child's teacher is an essential resource in successfully managing medication issues—providing information that can help your child's treatment team decide whether to initiate medication, adjust the dosage, and so on. Your child's pediatrician should be in close contact with your child's teacher, calling him before each follow-up visit or reviewing the teacher's current written narrative or rating scales that reflect your child's academic, behavioral, and social functioning at school. Teachers need to be aware of what medications can and cannot be expected to do, as well as the possible adverse effects of any given medication. Your child's pediatrician may be able to provide his teacher with handouts explaining approaches to medication management as well as positive effects and side effects. As a parent, you can play a key case-management role by encouraging this communication between your child's teacher and physician to make sure that they each get the information they need.

In most states, medications must be administered to students by a licensed medical provider, most often the school nurse—particularly because stimulant medications are legally considered controlled substances (see Chapter 4). Because many of the stimulant medications have "street value," it is usually not appropriate (or legal) for your child or adolescent to take them to school or to self-administer them, even if a particular school may be lenient in its policies. If medications are to be taken during the school day, make sure that you have filled out the appropriate consent forms for medication administration and that school personnel are informed immediately about any changes in dose or in the timing of doses. Several new once-a-day formulations of medications are now available (Concerta,

Metadate-CD, Ritalin LA, Adderall XR, Strattera), allowing your child to avoid the problems of embarrassment and compliance associated with the administration of medication at school.

A Personal Coach/Trainer

If parents and teachers can be said to share one goal regarding children with ADHD, it is to help them learn to manage their own behavior so that they can enjoy an independent, happy adulthood. At first, most children with ADHD require a great deal of external monitoring because they are unable to provide it themselves. Gradually, with support and encouragement, they will begin to internalize this role. Dr Edward M. Hallowell, author of the book *Driven to Distraction,* has developed a potentially useful method for providing this support. Called "life coaching," the technique involves identifying a single person to serve as the child's daily monitor—briefly chatting with her each day, asking her what her most important tasks are for that day and how she plans to accomplish them, and praising her for working toward her goals. While parents have such conversations with their children as a matter of routine, Hallowell believes that a non-parent—a school employee, neighbor, friend's parent, responsible classmate, or even a hired college student or retired person—can sometimes have a greater impact simply because of his outsider status. The daily conversation between your child and her coach is brief and can take place by telephone. It might take place in the morning before the school day begins, in the evening before the child starts her homework, or at any other time that the child feels is most appropriate. Its effectiveness seems to spring from its combination of practical assistance with emotional support as well as the consistency and reliability of its presence in the child's life. While this brief, daily form of coaching does not replace the role of a parent, psychologist, pediatrician, or medication, it may make a substantive difference in a child's functioning at school. It can also take some of the tension out of day-to-day parent-child interactions when a more neutral party is helping to facilitate charged issues like homework flow. When meeting with your child's teacher, consider asking him to recommend someone at school—a counselor, office clerk, or even a responsible student—who might be willing to act as coach for your child.

Support at Home

There is no denying that children with ADHD can make teaching, learning, and even playing more difficult at times. There is also no question that children with ADHD often have a special type of intensity, energy, and enthusiasm that can enhance everyone's daily experience. As you support your child through her academic career, make a point of focusing on these positive qualities, and asking others to do so as well. Your child has much to contribute to her classroom and her school. Do what you can to help improve her chance for success in this challenging but potentially rewarding environment.

By the time they enter college, many students with ADHD have grown accustomed to seeking outside support such as special tutoring, coaching, altered testing conditions, or study environments when necessary, and tailoring their medication schedule to the demands of each semester's academic schedule. As these students demonstrate, the presence of ADHD does not spell the end of academic success, but will likely require careful planning in a well-informed and positive way.

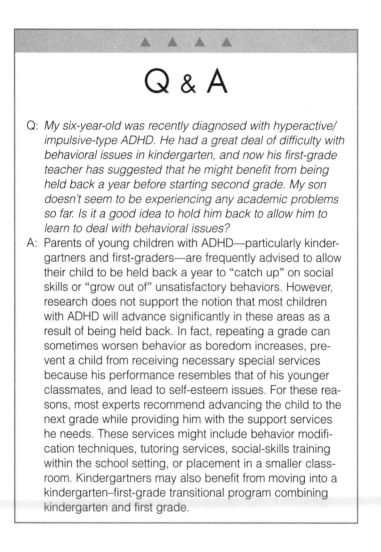

Q & A

Q: *My six-year-old was recently diagnosed with hyperactive/ impulsive-type ADHD. He had a great deal of difficulty with behavioral issues in kindergarten, and now his first-grade teacher has suggested that he might benefit from being held back a year before starting second grade. My son doesn't seem to be experiencing any academic problems so far. Is it a good idea to hold him back to allow him to learn to deal with behavioral issues?*

A: Parents of young children with ADHD—particularly kindergartners and first-graders—are frequently advised to allow their child to be held back a year to "catch up" on social skills or "grow out of" unsatisfactory behaviors. However, research does not support the notion that most children with ADHD will advance significantly in these areas as a result of being held back. In fact, repeating a grade can sometimes worsen behavior as boredom increases, prevent a child from receiving necessary special services because his performance resembles that of his younger classmates, and lead to self-esteem issues. For these reasons, most experts recommend advancing the child to the next grade while providing him with the support services he needs. These services might include behavior modification techniques, tutoring services, social-skills training within the school setting, or placement in a smaller classroom. Kindergartners may also benefit from moving into a kindergarten–first-grade transitional program combining kindergarten and first grade.

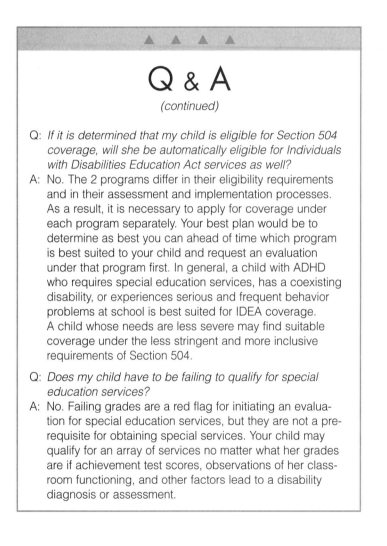

▲ ▲ ▲ ▲

Q & A
(continued)

Q: *If it is determined that my child is eligible for Section 504 coverage, will she be automatically eligible for Individuals with Disabilities Education Act services as well?*

A: No. The 2 programs differ in their eligibility requirements and in their assessment and implementation processes. As a result, it is necessary to apply for coverage under each program separately. Your best plan would be to determine as best you can ahead of time which program is best suited to your child and request an evaluation under that program first. In general, a child with ADHD who requires special education services, has a coexisting disability, or experiences serious and frequent behavior problems at school is best suited for IDEA coverage. A child whose needs are less severe may find suitable coverage under the less stringent and more inclusive requirements of Section 504.

Q: *Does my child have to be failing to qualify for special education services?*

A: No. Failing grades are a red flag for initiating an evaluation for special education services, but they are not a prerequisite for obtaining special services. Your child may qualify for an array of services no matter what her grades are if achievement test scores, observations of her classroom functioning, and other factors lead to a disability diagnosis or assessment.

CHAPTER EIGHT

When It Is Not Just ADHD: Identifying Coexisting Conditions

▲   ▲   ▲   ▲

One source of confusion about attention-deficit/hyperactivity disorder (ADHD) diagnoses and treatment is that ADHD frequently occurs not alone, but with other, coexisting conditions. As many as 50% to 60% of all children with ADHD also have at least 1 coexisting condition, and more than 10% have 3 or more. Disruptive behavior disorders (disorders involving behavior and conduct problems), anxiety and depressive disorders, learning disabilities, and language impairments are the most common. In addition to diagnosed disorders, many children with ADHD experience coexisting "problems"—functioning difficulties that are not formally defined as disabilities but that still require special attention. For example, up to 60% of children with ADHD experience some form of academic problem in school subjects (reading, math, social studies, etc), skills (such as handwriting), or productivity (completing assignments accurately and on time), and most of these children do not have learning disorders. Coexisting conditions may share many of the same symptoms or mimic the symptoms of ADHD. Coexisting conditions in young children with ADHD are particularly hard to identify correctly because children's behavior changes quickly and certain conditions only become diagnosable over time. What seemed at age 4 years to be a developing mood disorder may turn out to be aspects of ADHD.

In many cases—as with learning disorders that impede school performance—a coexisting condition or problem may affect your child's functioning in ways that require changes in his education or treatment plan. Sometimes, as can be the case with major depressive disorder, the symptoms of the coexisting condition may be more problematic than those of the ADHD and must be treated first, even if the ADHD was the original cause of your child's referral for treatment. Some conditions, such as conduct disorder, which involves extreme defiance and flaunting of rules, carry increased risks for substance abuse, criminal behavior, or other difficulties later in life—risks that may be diminished or even avoided if the condition is identified early and treated. For all of these reasons, it is always necessary to consider whether any of these coexisting conditions are present when your child is being evaluated for ADHD, and a comprehensive evaluation and ongoing monitoring are needed to diagnose any additional conditions that can accompany ADHD. Continued monitoring is vital throughout childhood and adolescence because some coexisting conditions may develop long after the original ADHD diagnosis and others may diminish over time.

In this chapter you will find up-to-date information on how best to recognize and treat the types of coexisting conditions that most commonly accompany ADHD, including

- **Disruptive behavior disorders,** including oppositional defiant disorder (ODD) and conduct disorder (CD)
- **Anxiety disorders,** such as generalized anxiety disorder, separation anxiety disorder, and phobias
- **Mood disorders,** including major depressive disorder, dysthymia, and bipolar disorder
- **Tics, Tourette syndrome, and obsessive-compulsive disorder (OCD)**

- **Learning, motor skills, and communication disorders**
- **Mental retardation and pervasive developmental disorders,** such as autism and related disorders
- **Coexisting problems** that, while not reaching the severity required for a specific diagnosis, may still significantly stand in the way of your child's progress

When viewed all together, this list of disorders may seem daunting, and even frightening. Keep in mind, however, that no child has all of these conditions, and that most are treatable. With early identification and a systematic evidence-based treatment program, you and your child may be able to avoid or minimize many of the effects of disorders that do appear.

What Else Is Going On?: Recognizing and Diagnosing Coexisting Disorders

Identifying a coexisting condition can be difficult because many behaviors suggestive of these conditions—such as sadness, anxiety, or frequent rule breaking—could also stem from ADHD-related difficulties, responses to conflict at home or at school, or just a normal part of the process of growing up. Your child may frequently seem defiant and uncooperative for many reasons (for example, because she has a disruptive behavior disorder, because her ADHD-related impulsiveness is causing her to act inappropriately before she thinks at school, because her parents are divorcing, or just because she is 15 years old). As with ADHD, there are no laboratory tests to determine whether her behavior is due to a coexisting condition. Accurate diagnosis may involve a combination of factors including a review of your careful observations of your child's behavior, an interview with your child, regular discussions among all members of her treatment and education teams, a review of your family's medical history, and the use of other tests or standardized rating scales as appropriate. Even with these aids, categorizing your child's cluster of behaviors as ADHD alone, as ADHD plus a coexisting condition, or even as a separate condition without ADHD may require multiple perspectives and regular review.

If your child has already been diagnosed with ADHD but has shown little or no response to systematic trials of medication and behavior therapy techniques, or you have increasingly observed symptoms of the specific disorders described later in this chapter, your child may have 1 or more coexisting conditions or problems in addition to ADHD. If your child was very young when she was diagnosed with ADHD, it may even turn out that she has the other disorder and *not* ADHD. If you are beginning to question whether your child has a coexisting disorder and is not just functioning poorly due to stresses or frustrations directly related to ADHD, ask yourself

- **How long has the troublesome behavior lasted?** Has oppositional behavior been going on for longer than about 6 months? Particularly in younger children, troublesome behavior can come and go quickly—but if your child's difficulties persist beyond half a year, she may need assessment for a coexisting condition. In the case of depressive or anxious symptoms, an even shorter observation period is recommended.
- **Is the behavior typical of her age group?** Troublesome behavior occurs in all children during various stages of development. Assessment may be necessary, however, if your child's problems develop or persist long past the age when others her age have outgrown such behavior.
- **How intense is the behavior?** All children test boundaries, act fearful, or are depressed now and then, but children with a diagnosable condition act in more prolonged and intense ways than others their age.
- **How much of a problem is it causing in her day-to-day functioning?** Is the behavior significantly interfering with

your child's academic progress, social relationships, or other important aspects of daily life? If so, a coexisting condition may be the cause.

- **Do you see any developmental delays?** Particularly during your child's preschool and early school years, keep track of whether she reaches the standard developmental milestones listed in on child development charts at or around the ages indicated. Your child's pediatrician will be checking on these during your well-child visits, and they are included in most child care books. Watch especially for any significant delays in language development, social skills, motor skills, or academic progress.

- **Do others in your child's family have ADHD or one or more of the conditions listed in this chapter?** Many co-existing conditions run in families. A child with ADHD and a close relative with conditions such as an anxiety disorder, depression, learning disorders, oppositional behavior, or a more serious conduct disorder has a greater chance of having ADHD and/or a coexisting condition herself.

If your answers to any of these questions have left you with doubts or even questions about your child's functioning, be sure to discuss your observations with your child's pediatrician, and any other professionals involved with your child. Following, you will find which types of behaviors are likely to signal each type of coexisting disorder, and what changes in treatment may be necessary to address the coexisting disorder and the ADHD.

Disruptive Behavior Disorders

Disruptive behavior disorders are among the easiest to identify of all coexisting conditions because they involve behaviors that are readily seen such as temper tantrums, physical aggression such as attacking other children, excessive argumentativeness, stealing, and other forms of defiance or resistance to authority. These disorders, which include ODD and CD, often first attract notice when they interfere with school performance or family and peer relationships, and frequently intensify over time.

Behaviors typical of disruptive behavior disorders can closely resemble ADHD—particularly where impulsivity and hyperactivity are involved—but ADHD, ODD, and CD are considered separate conditions that can occur independently. About one third of all children with ADHD have coexisting ODD, and up to one quarter have coexisting CD. Children with both conditions tend to have more difficult lives than those with ADHD alone because their defiant behavior leads to so many conflicts with adults and others with whom they interact. Early identification and treatment may, however, increase the chances that your child can learn to control these behaviors.

Oppositional Defiant Disorder

Many children with ADHD display oppositional behaviors at times. Oppositional defiant disorder is defined in the American Psychiatric Association's *Diagnostic and Statistical Manual of Mental Disorders, Fourth Edition (DSM-IV)* (see Chapter 2) as including persistent symptoms of "negativistic, defiant, disobedient, and hostile behaviors toward authority figures." A child with ODD may argue frequently with adults; lose his temper easily; refuse to follow rules; blame others for his own mistakes; deliberately annoy others; and otherwise behave in angry, resentful, and vindictive ways. He is likely to encounter frequent social conflicts and disciplinary situations at school. In many cases, particularly without early diagnosis and treatment, these symptoms worsen over time—sometimes becoming severe enough to eventually lead to a diagnosis of conduct disorder.

Conduct Disorder

Conduct disorder is a more extreme condition than ODD. Defined in the *DSM-IV* as "a repetitive and persistent pattern of behavior in which the basic rights of others or major age-appropriate social rules are violated," CD may involve serious aggression toward people or the hurting of animals, deliberate destruction of property (vandalism), stealing, running away from home, skipping school, or otherwise trying to break some of the major rules of society without getting caught. Many children with CD were or could have been diagnosed with ODD at an earlier age—particularly those who were physically aggressive when they were younger. As the CD symptoms become evident, these children usually retain their ODD symptoms (argumentativeness, resistance, etc) as well. This cluster of behaviors, combined with the impulsiveness and hyperactivity of ADHD, sometimes causes these children to be viewed as delinquents, and they are likely to be suspended from school and have more police contact than children with ADHD alone or ADHD with ODD.

Children with ADHD whose CD symptoms started at an early age also tend to fare more poorly in adulthood than those with ADHD alone or ADHD with ODD—particularly in the areas of delinquency, illegal behavior, and substance abuse.

ODD and CD: What to Look For

A child with ADHD and a coexisting disruptive behavior disorder is likely to be similar to children with ADHD alone in terms of intelligence, medical history, and neurological development. He is probably no more impulsive than children with ADHD alone, although if he has conduct disorder, his teachers or other adults may misinterpret his aggressive behavior as ADHD-type impulsiveness. (Attention-deficit/hyperactivity disorder behavior without CD, however, does not typically involve this level of aggression.) A child with ADHD and CD does have a greater chance of experiencing learning disabilities such as reading disorders and verbal impairment. But what distinguishes children with ODD and CD most from children with ADHD alone is their defiant, resistant, even (in the case of CD) aggressive, cruel, or delinquent, behavior. Other indicators to look for include

- **Relatives with ADHD/ODD, ADHD/CD, depressive disorder or anxiety disorder.** A child with family members with ADHD/ODD or ADHD/CD should be watched for ADHD/CD as well. Chances of developing CD are also greater if family members have experienced depressive, anxiety, or learning disorders.
- **Stress or conflict in the family.** Divorce, separation, substance abuse, parental criminal activity, or serious conflicts within the family are quite common among children with ADHD and coexisting ODD or CD.
- **Poor or no positive response to the behavior therapy techniques at home and at school (see chapters 6 and 7).** If your child defies your instructions, violates time-out procedures, and otherwise refuses to cooperate with your use of appropriate behavior therapy techniques, and his aggressive behavior continues unabated, he should be evaluated for coexisting ODD or CD.

Treatment

Children with ADHD and disruptive behavior disorders often benefit from special behavioral techniques that can be implemented at home and at school. These approaches typically include methods for training your child to become more aware of his own anger cues, use these cues as signals to initiate various coping strategies ("Take five deep breaths and think about the three best choices for how to respond before lashing out at a teacher."), and provide himself with positive reinforcement (telling himself, "Good job, you caught the signal and used your strategies!") for successful self-control. You and your child's teachers, meanwhile, can learn to better manage ODD- or CD-type behavior through negotiating, compromising, problem-solving with your child, anticipating and avoiding potentially explosive situations, and prioritizing goals so that less important problems are ignored until more pressing issues have been successfully addressed. These highly specific techniques can be taught by professional behavior therapists or other mental health professionals recommended by your child's pediatrician or school psychologist, or other professionals involved with your family.

If your child has a diagnosis of coexisting ODD or CD, and well-planned classroom behavioral techniques in his mainstream classroom have been ineffective, this may lead to a decision to place him in a special classroom at school that is set up for more intensive behavior management. However, as pointed out in Chapter 7, schools are mandated to educate your child in a mainstream classroom if possible, and to regularly review your child's education plan and reassess the appropriateness of his placement.

There is growing evidence that the same stimulant medications that improve the core ADHD symptoms may also help coexisting ODD and CD. Stimulants have been shown to help decrease verbal and physical aggression, negative peer interactions, stealing, and vandalism. Although stimulant medications do not teach children new skills, such as helping them identify and respond appropriately to others' social signals, they may decrease the aggression that stands in the way of forming relationships with others their age. For this reason, stimulants are usually the first choice in a medication treatment approach for children with ADHD and a coexisting disruptive behavior disorder.

The earlier stimulants are introduced to treat coexisting ODD or CD, the better. A child with a disruptive behavior disorder whose aggressive behavior continues untreated may start to identify with others who experience discipline problems. By adolescence, he may resist treatment that could help him change his behavior and make him less popular among these friends. He will have grown accustomed to his defiant "self" and feel uncomfortable and "unreal" when stimulants help check his reckless, authority-flaunting style. By treating these behaviors in elementary school or even earlier, you may have a better chance of preventing your child from creating a negative self-identity.

If your child has been treated with 2 or more types of stimulants and his aggressive symptoms are the same or worse, his pediatrician may choose to reevaluate the situation and replace the stimulant with other medications. If stimulant medication alone led to some but not enough improvement, his pediatrician may continue to prescribe stimulants in combination with one of these other agents.

Anxiety Disorders

As with disruptive behavior disorders, there is a great deal of overlap between anxiety disorders and ADHD. About one fourth of children with ADHD also have an anxiety disorder. Likewise, about one fourth of children with anxiety disorders have ADHD. This includes all types of anxiety disorders—generalized anxiety disorder, obsessive-compulsive disorder, separation anxiety, and phobia (including social anxiety). Younger children with overanxious disorder or separation anxiety are especially likely to also have ADHD.

Anxiety disorders are often more difficult to recognize than disruptive behavior disorders because the former's symptoms are *internalized*—that is, they often exist within the mind of the child rather than in such outward behavior as verbal outbursts or pushing others to be first in line. An anxious child may be experiencing guilt, fear, or even irritability and yet escape notice by a parent, teacher, or pediatrician. Only when her symptoms

are expressed in actual behavior, such as weight loss, sleepless-
ness, or refusal to attend school, will she attract the attention
she needs. It is important to ask your child's pediatrician or
psychologist to talk with your child directly if you suspect the
presence of persistent anxiety in addition to her ADHD.

What to Look For

Identifying an anxiety disorder in your child can be difficult
not only because her symptoms may be internal, but because
certain signs of anxiety—particularly restlessness and poor
concentration—may be misinterpreted as symptoms of ADHD.
Children with an anxiety disorder, however, experience more
than a general lack of focus or a restless response to boredom.
Their anxiety and worry are clear-cut, often focusing on specific situations or thoughts. They may seem tense, irritable, tired,
or stressed out. They may not sleep well, and may even experience brief panic attacks—involving pounding heart, difficulty
breathing, nausea, shaking, and intense fears—that occur for
no apparent reason. While their school performance may be
equivalent to that of children with ADHD alone, they tend to
experience a wider variety of social difficulties and have more
problems at school than children with ADHD alone. At the
same time, they may behave in less disruptive ways than children with ADHD alone because their anxiety inhibits sponta-
neous or impulsive behavior. Instead they may tend to seem
inefficient or distracted—having a great deal of difficulty
remembering facts or processing concepts or ideas.

Your child can be an important source of information that
may lead to a diagnosis of anxiety disorder, although some
children are reluctant to admit to any symptoms even if they
are quite significant. If the possibility of an anxiety disorder
concerns you, be sure to discuss any fears or worries she has
and listen carefully to her response. Report her comments to
her pediatrician and/or psychologist, and encourage her to

speak directly with these professionals. In the meantime,
ask yourself

- **Does she seem excessively worried or anxious about
  a number of situations or activities (such as peer relationships or school performance)?** Are her fears largely
  irrational—that is, overly exaggerated or unrealistic—
  rather than realistic worries about punishment for negative
  behavior? Does she find it difficult to control her worrying?
- **Does her anxiety lead to restlessness, fatigue, difficulty
  concentrating, irritability, muscle tension, and/or sleep
  disturbance?**
- **Does her anxiety or its outward symptoms significantly
  impair her social, academic, or other functioning?**
- **Does her anxiety occur more days than not, and continue
  for a significant duration?** Have her anxiety symptoms
  lasted for at least 6 months? Do her bouts of anxiety occur
  at least 3 to 5 times per week and last for at least an hour?
- **Is her anxiety unrelated to another disorder, substance
  abuse, or other identifiable cause?** A child who is distressed
  over a life event, who is abusing drugs, or whose family is in
  conflict may exhibit some of the symptoms of anxiety disorder. It is important to consider these other causes as the
  reason for anxiety instead of a formal anxiety disorder.
- **As a young child, did she experience developmental delays
  or severe anxiety at being separated from a parent, express
  frequent or numerous fears, or experience unusual stress?**
  Children with ADHD and a coexisting anxiety disorder are
  more likely to have experienced developmental delays in
  early childhood and more stressful life events such as
  parental divorce or separation.
- **Have others in her family been diagnosed with anxiety
  disorders?** Anxiety disorders tend to run in families. A
  careful review of your family's medical history may provide
  insight into your child's condition.

These are some symptoms of anxiety disorders, and their presence may indicate a need to have your child evaluated by her pediatrician or mental health provider. The sooner your child is properly treated for anxiety, the sooner she can improve her functioning and balance in her daily life.

Treatment

Treatment for children with ADHD and an anxiety disorder relies on a combination of approaches geared to each child's specific situation—including educating the child and her family about the condition, encouraging ongoing input from school personnel, initiating behavior therapy including cognitive-behavioral techniques, as well as traditional psychotherapy, family therapy, and medication management.

Behavior therapies are among the most proven and effective non-medication treatments for anxiety disorders. (The effectiveness of traditional psychotherapy has been less well studied.) As you learned in Chapter 6, behavior therapies target *changing the child's behaviors* caused by the anxiety rather than focusing on the child's internal conflicts. Cognitive-behavioral therapy techniques help children *restructure their thoughts* into a more positive framework so that they can become more assertive and increase their level of positive functioning. For example, a child can learn to identify anxious feelings and thoughts, recognize how her body responds to anxiety, and devise a plan to cut down on these symptoms when they appear. Other behavioral techniques that can be used for treating anxiety include modeling appropriate behaviors, role-playing, relaxation techniques, and gradual desensitization to the specific experiences that make a given child anxious.

Decisions about medication treatment of ADHD and a coexisting anxiety disorder depend largely on the relative strength of each condition. In the Multimodal Treatment Study of Children with Attention Deficit Hyperactivity Disorder (MTA) study of large numbers of children with ADHD and various coexisting conditions (discussed in detail in Chapter 3), behavioral treatments were equally as effective as medication treatment for children with ADHD and parent-reported anxiety symptoms. It was not known, however, how many of these children had true anxiety disorders.

In general, if your child's ADHD symptoms impede her functioning more than the anxiety does, and a medication approach is recommended, her pediatrician may choose to begin treating her with stimulants first. As he adjusts her dosage for maximal effect, he will monitor her for side effects such as jitteriness or overfocusing—possible responses to stimulants among children with ADHD and an anxiety disorder. If your child's ADHD symptoms improve with stimulant medication and her anxiety diminishes as well, her pediatrician may want to review her diagnosis to discern whether the anxiety stemmed from the ADHD-related behavior and was not a sign of an anxiety disorder. If the ADHD symptoms improve but your child's anxiety remains, her pediatrician may decide to add another type of medication. These medications can include a selective serotonin reuptake inhibitor (SSRI) or a tricyclic antidepressant (TCA).

Mood Disorders

Like anxiety disorders, mood disorders such as depression and bipolar disorder often involve subtle, internalized symptoms that can be difficult to recognize until they are expressed in outward behavior. Mood disorders occur in 15% to 20% of children with ADHD. Children with ADHD often have difficulty with irritability, moodiness, and emotional immaturity and tend to overreact to disappointments or frustration. If these problems are severe or interfere with functioning, evaluation for a mood disorder is recommended.

Types of Mood Disorders
The mood disorders most likely to be experienced by children with ADHD include dysthymic disorder, major depressive disorder (MDD), and bipolar disorder. Dysthymic disorder can be characterized as a chronic low-grade depression, persistent irritability, and a state of demoralization, often with low self-esteem. Major depressive disorder is a more extreme form of depression that can occur in children with ADHD and even more frequently among adults with ADHD. Dysthymic disorder and MDD typically develop several years after a child is diagnosed with ADHD and, if left untreated, may worsen over time. Bipolar disorder is a severe mood disorder that has only recently been recognized as occurring in children. Unlike adults who experience distinct periods of elation and significant depression, children with bipolar disorder present a more complex disturbance of extreme emotional instability, behavioral difficulties, and social problems. There is significant overlap with symptoms of ADHD, and many children with bipolar disorder also qualify for a diagnosis of ADHD.

What to Look For
Every child feels discouraged or acts irritable once in a while. Children with ADHD, who so often must deal with extra challenges at school and with peers, may exhibit these behaviors more than most. If your child claims to be depressed, however, or seems irritable or sad a large portion of each day, more days than not, she may have a coexisting dysthymic disorder. To be diagnosed with dysthymic disorder, a child must also have at least 2 of the following symptoms:

- Poor appetite or overeating
- Insomnia or excessive sleeping
- Low energy or fatigue
- Low self-esteem
- Poor concentration or difficulty making decisions
- Feelings of hopelessness

Before dysthymic disorder can be diagnosed, children must have had these symptoms for a year or longer, although symptoms may have subsided for up to 2 months at a time within that year. The symptoms also must not be caused by another mood disorder, such as MDD or bipolar disorder, a medical condition, substance abuse, or just related to ADHD itself (low self-esteem stemming from poor functioning in school, for example). Finally, the symptoms must be shown to significantly impair your child's social, academic, or other areas of functioning in daily life.

Major depressive disorder is marked by a nearly constant depressed or irritable mood or a marked loss of interest or pleasure in all or nearly all daily activities. In addition to the symptoms listed previously for dysthymic disorder, a child with MDD may cry daily; withdraw from others; become extremely self-critical; talk about dying; or even think about, plan, or carry out a suicide attempt. Unlike the brief outbursts of temper exhibited by a child with ODD who does not get her way, a depressed child's irritability may be nearly constant and not linked to any clear cause. Her inability to concentrate differs from ADHD-type inattention in that it is accompanied by other symptoms of depression, such as loss of appetite or loss of interest in favorite activities. Finally, the depression itself stems from no apparent cause—as opposed to being demoralized as a result of specific obstacles posed by ADHD or becoming depressed in response to parental divorce or any other stressful situation. (In fact, research has shown that the intactness of a child's family and its socioeconomic status have little or no effect on whether a child develops MDD.) While children with ADHD/CD alone are not at higher than normal risk for attempting suicide, children with ADHD/CD who also have an MDD and are involved in substance abuse are more likely to make such an attempt and should be carefully watched.

Talk of suicide (even if you are not sure whether it is serious), a suicide attempt, self-injury, any violent behavior, or severe withdrawal should be considered an emergency that requires the immediate attention of your child's pediatrician, psychologist, or local hospital.

A depressed child may admit to feeling guilty or sad, or she may deny having any problems. It is important to keep in mind the fact that many depressed children refuse to admit to their feelings, and parents often overlook the subtle behaviors that signal a mood disorder. By keeping in close contact with her teacher, bringing your child to each of her treatment reviews with her pediatrician, and including her in all discussions of her treatment as appropriate to her age, you can improve the chances that her pediatrician or mental health professional will detect any signs of developing depression, and that she will have someone to talk to about her feelings.

A child with bipolar disorder and ADHD is prone to explosive outbursts, extreme mood swings (high, low, or mixed mood), and severe behavioral problems. Such a child is often highly impulsive and aggressive, with prolonged outbursts typically "coming out of nowhere" or in response to trivial frustrations. She may have a history of anxiety. She may also have an extremely high energy level and may experience racing thoughts and inflated self-esteem or grandiosity, extreme talkativeness, physical and emotional agitation, overly sexual behavior, and/or a reduced need for sleep. These symptoms can alternate with periods of depression or irritability, during which her behavior resembles that of a child with MDD. A child with ADHD/ bipolar disorder typically has poor social skills. Family relationships are often strained because of the child's extremely unpredictable, aggressive, or defiant behavior. Early on the symptoms may only occur at home, but often begin to occur in other settings as the child gets older. Bipolar disorder is a serious psychiatric disorder that can sometimes include psychotic symptoms (delusions/hallucinations) or self-injurious behavior such as cutting, suicidal thoughts/impulses, and substance abuse. Many children with bipolar disorder have a family history of bipolar disorder, mood disorder, ADHD, and/or substance abuse. Children with ADHD and bipolar disorder are at higher risk than those with ADHD alone for substance abuse and other serious problems during adolescence.

If your child has ADHD with coexisting bipolar disorder, her pediatrician will generally refer her to a child psychiatrist for further assessment, diagnosis, and recommendations for treatment.

Treatment

As with ADHD with anxiety disorders, treatment of ADHD with depression usually involves a broad approach. Treatment approaches may include a combination of cognitive-behavioral therapy, interpersonal therapy (focusing on areas of grief, interpersonal relationships, disputes, life transitions, and personal difficulties), traditional psychotherapy (to help with self-understanding, identification of feelings, improving self-esteem, changing patterns of behavior, interpersonal interactions, and coping with conflicts), as well as family therapy when needed.

Medication management approaches, as with ADHD and other coexisting conditions, include treating the most disabling condition first. If your child's ADHD-related symptoms are causing most of her functioning problems, or the signs of depression are not completely clear, your child's pediatrician is likely to start with stimulant medication to treat the ADHD. In cases when the depressive symptoms turn out to stem from poor functioning due to ADHD and not to a depressive disorder, they may diminish as the ADHD symptoms improve. If the ADHD and depressive symptoms improve, your child's pediatrician will probably maintain stimulant treatment alone. If her ADHD symptoms improve but her depression remains the same, even after a reasonable trial of the type of broad psychotherapeutic approach described previously, her pediatrician may add another medication, most commonly an SSRI—a class of medications including Prozac, Zoloft, Paxil, Luvox, and Celexa. Selective serotonin reuptake inhibitors can make the symptoms of bipolar disorder worse, so a careful evaluation must be completed before starting medication. If this approach is unsuccessful, you may be referred to a developmental/behavioral pediatrician or a psychiatrist, who may try other classes of medications.

Tics, Tourette Syndrome, and OCD

Tics are rapid, repetitive movements or vocal utterances. They may be motor (like excessive eye blinking) or vocal (such as a habitual cough or chronic repetitive throat clearing noises), chronic (continuing throughout childhood), or transient (lasting less than 1–2 years). In children who eventually develop tic disorders and ADHD, the ADHD usually develops 2 to 3 years before the tics.

Tourette syndrome, which is quite rare, is a more severe form of tic disorder involving motor and vocal tics that occur many times per day. The average age at which it appears is 7 years. While children with Tourette syndrome may develop ADHD, the 2 disorders are separate and independent conditions. Attention-deficit/hyperactivity disorder is not a variant of Tourette syndrome, and Tourette syndrome is not just a variety of ADHD. Research has shown that chronic tic disorders, Tourette syndrome, and OCD may stem from some common factors, and a child with any of these conditions is quite likely to also have ADHD.

Obsessive-compulsive disorder involves such symptoms as obsessive thoughts (such as a highly exaggerated fear of germs) and compulsive behaviors (for example, excessive hand-washing in an attempt to reduce the fear of germs) that the child is unable to control or limit. In this sense, OCD is similar to tic disorders and Tourette syndrome, and creates additional functioning problems for children with ADHD.

What to Look For

Tics tend to resemble certain ADHD-related symptoms—fidgeting and making random noises in particular—and may occasionally be mistaken for signs of ADHD. True tics, however, differ from ADHD-type fidgetiness or hyperactivity in that they almost always involve rapid, repeated, identical movements of the face or shoulders or vocal sounds or phrases—they may cause a child to become socially isolated. To receive a diagnosis of Tourette syndrome, the tics need to have developed before 18 years of age, include motor and vocal tics, occur many times each day, and continue for at least a year. Though the intensity of the tics may increase or decrease periodically, a child with active Tourette syndrome is rarely completely tic-free for more than 3 months at a time.

While tic disorders and Tourette syndrome involve outbursts of simple movements or vocalizations, OCD consists of obsessive thoughts and compulsive behaviors. In contrast to the common childhood "obsessions" with computer games or television, OCD-type obsessive thoughts and behaviors provide no pleasure and stem from no rational desire or motivation. Rather they occur because the child is unable to stop them, even when he realizes that they are inappropriate—and they can interfere with a child's functioning for literally hours a day.

Treatment

Mild or transient tics may not need to be treated with any medication. Until recently, stimulant medication was not recommended for children with ADHD and a coexisting tic disorder because the stimulants were thought to be a possible cause of Tourette syndrome. It is now known that starting stimulants does not cause Tourette syndrome or even increase tics in most children with ADHD. Stimulants may actually result in improvements in the tics in some cases. However, stimulants at high doses may bring out or exaggerate tics in a child with ADHD, who would have eventually developed them even without stimulants. The potential disadvantage of mildly increased tics is often outweighed by stimulants' effectiveness in treating the symptoms of ADHD. Meanwhile, lowering the stimulant dose or switching to a different medication can sometimes decrease or eliminate some tics altogether. If your child's tics are especially severe or socially disruptive, a combination of stimulants and clonidine, guanfacine, or other medications (including TCAs, pimozide, and haloperidol) or newer medications (such as risperidone) may also be considered. Possible side effects must be taken into account when using these medications.

Children with ADHD and coexisting OCD are generally prescribed an SSRI or the tricyclic medication clomipramine. Stimulants and SSRIs or clomipramine can be combined to treat OCD and ADHD.

Learning, Motor Skills, and Communication Disorders

Most learning problems encountered by children with ADHD are not due to learning disabilities. About 40% of children with ADHD experience such learning challenges as work production problems and organizing difficulties that are categorized as learning "problems," not disabilities. Learning disabilities are generally thought of as a child's failure to develop specific academic skills at the expected level in spite of adequate intelligence and education. Attention-deficit/hyperactivity disorder itself is not a learning disorder—with proper treatment and support, many children with ADHD can perform as well as their peers academically. The true incidence of coexisting learning disabilities is not clear because of discrepancies in how they are defined, and estimates vary widely.

Although there is increasing controversy about how learning disorders should be defined, they are generally diagnosed by showing that there is a significant discrepancy between a child's cognitive abilities, as measured by standard IQ tests, and her actual learning, as measured on standardized individual achievement tests in reading, mathematics, and written expression. Nonverbal learning disabilities are not generally included in the standard definitions of learning disability, but are important to consider especially when children have coexisting problems with attention. Other recognized disabili-

▲   ▲   ▲   ▲

DISORDERS THAT INTERFERE WITH ACADEMIC FUNCTIONING

Learning Disorders
- Reading disorder
- Mathematics disorder
- Disorder of written expression
- Nonverbal learning disability*

Motor Skills Disorder
- Developmental coordination disorder

Communication Disorders
- Expressive language disorder (difficulties with using language to express oneself, including having a limited amount of speech, limited range of vocabulary, difficulty acquiring new words, using appropriate grammar, etc)
- Mixed receptive-expressive language disorder (difficulty understanding and using language, words, sentences, or specific types of words)
- Phonological disorder (difficulty with pronunciation or articulation of speech sounds)
- Stuttering

*Not included in the formal *Diagnostic and Statistical Manual of Mental Disorders, Fourth Edition* diagnostic categories

ties that can interfere with academic functioning include motor skills disorder (developmental coordination disorder) and communication disorders.

Learning Disorders

Reading Disorders

Reading disorders, the most common and best studied of the learning disabilities, account for 80% of all children diagnosed as learning disabled. Children with reading disorders are able to visualize letters and words, but have difficulty recognizing that letters and combinations of letters represent different sounds. Most reading disorders involve difficulties with recognizing single words, rather than with reading comprehension. The cause often lies in the area of the child's "phonologic awareness"—difficulty perceiving how sounds make up words. Reading disorders—even including letter reversals—have little to do with vision. These problems make it quite difficult for children to add new words to their reading repertoire and become good readers. While their listening and speaking skills may be adequate, they may have trouble naming objects (such as quickly coming up with the word for "computer" or "backpack") and/ or remembering verbal sequences (such as "The boy saw the man who was driving the red car."). A smaller group of children also have reading disabilities that involve comprehension, and these children tend to have poor receptive language skills—that is, difficulty understanding language even when it is spoken to them. A reading disorder, depending on how it is defined, is not necessarily a lifelong condition, but these problems do persist into adulthood in at least 40% of children.

Like all other learning disabilities, reading disorders cannot be detected through neurological tests such as special examinations, electroencephalograms (brain wave tests), or brain scans (such as computed tomographic scans and magnetic resonance imaging). They are identified by educational testing when a child's reading level or language achievement scores are significantly lower than her abilities would indicate, lower than her achievement in other academic areas, or lower than those of her classmates. In assessing reading disabilities, it is important to identify each component of your child's problem so that specific treatment measures can be applied. It is also important to address the attentional and behavioral aspects of the ADHD so that your child can make optimal progress at school.

Mathematics Disorder

Mathematics disorder can be thought of as a type of learning disability in which spoken language is not affected, but computational arithmetic is. Children with mathematics disorder also may have difficulties with motor and spatial, organization, and social skills. Children with coexisting ADHD, or even ADHD alone, can have additional problems in mathematics—such as delays in committing math facts to memory, the making of careless mathematical errors, rushing through problems and impulsively putting down the wrong answers or not showing

their work, and making errors because they misaligned columns during addition or long division.

Written Expression Disorder

Children with written expression disorder can have difficulty composing sentences and paragraphs; organizing paragraphs; using correct grammar, punctuation, and spelling in their written work; and writing legibly. Children with spoken-language problems can develop problems with written language as well as math. Children with ADHD can also have difficulty with taking the mental time to plan their writing, and their handwriting can be sloppy and sometimes unreadable without necessarily having a written expression disorder. When handwriting problems are more a function of ADHD than a written expression or motor skills disorder, they sometimes improve rapidly and dramatically with appropriate stimulant medication treatment.

Nonverbal Learning Disorder

Nonverbal learning disorder (NVLD) is a condition that is not yet formally categorized as a disorder but that has been the subject of increasing interest. It is particularly important to consider in children with ADHD because it relates to attentional functioning. It is often difficult to decide whether a child with ADHD has coexisting NVLD or whether she just has an NVLD that mimics ADHD—especially the inattentive symptoms. Nonverbal learning disorder accounts for about 5% to 10% of children with learning disabilities. It consists of a cluster of deficits, including poor visuospatial skills, problems with social skills, and impaired mathematics ability. Problems with disorganization, inconsistent school performance, and social problems may lead to an evaluation for ADHD. Children with NVLD may experience mild early language delays, but by kindergarten their vocabulary, early reading skills, and understanding of information that they hear are often developing normally, and their verbal memory skills can be excellent. Their verbal expression, however, is often delayed or poorly organized. They often have weak hand-eye coordination skills (such as copying pictures) and are easily confused by visual or spatial information. They have poor motor coordination and tend to dislike physical activity, particularly as they get older. Their difficulties in mathematics can be very significant, with difficulty understanding math concepts, lining up columns of numbers correctly, or visualizing geometry or word problems. They can also have problems with peer relations because they tend to miss many nonverbal social cues in interactions with others, causing them to seem withdrawn or awkward. They often feel overwhelmed by new situations or complex information, preferring their routines, and avoid taking risks. Children with NVLD are often not identified until late elementary school or middle school, when the peer problems increase and academic tasks become more complicated. They frequently develop symptoms of depression and anxiety.

Motor Skills Disorder
Motor skills disorder, also known as developmental coordination disorder, is diagnosed when motor skills problems significantly interfere with academic achievement or activities of daily living. It is frequently overlooked in children with ADHD due to its nonspecific cluster of symptoms—yet it can affect children's lives by interfering with writing and other academic activities or preventing children from participating at their classmates' level in sports and play. Children with ADHD and other learning disabilities frequently have motor skills disorder as well. Motor skills disorder involves a developmental delay of movement and posture that leaves children with coordination substantially below that of others of their age and intelligence level. These children seem so clumsy and awkward they are rarely picked for teams at school. As the years pass, they tend to fall further behind in terms of motor skills, and their confidence

diminishes as a result. By adolescence, most children with motor skills disorder not only perform poorly in physical education classes, but may also have a poor physical self-image and perform below expectations academically.

Motor skills disorder may be first identified when a preschooler or kindergartner is unable to perform age-appropriate skills such as buttoning buttons and catching a ball, or an elementary-school child struggles with writing or sports activities. A child with motor skills disorder may have difficulty with the mechanics of writing, with planning motor actions, or with memorizing motor patterns. While many young children with ADHD but no motor skills disorder may seem clumsy in their younger years, their awkwardness is related more to inattentiveness or impulsivity than to poor motor control and is frequently outgrown. A child with ADHD and coexisting motor skills disorder may not outgrow her clumsiness.

If your child is diagnosed with developmental coordination disorder, she may be referred to a pediatric occupational therapist for individualized therapy and, particularly if her deficits negatively affect her academic performance or daily skills, be recommended for special gym activities at school to promote hand-eye coordination and motor development and improve specific skills.

Communication Disorders

Communication disorders—conditions that interfere with communications with others in everyday life—involve not only the ability to appreciate language sounds (phonologic awareness) but also to acquire, recall, and use vocabulary (semantics) and to deal with word order and appropriately form or comprehend sentences (syntax). Subcategories of disorders have been identified, including expressive language disorder, mixed receptive-expressive disorder, phonological disorder, articulation (word pronunciation) disorder, and stuttering. Because there is such a close association between communication and social relationships, these language deficits are often accompanied by social skills difficulties. Children with ADHD without a language disorder may also have difficulties in using language, particularly in social situations. You may notice that your child has problems with excessive talking, frequent interruption, not listening to what is said, blurting out answers before questions are finished, and having disorganized conversations.

Treatment

Children with a learning, motor skills, or communication disability may require tutoring, an in-class aide or other classroom support, an altered curriculum, special education classes, pull-out time, speech/language therapy, occupational therapy, or adaptive physical education. Many children with ADHD benefit from a positive behavior management plan. As described in Chapter 7, many of these services must be provided free of charge by your school district if your child qualifies for coverage by the Individuals with Disabilities Act or Section 504. Your child's pediatrician can also refer your child to private sources for evaluation and help.

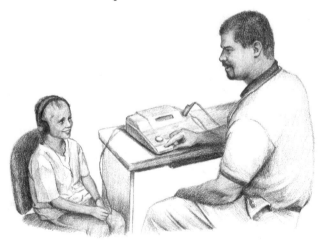

While stimulant medication does not improve the academic achievement of children with learning disabilities alone, it can help children who have both learning disabilities and ADHD improve their reading performance and seatwork completion by helping them improve their attention and focus during these tasks. This is most likely due to stimulants' positive effect on children's attentiveness, which allows them to benefit more from special tutoring and other forms of therapy. Thus use of stimulants to treat ADHD symptoms is often recommended as an important part of treatment for ADHD/learning disabilities.

Mental Retardation and Pervasive Developmental Disorders

Most forms of mental retardation and the more severe forms of pervasive developmental disorders (PDDs) are recognized early in a child's life, as children fail to achieve standard developmental milestones at appropriate ages or clearly display unusual behaviors. Mental retardation is diagnosed in the 2% to 3% of children who score the lowest on a standard IQ test and are delayed to the same extent in such life skills as self-care, self-direction, and the use of academic skills. Eighty-five percent of children with mental retardation fall into the mild range, with IQ scores from 50 to 70. Pervasive developmental disorders, also known as autistic spectrum disorders, are diagnosed in children who have serious problems with social interactions; delayed and/or unusual communication; and repetitive and unusual behaviors, rituals, interests, or activities. Both of these conditions are usually diagnosed within the first few years of life. Children with milder forms of mental retardation or PDD may escape detection until their school years, when parents or teachers begin to wonder if their symptoms signal the presence of ADHD or learning disabilities and bring them to a pediatrician for evaluation.

Mental Retardation

Until recently, physicians did not believe that ADHD occurred in children with mental retardation, but assumed that these children's hyperactive or other ADHD-type behavior was an aspect of mental retardation. As a result, stimulant medications were rarely used to treat children who actually had ADHD and coexisting mental retardation. But recent research reveals that as many as 25% to 40% of children with mental retardation also have ADHD—significantly more than in the general population.

Pervasive Developmental Disorders—Autism and Related Disorders

The number of children with PDD and ADHD is difficult to determine because children with PDD alone often have elements of impulsiveness and hyperactivity. A child with PDD may also have mental retardation, but even if he does not, his PDD is likely to prevent him from participating fully socially and in many school and home activities. The most severe form of PDD, autistic disorder (autism), involves severe language and social impairment and abnormal, repetitive, and unusual patterns of behavior. Autistic disorder usually becomes manifest by age 3 years. Autistic children are unable to form normal relationships with others. Coexisting ADHD can add a significant overlay of aggressive, impulsive, or hyperactive symptoms to the behavior of a child with autism, although it is not always easy to separate the ADHD behaviors from those related to the autism itself.

Asperger syndrome is a recently recognized form of PDD. Children with this condition are of average to above-average intelligence and are able to function adequately in many aspects of daily life. They do not have language delays but have difficulty making conversation and using polite manners, and may have an unusual tone of voice. They experience significant disabilities in social interaction with peers and display unusually intense and narrow interests or obsessions. Children with Asperger syndrome may have coexisting ADHD and are at increased risk of developing anxiety or depressive disorders.

Treatment

Individualized educational programming, behavior therapy, and family support are essential elements in the treatment of children with mental retardation or PDD. Medication may be helpful for specific symptoms. Stimulants can usually be used to treat ADHD symptoms in children with ADHD and mental retardation or PDD, though the rates of side effects and nonresponse are somewhat greater than in those with ADHD alone.

Most children with mental retardation/ADHD or PDD/ADHD will be able to remain in a regular public school, but may need special education–related services such as speech/language therapy and behavior management programs. (See Chapter 7 for descriptions of resources and laws relating to student disabilities.) Children with more serious forms of PDD, including autism, require a more intense program of behavior therapy than that used for children with ADHD alone. You can further support your child's progress by educating yourself about his condition, monitoring the latest research on his areas of disability, and advocating for his rights and appropriate services within the public school system. Review Chapter 7 for information on how to work with your child's teachers to create an Individualized Education Program for him, and contact the appropriate local and online family support groups for more information and help.

Coexisting Problems

Academic Problems

As was pointed out earlier in this chapter, children with ADHD frequently experience significant challenges at school and elsewhere that cannot be formally categorized as disabilities or formal disorders. Forty percent of children with ADHD, for example, who do not qualify for a diagnosis of learning disability experience learning problems that lead to underachievement at school. These learning problems may include

- Inattention and distractibility
- Lack of persistence and inconsistent performance
- A tendency to become easily bored or to rush through or not complete work
- Impulsive responses and careless errors
- Difficulty self-correcting mistakes
- A limited ability to sit still and listen
- Difficulty with time-limited tasks and test taking
- Problems with planning, homework flow, and work completion
- Difficulty taking notes or performing other forms of multitasking
- Difficulty memorizing facts
- Difficulty organizing and producing written work
- Sloppy and slow handwriting that can also create obstacles in expressive writing
- Difficulty with reading comprehension

Stimulant medications that decrease your child's ADHD symptoms are likely to help her address many of these problems. Behavior therapy techniques aimed at increasing or decreasing specific behaviors at home and in school can also prove beneficial. As discussed in chapters 5 and 7, specific behavioral goals, such as improving completion of assignments, can be addressed by understanding your child's individual strengths and weaknesses and collaborating with school staff in using positive reinforcement, appropriate behavioral techniques, daily report cards, and ongoing monitoring.

Recognizing Coexisting Strengths

Finally, but most importantly, do not forget to pay attention to your child's coexisting strengths. The main focus should always be on your child, and not on his challenges, disabilities, and coexisting conditions. Children with ADHD frequently meet with disapproval, social rejection, and other forms of discouragement. However, if encouraged to grow up aware of and invested in their own talents, strengths, positive energy, and achievements, they can mature with a more healthy and balanced perspective and better self-esteem as they head toward productive and successful adult lives.

CHAPTER NINE

Unproven Treatments for ADHD

▲   ▲   ▲   ▲

In this book you have been introduced to the treatment approaches that have been proven most effective for children with attention-deficit/hyperactivity disorder (ADHD). Yet you are likely to read or hear about "alternative" types of treatment that proponents claim can diminish or eliminate ADHD symptoms or the conditions that may accompany them. These approaches may seem particularly attractive to parents or children who have not experienced sufficient improvement in spite of standard treatments, who are uncomfortable with the idea of daily medication use, or who feel overwhelmed by the effects of ADHD on their daily lives. Some of them have the additional attraction of being proposed as "cures" or "natural treatments." The theories on which they are based may make a great deal of intuitive sense as well—for example, when they target a child's diet to treat hyperactivity or his hearing to help attention. However, as you will learn in this chapter, none of the alternative approaches discussed here have been shown to reliably produce positive and sustained effects for most children with ADHD. Some have actually been proven ineffective. Others may or may not eventually be demonstrated to have a positive effect, but have not yet been studied sufficiently for their use to be recommended at this time.

Because the claims for ADHD treatments are so vast and so varied, it is important to subject any report of a new or unconventional treatment approach to the same scrutiny and consideration you would apply to any major decision affecting your family: by considering the source of the information, reasonableness of its claims, and scientific evidence that backs them up, and by discussing the treatment with experts in the field such as your child's pediatrician or psychologist. In this chapter you will learn how to consider the validity of claims for ADHD treatments by

- Understanding how a proposed treatment is scientifically evaluated, and what steps must be taken to prove that a treatment is sound
- Reviewing the evidence for and against such proposed ADHD treatments as dietary changes; visual, auditory, and sensory integration approaches; hypnotherapy; biofeedback; applied kinesiology; homeopathy; and various other methods
- Considering the types of questions you should ask, and the steps you should take, before committing effort, time, and money to a new form of treatment, however promising it may seem

How Treatments Are Proven Effective

You may have noticed that the media seem to report on a new treatment for ADHD every other week. If so, you may wonder why so many alternative treatments exist for ADHD, and why they so easily gain credibility with the general public. One reason is that, as opposed to such medical conditions as diabetes, the results of a given treatment for ADHD are difficult to measure objectively—that is, there is no blood, urine, or other laboratory test that can prove conclusively that the treatment has worked. Instead, as you will see, the effectiveness of treatments for ADHD are judged through rigorous studies of groups undergoing the treatment compared with those who are not.

Because effects of these treatments are determined through relatively subjective methods such as changes in teachers' and parents' observations, and ratings of behaviors over time— not by objective blood or urine tests—it is often more difficult, even with careful statistical analysis, to clearly establish that any proposed standard or alternative treatment for ADHD is well-founded. If a treatment cannot quickly and objectively be proven effective, it is easier for its proponents to just claim that it works. Thus claims for a particular approach can be greatly exaggerated and widely disseminated long before they have been sufficiently studied.

Yet there is a standard, reliable process for deciding whether a new treatment is effective. This process is called the *scientific method,* and through it scientists can subject any treatment approach to a reliable series of tests or studies to evaluate its effectiveness. Studies of ADHD conducted according to the scientific method make use of research tools including structured observations, rating scales, and objective tests of the child's functioning whenever possible. They are structured so that extraneous factors that might influence results are taken into account and designed so that they can be reproduced by other researchers to make sure similar results are achieved.

According to the scientific method, we can only rely on the results of studies relating to a particular treatment if the researchers have

- **Formulated a clear hypothesis.** The researcher must state what she wants to determine through the study. For instance, she might state the hypothesis, "Because diet and nutrition are known to affect brain development, might a diet fortified with extra vitamins have a positive effect on ADHD symptoms?"
- **Created a detailed plan to test the hypothesis.** The researcher must define the nature of the treatment (for example,

state which vitamins will be administered, at what dose, and
how frequently), how it will be administered (by parents,
by a physician, by the children themselves), how it will be
monitored (by counting the number of pills left in the bottle
at the end of the study), and how the effects will be measured (through a daily dosage checklist, parents' reports,
physicians' records). In this way, the study results can be
systematically explained (perhaps it did not work because
the children reported taking the vitamins but did not always,
for example), and other researchers can confirm the results
by using the same methods with different sets of children.

- **Defined the group to be tested.** This is an important and
  sometimes difficult part of creating a reliable study. Can a
  child be allowed to participate in the study solely on the
  basis of whether he looks hyperactive to the researchers?
  Must he have been diagnosed by his pediatrician? Or have
  the researchers made their own diagnosis according to rigorous research criteria? The group under study must also
  be large enough for the treatment results to apply to the
  population as a whole—1, 6, or even 100 children may
  not be enough, depending on the research question. The
  group receiving treatment must be compared with a group
  not receiving the treatment, and/or another group or
  groups receiving a different type of treatment for ADHD.
  The members of the groups under study should otherwise
  be as similar as possible, and children who might be affected by extraneous influences such as coexisting disorders,
  high or low extremes in intelligence, and unusual family
  circumstances are sometimes screened out. Depending on
  the question to be answered, the researcher must limit as
  many other variables as possible, aside from the treatment
  under study.

- **Eliminated the power of suggestion.** One way to test whether a treatment is effective is to compare the proposed treatment with a "placebo" treatment. People often tend to respond to placebos—inactive medications or treatments they believe may work—whether the treatment is actually effective in the long run. A person with a headache who is given a sugar pill, believing it is pain medication, may report that the headache is gone a short time later. One way to test whether a treatment for ADHD is effective, for example, is to make sure that the subjects do not know whether they are really receiving the proposed treatment or a placebo treatment. In the vitamin treatment example, then, half of the subjects in the study might receive actual megavitamins and the other half would receive an inactive, neutral, but identical-looking pill. Depending on the type of investigation, the study design may work even better if used in a "double-blind" experiment—that is, if the subject, her family, her teacher, and the researcher do not know whether the actual pill or a placebo was used until the study has ended. That way there is no danger that the researcher has inadvertently communicated this information to the subject, her family, or teacher, or that he misinterpreted the results because of what he knew.

Placebo treatments are more difficult to create when the treatment involves a procedure, such as psychotherapy, rather than a pill. Still researchers must make every effort to make the real treatment and the placebo treatment equally convincing to the subject. At least having independent evaluators who are "blinded" improves the accuracy of the study.

- **Provided a valid means of evaluating the results.** Some treatment results are easier to evaluate than others. In the case of ADHD, results can be difficult to evaluate because they cannot be measured through laboratory tests or other fully objective measures. Still, researchers can standardize test results through such techniques as quantifying behaviors (having teachers report how many times per day a child interrupted a conversation, got out of his seat without permission, or failed to hear someone talking to him), using standard rating scales, comparing the study subjects' performance to that of the other groups in the study who received different treatments, and measuring changes in the behaviors being studied at predetermined intervals through-out the course of the investigation. Treatments can be evaluated by standardized tests (performance on standardized math tests), as well as in terms of the child's performance in the real world (measures of classroom behavior or improvements in family relationships). Rigorous statistical techniques are then used to find any significant differences in results among the groups in the study. The methods and results of any study are then reviewed by other experts in the field—a process required before the study is published in a reputable scientific journal. If a treatment proves successful, it is also helpful to follow children on the treatment for a longer time than the period that was studied to make sure that the beneficial results continue and do not cause any serious long-term side effects.

Which Treatments Have Been Shown to Work?

As has been pointed out throughout this book, the most proven treatments for ADHD are stimulant medications and behavior therapy techniques, often used together. These forms of treatment have been the most studied and validated by the types of rigorous scientific research described previously. For this reason, pediatricians can feel secure in recommending these approaches as proven, safe, and effective first-line treatments for ADHD.

Many other forms of treatment for ADHD have been tested in studies using the scientific method. Some, such as traditional psychotherapy and cognitive therapy, have been shown through convincing research not to demonstrate results in treating the condition's core symptoms. Another group of potential treatments for ADHD has been tested to some extent, but the studies have been too few in number or were conducted with some major flaws in the study design, or the results were too ambiguous to prove that the treatment works. Evidence of a treatment's effectiveness may be insufficient if the

- Studies involve too few subjects, so that results cannot be generalized to the ADHD population at large
- Proof relies on anecdotal evidence, such as parents' testimonies or one physician's experience with his own clients, rather than on a large group that has been part of a well-designed scientific study
- Study results have not been subjected to the scrutiny of experts who would have reviewed the study prior to publication to identify any possible flaws in the study design or the results

Following, you will find discussions of the evidence supporting or refuting the usefulness of a number of the most popular alternative approaches to treating ADHD and associated problems. Some of these approaches have simply not been studied. Others are based on inaccurate assumptions about the nature of ADHD or its causes, and are therefore unlikely ever to lead to an effective treatment. Still, others may eventually be shown to have a significant positive effect, though the current supporting evidence is insufficient. In examining the facts behind the theories, you can not only learn more about these particular treatments, but can also become more comfortable in critically assessing future proposed ADHD treatments on your own.

Your Child's Diet: A Cause and a Cure?

"You are what you eat" is a belief so prevalent in our culture—and true to some extent—that it is easy to understand the temptation to attribute ADHD-type behaviors to some dietary causes, or to believe that particular changes in diet can diminish the symptoms related to the condition. In fact, recent scientific research has supported the belief that diet and nutrition are related to mood and behavior, and that they can affect brain development in the early years. Add to this a widespread concern about the effects of sugar, artificial additives, and other elements in children's diets and it is no wonder that special diets have become the most popular alternative to medication and behavior therapy treatment for ADHD.

Certainly, concerns about nutrition are valid for all children and should not be dismissed. It is also true that some forms of dietary management, and the addition of some trace elements through special supplements, may help with some specific health- or behavior-related problems. However, as you will see, none of the special diets designed to treat the symptoms of ADHD have yet been conclusively shown to be effective for most children with the condition.

Supplemental Diets

It stands to reason that an adequate diet is necessary for a child's healthy growth. Proper nutrition, including an array of vitamins, minerals, amino acids, and essential fatty acids (EFAs), is particularly necessary in the first few years of life to support brain development and prevent certain neurological disorders. Even among older children, a lack of certain dietary components such as protein, or an insufficient number of calories, can negatively affect a child's learning and behavioral abilities, and vitamin or mineral deficiencies can certainly interfere with learning over the course of a school year. Research shows, however, that a young child must be significantly malnourished in proteins and calories before brain development is seriously affected, and this level of malnutrition is rare in the United States. To date no convincing evidence has shown that a poor diet causes ADHD, or that dietary supplements can be used to successfully treat the condition.

Megavitamin Therapy

In the 1950s Drs Abram Hoffer and Humphry Osmond began using megavitamins containing large amounts of vitamin B_3, vitamin C, and, later, pyridoxine (vitamin B_6), to treat schizophrenia. This treatment was based on the theory that schizophrenia and some other forms of mental illness are caused by a genetic abnormality that greatly increases the body's vitamin and mineral requirements. By providing patients with enormous doses (megadoses) of these substances, Hoffer and Osmond felt that psychiatrists could provide an "optimum molecular environment for the mind" in which the symptoms of mental illness would diminish or disappear.

In the 1960s the chemist and Nobel Laureate Linus Pauling put his support behind this theory, giving it the name *orthomolecular psychiatry* and greatly increasing its visibility among experts and the general public. In the 1970s Dr Allan Cott claimed that hyperactivity and learning disabilities were also the result of vitamin deficiencies and could be alleviated with megavitamins and large doses of minerals. Treating ADHD symptoms in children with nutritional supplements—supplements that contained at least 10 times the recommended daily allowance of vitamins, minerals, and other necessary elements—became an increasingly popular alternative to stimulant medication, particularly among families who considered megavitamins the more "natural" approach.

Research has failed, however, to reveal significant positive
results from megavitamin therapy. While some early studies
resulted in improved classroom attention ratings for subjects
taking megavitamins, these studies were marred by the fact that
the children, their parents, their teachers, and the researchers
were all aware that a given subject was being given this new
form of treatment. When the studies were repeated using the
double-blind method discussed earlier, so that no one knew
whether a particular child was taking a megavitamin or a placebo, no behavioral improvement was shown. In fact, it was dis-
covered that disruptive behavior increased in a significant
number of the children given the megavitamins. Studies have
also suggested certain abnormalities in the way the liver functions among children on megavitamin therapy, signaling possible toxic effects of this high level of vitamin intake—a strong
reminder that "natural" substances are not always safe, especially in the highly "unnatural" doses prescribed here. As a result,
experts have concluded that megavitamin therapy for ADHD
is of little benefit for nearly all children with the condition—
and potentially harmful. In 1976 the American Academy of
Pediatrics Committee on Nutrition issued a formal statement to
that effect. This is not to say that children with ADHD should
not take any vitamins, just that vitamins at normal doses and
even megadoses are not in any way an effective treatment
for ADHD.

Other Vitamin and Mineral Supplements

In the wake of the enthusiasm for megavitamin therapy, a
number of specific nutritional elements have been studied
regarding their possible role in the development of ADHD
and their potential for treating the condition. These elements
include iron, magnesium, pyridoxine (vitamin B_2), zinc, and
certain EFAs including linoleic acid and linolenic acid. All of
these elements are known to be necessary for optimal brain

development and function. Some studies comparing the levels of these substances in the blood of children with ADHD to their peers without the condition have even revealed lower levels of zinc or EFAs. (No difference between children with or without ADHD has been shown for levels of iron, magnesium, or vitamin B_2). Despite this evidence, no links between these low levels and ADHD-type behavior have been established to date, and no significant improvement in ADHD behaviors has been demonstrated when supplemental doses of these substances are provided. As with all children, any nutritional deficiency should be corrected with a standard supplement or change in daily diet. But supplementation should not exceed the daily recommended allowance because higher levels of some elements (zinc in particular) can prove toxic.

Additional Supplements to Improve Performance

A number of other dietary supplements have been proposed to replace the use of stimulants in treating ADHD. Principal among these are *nootropics, antioxidants,* and *herbs.* Nootropics, specifically a substance called *piracetam,* have been advocated as cognitive enhancers for children with Down syndrome, dyslexia, and ADHD. While there is no scientific proof of positive effects relating to Down syndrome, one convincing study did show improvement in reading ability and comprehension among children taking piracetam supplements. While there is a rational basis for theorizing that piracetam may also improve ADHD-type behaviors because it is believed to enhance the transmission of the same brain chemicals influenced by stimulant medication (dopamine and noradrenaline), no controlled studies have yet been published, so this treatment cannot be recommended.

Deanol (DMAE), lecithin, and phosphatylserine are other nootropics frequently found in over-the-counter ADHD remedies available in health food stores or on the Internet. Lecithin and phosphatylserine have not yet been sufficiently studied as treatments for this condition, but DMAE has seemed in one reliable study to be as effective as the stimulant methylphenidate in treating target behaviors. It is clear, then, that though these nootropics cannot currently be recommended as a substitute for stimulants due to insufficient evidence, they are currently being seriously researched and warrant further study as a potential future treatment for the symptoms of ADHD.

Antioxidants and herbs, used for many centuries in traditional medicine, have only recently come under scientific study. Some of the substances that have been marketed as treatments for ADHD include *pycnogenol,* an antioxidant derived from pinebark; *melatonin,* another antioxidant known to successfully treat sleep cycle disturbances in certain children; *gingko biloba extract,* often used in Europe to treat circulatory and memory disorders; and such herbs as *chamomile, valerian, lemon balm, kava, hops,* and *passion flower.* While melatonin can be useful in addressing sleep disturbances in a child with ADHD, and the herbs mentioned may also be useful as mild sleep aids, the reported positive effects of these antioxidants and herbs as treatments for ADHD's core symptoms has been solely anecdotal so far, and there is insufficient scientific evidence to support their use.

If you do decide to administer any of these substances to your child, it is imperative to inform your child's pediatrician and then carefully limit and monitor their use because some can lead to harmful effects if used in combination with other medications. Gingko biloba extract, for example, must not be taken with aspirin, anticoagulants, or antidepressants, and the herbs listed should not be used when taking sedative medications due to the danger of compounding the sedative's effects. It is necessary to keep in mind that these substances can vary considerably in potency from one preparation to another, and that they are not standardized or regulated by the US Food and Drug Administration.

Elimination Diets

Other theories about the causes of, and treatment for, ADHD have evolved from the hypothesis that certain substances that are *present,* rather than absent, in a child's diet may lead to or worsen the condition. The suspected harmful substances include artificial food additives, preservatives, sugar, or other elements speculated to cause allergic responses or yeast infections that can lead to the development of ADHD. According to these theories, eliminating such elements may eliminate or diminish the symptoms of ADHD.

Feingold Diet

In the mid-1970s a groundswell of concern about the effects of food additives, artificial flavorings, and dyes in the American diet accounted for, in part at least, the huge popularity of the

Feingold Diet as a treatment for ADHD. Dr Benjamin Feingold, a practicing allergist, theorized that these food additives, as well as substances called *salicylates* (contained in many fruits and vegetables), were causing hyperactivity and learning disabilities in many children. In his book, *Why Your Child Is Hyperactive,* Dr Feingold claimed that when these children were given a special "elimination diet" that omitted these substances, half of them showed a dramatic improvement in behavior. When the elements were reintroduced into the children's diet, the symptoms returned.

The Feingold Diet became hugely popular in the United States, not only in the population at large but among some ADHD experts and politicians as well. A National Advisory Board on Hyperkinesis and Food Additives was created, and The Feingold Association of the United States was established to support and provide information to parents. All of this activity occurred despite the fact that Feingold's theory was based solely on anecdotal accounts and conjecture rather than conclusive scientific evidence—and the reality that these types of elimination diets are very difficult to carry out, particularly when the child is not at home where his parents can supervise his diet.

The good news was that the theory's popularity increased public awareness of the presence of artificial additives in the diet and motivated more productive scientific inquiry into the relationship between diet and behavior. The disappointing news came in a subsequent series of studies revealing that only about 10% of children with ADHD demonstrated the predicted allergy to food dyes, and a mere 2% on the Feingold Diet showed consistent behavioral improvement when these food dyes were eliminated. Later studies provided a somewhat more positive slant: the small number of children who did respond negatively to food dyes benefited from them being eliminated (usually through decreased irritability and restlessness and improved sleep cycles), and most subjects' parent ratings reflected some improvement in behavior even though their teacher and laboratory ratings did not. As a result, experts now recommend screening certain selected children for food sensitivities, although they do not support the use of the Feingold Diet to treat ADHD.

Diets Eliminating Sensitizing Food Substances

In the decades since the Feingold Diet was introduced, studies of the impact of diet on behavioral disorders have become more sophisticated and reliable. Newer research has shown that behavioral improvement using elimination diets is more likely in children who have inhaled and food allergies, a family history of migraines, and food reactivity. Younger children seem to be the most responsive. Whole foods like milk, nuts, wheat, fish, and soy have been implicated in addition to additives. Elimination diets can sometimes influence sleep and mood disturbances as well as ADHD symptoms. Sensitivities to substances in the environment—in medicines, clothes, water, our homes, the air, and so on—have also been studied as they relate to children's health and behavior. The results have shown a link between sensitizing foods and some health and behavior problems in a small percentage of children with ADHD. In most cases, these children experience a variety of coexisting health and behavioral difficulties in addition to ADHD—particularly sleep-related and neurological problems. They are also likely to have a family history of food sensitivities or migraine headaches.

Because this link has been established, if food or additive sensitivities are highly suspected in your child, she may be tested for them by first eliminating an entire range of common foods (typically milk, soy, wheat, corn, citrus, and peanuts) for 2 to 4 weeks. If her symptoms improve—signaling the possible presence of a food sensitivity—the range of foods can be restored to her diet, then one food at a time can be removed for a short period, with the results being monitored. This process can continue until the correct substance has been identified or all likely possibilities have been exhausted.

Elimination diets are often easier to introduce with young children, whose tastes in food may be easier to change. (Older children and adolescents are less likely to stick to a special diet.) They work best if you carefully target and quantify the behaviors you are hoping to improve. If these dietary changes prove to be extremely useful, a nutritionist can introduce you to tasty dishes that omit the offending food, and an appropriate support group can help with such issues as teaching your child to avoid the food away from home. As with the Feingold diet, these diets are difficult to integrate into daily routines. Children tend to resist diets that make them stand out from their peers, and it is often difficult for parents to devote the extra time to food preparation that these diets demand. As a result, you may experience considerable parent-child conflict when implementing one of these types of diets.

Meanwhile, it is important to understand that for most children with ADHD who do not have food sensitivities (and for some who do), elimination diets are not effective treatments for ADHD itself. If your child is on a special diet, you will need to make sure it is not replacing a more effective treatment for her ADHD. In most cases, stimulant medication, behavior therapy, and the other measures described in previous chapters will have a much clearer positive effect on your child's ADHD-related behaviors, while a well-balanced diet with few processed foods may improve her general health and attitude.

Sugar-Free Diets

Humans are naturally attracted to sugar because it tastes good and because our bodies rely on glucose—the form of sugar

found in natural foods—for metabolic processes. Like many other children, children with ADHD often have strong sugar cravings, and this has contributed to the belief that sugar and candy consumption can cause hyperactive behavior. A great deal of objective evidence, however, has shown that this assumption is untrue for most children with or without ADHD. While one early study did reveal a link between high sugar consumption and hyperactive behavior, there was no evidence that one *caused* the other or that the behavior problems were not due to different parenting styles or other factors. A number of subsequent scientifically rigorous studies could not demonstrate any adverse effects of sugar on the behavior of children. As for children with ADHD, sugar consumption has not been shown to cause or enhance ADHD-related behavior.

Of course allowing sugar only in moderation makes sense for any child. Major reductions or the elimination of sugar altogether, however, may create unnecessary conflicts with your child while providing few or no benefits. If your child shows an uncontrollable craving for sugar and carbohydrates, discuss this with her pediatrician. Aside from issues relating to general health, a sugar-free diet is not considered a useful tool in treating ADHD.

Aspartame-Free Diet

Aspartame, an artificial sweetener that became available in the early 1980s, consists of amino acids that cross from the bloodstream into the brain to affect brain function. (Interestingly, it was used as the placebo in some of the studies of sugar's effects on behavior.) It was believed that among individuals susceptible to this substance, aspartame might lead to seizures or ADHD-type behaviors. No such effects have been demonstrated, however, and elimination of aspartame for children with ADHD is not considered an effective treatment except for children with phenylketonuria, a chemical disorder that prevents some people from being able to break down or metabolize aspartame.

Yeast- or Fungus-Free Diets

In the mid 1980s, Dr William Crook, a practicing pediatrician and allergist, popularized the theory that hyperactivity, irritability, and learning disorders in children could be caused by chronic candida (yeast) infection—the same type of yeast overgrowth that leads to vaginal infections in women. Crook pointed out that frequent or prolonged use of antibiotic treatment could pave the way for this type of infection because the antibiotics killed the bacteria that normally control the spread of yeast. To prevent this from happening, Crook devised a special diet eliminating all sources of sugar (because sugar leads to yeast growth) and all foods made with or contaminated by molds and yeast (such as breads, cheeses, dried fruits, and processed foods). He also recommended decreasing levels of additives and potential allergens in the diet, clearing the child's environment of chemical pollutants and molds and providing vitamin and mineral supplements. For children with a history of antibiotic use, this elimination diet could be combined with such antifungal agents as nystatin or ketonazole to combat yeast without affecting useful bacteria. Finally, he recommended academic and behavior therapy support for all children with ADHD.

Crook claimed a success rate of 75% in reducing hyperactive behavior among his own patients with ADHD. However, his claims were based solely on his own professional observations rather than on any scientific study. While he speculated that yeast overgrowth produces toxins that weaken the immune system, thus leading to ADHD, he did not explain how the mechanism might work. (In fact, candida has not been shown to weaken the immune system, but to take advantage of an already weakened system to flourish.) Because there is insufficient objective research to validate Crook's claims, because yeast infections have not been shown to cause ADHD, and because the often-recommended megadoses of vitamins can be potentially dangerous to your child's health, this approach to treating ADHD is not recommended.

Vision, Inner-Ear, Auditory Integration, and Sensory Integration Problems

An entire class of theories about the causes of ADHD and effective treatments for it centers on the workings of the senses. Problems relating to sight, hearing, balance controlled by the inner ear, sensory integration, and so on have been proposed as underlying conditions that lead to ADHD and accompanying problems and disorders. Each theory is linked to a treatment approach, and each form of treatment is supported by a large number of vocal enthusiasts. Again, none of these theories or methods has yet been proven valid in diminishing or eliminating the behaviors related to ADHD.

Optometric Training

Optometric training, a kind of eye training for children with learning disabilities, is based on the theory that faulty eye movements and problems in visual perception can cause dyslexia, language disorders, and other learning problems that frequently accompany ADHD. Named *behavioral optometry* by the optometrists who developed and support this form of therapy, the treatment consists of teaching children specific visual skills as a way of improving learning. These skills include tracking moving objects, fixating on or locating objects quickly and accurately, encouraging both eyes to work together successfully, and changing focus efficiently. The skills are taught through the use of eye exercises and special colored or prismatic lenses. Optometric training is often supplemented with training in academic skills, nutrition, and personal relationships. This treatment is frequently quite expensive.

However, little research has supported the theory that dyslexia or other learning disabilities are caused by vision defects or problems, and thus vision training is an ineffective approach to reading and learning disabilities. In 1984 the American Academy of Pediatrics (AAP), along with the American Association for Pediatric Ophthalmology and Strabismus and the American Academy of Ophthalmology, issued a policy statement affirming that no known scientific evidence "supports the claims for improving the academic abilities of dyslexic or learning-disabled children with treatment based on visual training, including muscle exercises, ocular pursuit or tracking exercises, or glasses (with or without bifocals or prisms)." Because vision training is not only ineffective but may delay more effective treatment for coexisting learning disabilities, it is not recommended.

Motion-Sickness Medication

Dr Harold Levinson, a New York physician, is responsible for the popular theory that inner-ear problems can cause problems with balance, coordination, and energy regulation, which in turn can lead to ADHD and learning disabilities—as well as dyslexia, obsessive-compulsive disorder, panic disorder, and many other difficulties. In his book, *Total Concentration*, Levinson states that ADHD symptoms are often related to a kind of dizziness or motion sickness resulting from inner-ear problems. He recommends treatment with anti–motion-sickness medications, often in combination with antihistamines, tricyclic antidepressants, the antipsychotic drug thioridazine (Mellaril), vitamin B complex, gingerroot, or stimulants.

To date no studies have revealed a link between ADHD and inner-ear deficiencies, and Levinson's theory conflicts with much that is currently known about ADHD. His claims rest almost entirely on anecdotal information, and the published reports of his work consist of individual case studies rather than scientific research. Because insufficient research has been conducted to prove this treatment effective, and because it contradicts many of the known facts about the causes of ADHD, it is not recommended as a treatment option.

Sound Treatment

Difficulties with auditory integration—that is, organizing, attending to, and making sense out of information while listening—have also been suspected as a cause of ADHD. The Tomatis Method, devised by the French physician Alfred Tomatis, is perhaps the best-known treatment approach aimed at this proposed deficiency. A large number of individual accounts testify to the effectiveness of Tomatis' auditory-stimulation sessions—in which children listen to high-frequency modifications of the human voice, classical music, and Gregorian chant through special headphones called "electronic ears," and are given listening training to improve focus and attention. The effects of music and sound on brain function have been insufficiently studied to date, however. While one study did show that boys with ADHD were better able to solve arithmetic problems when listening to their favorite music—implying that auditory stimulation may help to improve performance on specific tasks—no scientifically controlled studies have yet supported the claim that the Tomatis Method improves ADHD. Any improvement that has been reported by individuals may be due to the treatment's emphasis on individual attention for each child, with at least 75 specially designed listening sessions and targeted training in social and academic skills.

Sensory Integration Training

Dr Jean Ayres, an occupational therapist, developed the theory that much of the hyperactivity in today's children is the result of poor sensory integration—that is, the failure of the brain to organize and make use of information derived from such senses as vision, hearing, smell, taste, touch, motion, and temperature. According to this theory, sensory integration dysfunction makes it difficult to concentrate and sit still, and puts children at risk for learning disabilities, problems with coordination, social difficulties, and touch sensitivity. Ayres claimed that sensory integration dysfunction is usually genetically inherited or acquired prenatally, during birth, or from environmental toxins. Recommended treatment includes exercises or experiences that provide the child with extrasensory stimulation and feedback—such as brushing and rubbing of the skin, deep-pressure exercises, vibration, stretching, and so on.

While this approach has some intuitive appeal, feels good to children, can be calming, and is said to address the poor coordination and social difficulties that many children with ADHD experience, no convincing evidence has surfaced to prove that deficits in sensory integration are a cause of ADHD or its related disorders. Studies have not shown that sensory integrative training succeeds as a treatment for children with ADHD or learning or behavior problems. While not known to be harmful in any way, the expense and time demands are such that this approach cannot be recommended as a treatment for ADHD.

Hypnotherapy, Guided Imagery, and Biofeedback

A number of proposed treatments for ADHD—including hypnotherapy, self-hypnosis, guided imagery, biofeedback, and relaxation training—are aimed at helping a child begin to regulate his own behavior and psychological state. The fact that these techniques can be used quite successfully for children in other areas of self-regulation (headache management, teaching bowel control, etc) increases their appeal as a form of treatment.

Hypnotherapy has not been shown to significantly improve the core symptoms of ADHD, though it may improve such accompanying problems as sleep problems and tics when used as part of an integrated treatment approach.

In biofeedback, changes in a child's heart rate, muscle tension, and rate of sweating are fed into a computer through sensors placed on the child's skin. Changes in these body functions are then displayed on the computer screen as charts, designs, or cartoons that change color or size as the child learns to regulate these functions. Eventually the child can learn how to control the functions voluntarily without the aid of the computer "feedback." Dr Joel Lubar and others have proposed that children with ADHD have more unalert brain waves than their peers, and can learn to increase the ratio of alert to unalert brain waves through biofeedback. If this could be demonstrated to work, it would provide more of a permanent cure for ADHD than the temporary help provided through medication. However, studies of this form of treatment have not yet proven it to be effective or distinguished between the effects of the biofeedback mechanism itself and other aspects of the treatment—including the subject's close relationship with his therapist, the high number of focused sessions (at least 30–40 sessions in most cases), and the training in academic skills that usually accompanies these sessions. It should also be pointed out that biofeedback treatment is an expensive approach to treating ADHD. While it has potential as a possible treatment and certainly warrants further study, at the present time it remains an unproven therapy for ADHD.

Applied Kinesiology

Advocates of this approach, also known as neural organization technique, believe that learning disabilities are caused by the misalignment of 2 specific bones in the skull—a misalignment that creates unequal pressure on different areas of the brain and leads to brain malfunction. This misalignment is also said to create "ocular lock," an eye movement malfunction that contributes to reading problems. Treatment consists of restoring the cranial bones to the proper position through specific body manipulations.

This theory is not consistent with either current knowledge about the causes of learning disabilities or knowledge of human anatomy. (Standard medical textbooks inform us that cranial bones do not move.) No research has been done to support the effectiveness of this form of treatment. Because it is based on false assumptions concerning the causes of learning disabilities, it is not recommended as a treatment for these disabilities, nor for ADHD.

Homeopathy

Homeopathy, a therapeutic approach developed in the 1800s that is especially popular in Europe, springs from the concept that illness results from a disorder of "vital energies," and that these energies must be restored if a patient is to recover. Vital energies can be restored through the use of dilute animal, plant, or mineral extracts designed to treat specific symptoms. These treatments have been shown to be more effective than placebos in reliable scientific studies, though the reason for this is not yet known. Homeopathic treatment for ADHD, increasingly widespread in the United States as individual accounts of success have spread, has also been demonstrated effective in an initial study in improving ADHD-type behavior, though the study failed to use a fully double-blind technique. Though the mechanisms underlying this treatment are still not scientifically defined, the success of this study merits further investigation of homeopathy as a treatment for ADHD, but it cannot be recommended as a proven therapy at this time. If you do become interested in using this approach, be sure to discuss your plans first with your child's pediatrician. Some extracts can interact negatively with medications your child may be taking.

New Remedies for ADHD: You Be the Judge

Claims about a new treatment can be difficult to resist. Who wouldn't love to find a "miraculous" new treatment that would completely eradicate the symptoms of ADHD and involve only healthy, "natural" substances that appear in our ordinary diet? Yet the very terms that tap into your longing to use them to conquer this condition—terms such as "cutting-edge," "amazing," "revolutionary"—should also serve as signals that it is time to take a hard look at the evidence that backs such claims up. Many of the proponents of these cures carry impressive initials after their names—many are "doctors" or "professors" of some kind. Many are sincere in their belief that they have found a major treatment or even a cure for this complex and often baffling disorder. Yet sincerity—even passionate belief—is not enough to render a treatment effective.

In reviewing the summaries of the popular ADHD-related theories and treatments described previously, you have seen how important it is to go beyond proponents' claims—no

matter how convincing or intuitively "right" they may seem—
to examine the scientific research backing up those assertions.
As you encounter news of new proposed treatments for ADHD,
ask yourself these questions, provided by the advocacy organization Children and Adults With Attention-Deficit/Hyperactivity
Disorder (CHADD). (See fact sheets at www.chadd.org.)

Will it work for my child?

Suspect an unproven remedy if it

- Claims it will work for everyone with ADHD and other
  health problems
- Uses only case histories or testimonials as proof
- Cites only one study as proof
- Cites a study without a control (comparison) group

How safe is it?

Suspect an unproven remedy if it

- Comes without directions for proper use
- Does not list contents
- Has no information or warnings about side effects
- Is described as harmless or natural (Remember, most
  medication is developed from natural sources. A "natural"
  treatment may still be ineffective or harmful.)

How is it promoted?

Suspect an unproven remedy if it

- Claims it is based on a secret formula
- Claims that it will work immediately and permanently for
  everyone with ADHD
- Is described as "astonishing," "miraculous," or an "amazing
  breakthrough"
- Claims it cures ADHD
- Is available from only one source

- Is promoted only through infomercials, self-promoting books, or by mail order
- Claims that treatment is being suppressed or unfairly attacked by the medical establishment

Even when an alternative treatment has been shown to be potentially useful for specific symptoms or behaviors that have been targeted for your child, it is important to consider, and to discuss with your child's pediatrician, whether it is more effective than already proven treatments, whether it may involve any uncomfortable or dangerous side effects or health hazards, how expensive it is, and how difficult it is for your family to implement. If your child's pediatrician is not knowledgeable about the approach in question, you will need to do much of the research yourself through the avenues discussed previously.

Also keep in mind that the first and most important step in choosing the best treatment for your child is obtaining a full and accurate diagnosis of his ADHD and any coexisting problems or conditions. A standard medical evaluation is also necessary to learn whether your child could benefit from special treatment for any nutritional, vision, hearing, or other problems. Standard treatments, such as stimulant medication and behavioral therapy, should always be considered as first-line approaches to ADHD. If you, your child, and his treatment team prefer an alternative treatment, the scientific validity of the treatment and its appropriateness for your child must be carefully reviewed, analyzed, and discussed.

▲ ▲ ▲ ▲

USING THE INTERNET

An excellent source of medical information and valuable advice, the Internet is also the source of a great deal of dubious health-related theories, "facts," and testimonials. In searching the Internet for information about a proposed ADHD treatment—or for any other information about ADHD and related conditions—it is always a good idea to start with the most reliable general information Web sites and expand from there. The Web sites listed in the Resources section of this book are excellent first steps. They can provide you with links to more specific information, support groups, and sources of government information.

A good way to quickly ascertain the reliability of an Internet resource is to look at the suffix of its Web site address. Government information Web site addresses end in ".gov." These include sites such as the National Institutes of Health and National Institute of Mental Health and have a wealth of health-related teaching materials for the general public. Nonprofit organizations, such as the AAP and CHADD, have Web sites ending in ".org"—however, not all organizations put out materials as reliable as the materials from these 2 organizations. Academic Web sites have ".edu" suffixes on their Internet addresses, and many of these have evidence-based educational materials geared toward parents. Web sites with the suffixes ".com" generally are commercial Web sites not necessarily affiliated with an educational entity or a source of reliable information.

Take some time to look at these sites—and be sure to explore any Web site first before recommending it to your child.

CHAPTER TEN

ADHD in Adolescence

▲   ▲   ▲   ▲

For every child, with or without attention-deficit/hyperactivity disorder (ADHD), adolescence is a time of profound change— a time of transitioning from full dependence on and identification with his family toward a separate, independent adult self. Although it was previously believed that most children outgrow ADHD by their teenage years, and that the condition rarely continues into adulthood, recent research has shown that ADHD persists into adolescence and beyond for *70% to 85%* of children diagnosed with the condition. As the parent of a teenager with ADHD, you will need to understand and prepare for the many ways in which this normal developmental process can affect your child's academic and social performance and his relationship with you—as well as how ADHD may affect his development. With the onset of adolescence, his treatment plan will need to be reviewed carefully. You may need to readjust your teenager's medication plan, for example, as his activities expand. His willingness to take medication may waver as he resists seeming "different" from his peers. The increasing academic demands of middle school and high school may require more attention to staying organized or to changes in his educational plan. At home your teenager may respond negatively to parenting techniques you once found effective—and insist on approving any new approaches you want to use. Meanwhile the presence of ADHD may be accompanied by delays in the development of skills necessary to support an increasingly independent life.

Clearly, these changes make adolescence a challenging time for your entire family. However, it is also a time of great promise as your teenager begins to explore his potential as a unique human being with a great deal to offer the world. Finding the ideal balance between protection and empowerment will be a difficult task for you as a parent, yet there is nothing more exciting than watching your adolescent with ADHD start to fully accept, manage, and master his own situation. Your earlier efforts to help your child take control of his own progress will start to pay off now as he enters early adulthood. This chapter will outline the additional steps necessary to

- Help your child meet new academic challenges.
- Help him manage new social and emotional pressures.
- Help you parent more effectively.
- Learn to take care of yourself as he works on becoming more independent.

ADHD and Your Teenager's Development

Every teenager's primary developmental task is to begin the process of "individuation," or the creation of a sense of self separate from her identity with her family. A child's sense of her own uniqueness begins early in life, of course, but kicks into high gear at around age 11 or 12 years. One early step in this individuation process—a step that will occupy much of your child's energy for the next few years—is to establish as clearly as possible the ways in which she is *not* like you. Once she feels that these differences or boundaries have been securely defined, she can move in later adolescence toward understanding who she *is*.

Establishing a separate sense of self is not easy for the younger teenager. Even *she* does not always understand why she so frequently tunes you out, slams her bedroom door when she is angry, or hides her journal—and her own behavior may frighten or upset her at times. Her personal identity, or ego, can be so fragile that any minor threat, such as a parent's criticism or a sibling's teasing, may lead to extremely defensive behavior. At the same time, her weak sense of who she is can leave her vulnerable to peer pressure and other potentially negative outside influences. As she gains more experience establishing her personality in the larger world, and enjoys confidence-boosting success in social, academic, and other realms, these more difficult benchmarks of adolescence will start to diminish.

In the meantime, however, the typical adolescent's developmental tasks—her need to separate from her parents, define herself, fit in with her peers—put her at greater risk than in earlier childhood for academic failure; experimentation with tobacco, drugs, or alcohol; early sexual activity; and all of the other types of activity that keep parents up at night. Most adolescents develop new strengths during these years that help them with decision making on their own as their parents' influence starts to fade. They improve their ability to think long term, resist momentary impulses, and regulate their own behavior. Teenagers with ADHD, however, often lag behind in these areas, while experiencing the same need for independence as their peers. At the same time, certain ADHD-related behaviors may actually increase the risk that your child will engage in some of the self-defeating activities that many other teenagers may avoid. In part, this is because adolescents with ADHD can lack insight into their own functioning and are less able to realistically assess their abilities than their peers. This makes self-management more difficult, and creates a key paradox because it occurs at exactly the time that they need to assume greater control of their lives.

The manner in which ADHD is manifested during adolescence depends on its severity, subtype (predominantly hyperactive/impulsive-, inattentive-, or combined-type ADHD), and

your teenager's particular symptoms. Her ADHD-related behavior is also strongly affected by her stage of development;
her risk-taking behaviors; and the presence of any coexisting
conditions such as depression, learning disabilities, or anxiety
disorder. The quality of her home and school environment can
also make an enormous difference in how well she functions in
her daily life. As a result, teenagers with ADHD tend to behave
in widely varying ways. A teenager with hyperactive/impulsive
ADHD and a coexisting disruptive behavior disorder may get
into fights constantly at school and be suspended several times
each semester, while another with inattentive-type ADHD and
depression may fall behind in school, lose self-esteem, and escape special notice until she starts "self-medicating" with marijuana or alcohol. An adolescent with good verbal and language
skills may have managed to keep up her grades and go undiagnosed for ADHD in elementary and middle school, but start
to fail her high school courses as the demands for a high level
of work production exposed her organizational weaknesses.
Another teenager who has participated in her ADHD treatment
all along and experienced successes may show marked improvement at school and with friends as she grows able to help manage her own medication and take greater control of her areas of
strength and weakness.

Each subtype of ADHD can present its own challenges during adolescence. By educating yourself about these issues and
how they come into play in different ways for different teenagers, you can better support your child as she proceeds
through this new developmental stage.

Poor Impulse Control

Most adolescents act impulsively now and then, and teenagers
are known for favoring short-term pleasures over long-term
benefits. Teenagers with hyperactive/impulsive- or combined-
type ADHD, however, can have much more difficulty than

▲   ▲   ▲   ▲

IS IT ADOLESCENCE OR ADHD?

When faced with a disruptive 14-year-old, a 10th-grader with a sudden drop in grades, or a high school junior who regularly ignores the curfews you impose, it can be difficult if not impossible to tell whether such behavior is part of normal adolescent development or an aspect of your child's ADHD. As was the case earlier in childhood, ADHD-related behaviors resemble those of teenagers without ADHD, but are at the more extreme end of the continuum and are likely to continue for months or years after they have diminished in individuals without ADHD.

In the end, it is not really important to know whether a particular behavior is or is not ADHD-related because your response in either case should be the same. Unacceptable behaviors need to be met with consistent limits and appropriate consequences. Your teenager's potentially greater difficulties with impulse control, focusing, and organizing and long-term planning may require extra consistency, structure, and thought on your part—but she would benefit from this form of positive parenting even if she did not have ADHD.

others in regulating their impulses, even when they know their behavior is self-destructive. As when younger, your child may still act first and think later—but now the stakes are higher and impulsiveness can potentially lead to substance abuse, aggressive behavior, unprotected sex, reckless driving, or other high-risk situations. Even minor impulsive behavior—interrupting others, fidgeting at his desk—may cause academic or social problems for your teenager as others expect more "mature" behavior despite the presence of ADHD.

It is important for you and your adolescent to understand that behaving impulsively is not a moral failure on his part, but an aspect of his ADHD that requires special attention during this period. Your adolescent will benefit from learning about ways to minimize the potentially damaging effects of this behavior. Later in this chapter, you will find a number of suggestions that may help with managing impulsiveness in your teenager's personal, academic, and social life.

Difficulty Focusing and Organizing

Teenagers with predominantly inattentive- or combined-type ADHD generally do not concentrate or sustain their attention as well as their classmates. At times they can find it almost impossible to focus on a class lecture, take good notes, complete homework or other tasks, or prioritize schoolwork and other activities. Others may characterize them as "flighty" or "daydreamy," but these behaviors are aspects of ADHD, not personality traits. Clearly, such difficulties can get in the way of your teenager's desire to take greater control of her own academic success. She may start the school year determined to bring home a "great" report card, and have no idea why she is struggling with her grades so much more than her peers. An inability to focus can also defeat her efforts to succeed socially or at a job. You will need to help your teenager understand that extra support may be necessary to help her achieve the higher performance demands of adolescence, and that this temporary support is a necessary step along the road toward independence.

Problems With Long-term Planning

The adolescent surge toward independence is accompanied by a burst of maturation that helps most teenagers achieve their eventual goal of full individuation. This development centers on complex thinking—the ability to plan ahead, conceptualize and prioritize the steps necessary to reach a goal, and move steadily toward that goal until it has been achieved. Teenagers with ADHD, however, can lag behind in this form of maturation. As a result, while your teenager may be as determined as her peers to "control her own destiny"—wanting to get a job or apply to colleges all on her own—she will often need extra support in achieving these goals. By discussing ahead of time how you and others can help her take the steps she needs to succeed, you can help her understand that a key to being a truly self-sufficient person includes knowing when and how to seek assistance—whether that involves scheduling a meeting with her teacher, asking a counselor for special guidance, or using a coach to help her organize and plan her homework.

Low Self-esteem

Teenagers with ADHD can experience a good deal of difficulty in academic, social, or personal realms. Even with your support and empathy, such experiences can decrease your child's confidence and self-esteem. Low self-esteem may lead him to refuse medication, avoid special educational activities, or do anything else that might make him appear or feel different from his peers. Lack of confidence may also leave teenagers with ADHD more vulnerable to peer pressure regarding drug use or other

dangerous behaviors as they try to prove they are as "cool" as anyone else. Finally, the sense that they are not as competent as their peers may sap their motivation as they try to compete for academic or social success. Later in this chapter, you will learn some strategies for addressing these issues with your teenager.

Dependence Issues

Like any other teenager, your adolescent will want and expect to attend parties, get a driver's license, and generally enjoy increasing amounts of privacy and independence with each passing year. Yet it is important for you and your adolescent to understand that having ADHD can potentially make some activities more risky, and these may need to be monitored more closely than for his peers without ADHD. A teenager dealing with inattention, for example, may need to agree to drive only while his stimulant medication is in effect. If your child's problems completing homework have led to failing grades, he may need help with reviewing his work each night to be sure he has met his goals. Of course, your teenager is likely to resent and resist some of these potentially helpful measures, but he will also rely on you to set and enforce necessary limits. You can make it easier for him to accept this continued dependence by problem-solving with him in a way that respects his needs by inviting him to help create the rules and routines he needs.

Your Teenager's Treatment Plan

The best strategy for preparing your child to successfully manage the challenges that ADHD imposes during adolescence is to have encouraged him to be actively engaged in all elements of his treatment plan in his preteen years. One parent writes, "We've always made it a point to have Seth be part of his school conferences and medical visits. When he was in grade school he dreaded his visits to his pediatrician to discuss his treatment. He would tell us that 'She always asks me the same questions about school and about my medicine, and always tells me the same things about how my medicine works.' Then when he was about 11 she started meeting with him alone for part of our visits, and he would usually come out with a list of three or four things that he was going to work on. Eventually we began to notice that Seth was beginning to take more responsibility on his own

▲   ▲   ▲   ▲

PREDICTORS OF SUCCESS DURING ADOLESCENCE

Some of the most important factors in teenagers with ADHD who do the best during adolescence include

- Early intervention
- An adolescent's self-understanding and acceptance of problems and issues
- A supportive family
- An understanding and developmentally attuned school system
- An appropriate Individualized Education Program if indicated
- A teenager's willingness to engage in appropriate counseling, mentoring relationships, and "coaching" surrounding production and completion of work

The highest-risk factors leading to negative outcomes for adolescents with ADHD include

- Delayed intervention
- An ongoing cycle of failure
- Serious behavior problems in school
- Significant substance abuse
- Medication refusal
- Damaged self-esteem resulting from the adolescent's problems being viewed as character flaws rather than ADHD-related behaviors
- Giving up or lack of motivation

for making sure that his homework got into his backpack before he left for school, and he would remind us if we forgot to put out his medication in the morning. By the time he was in 11th grade he had pretty much taken over the responsibility for his medication and even asked us if we could get him a tutor to help him organize one of his long-term projects. We feel like we did something right by keeping him involved in his own treatment."

Changing Treatment Needs

Throughout this book, you have been encouraged to continue addressing your child's functioning problems and to meet regularly with her treatment team to reassess her needs. Regular review sessions become especially important as your child enters adolescence and academic, social, and emotional pressures start to increase. As the parent of a teenager with ADHD, you will need not only to keep track of her homework production and grades, but also to arrange with her teachers for regular, brief meetings or telephone conferences about her progress. Weekly home-school report cards and other monitoring tools (see Chapter 7) used with younger adolescents can help reveal any academic or behavioral problems before they cause too much damage, and lead to helpful changes in her treatment or education program. Chances are your teenager may object at some point to this level of scrutiny, which is more than her peers without ADHD probably receive. To counterbalance this, make sure that you provide ample opportunities for her to assert her autonomy in as many appropriate situations as possible, and allow her to direct as much of the monitoring system as is developmentally appropriate.

Aside from changing academic needs, your adolescent may experience greater social conflict and increased emotional stress during middle school and high school. You may hear about some of these problems—particularly disruptive behavioral issues—from school personnel. Other important changes—increases in depression or anxiety, increasing social rejection, plunging self-esteem—may remain virtually invisible to you as a parent. As your child begins the normal adolescent process of individuation described previously, she is less likely to confide in you about these types of problems. For this reason, it is very important to allow time for her to meet privately with her doctor during every treatment review session to ensure that she receives a careful screening for these symptoms and additional diagnostic work or help if indicated.

Keep in mind that the older your child gets, the more aware she is of the special attention she is receiving and the more sensitive she will be to what this says about who she is and what her capabilities are. The more you can present monitoring techniques as proactive tools for her own self-empowerment, rather than limits to her personal growth, the more positive her attitude toward her treatment is likely to be.

Medication Management

You have already read about the specifics of medication management in Chapter 4. If your child has been successfully treated with medication in the past, your medication management plan should be carefully reviewed as adolescence begins. There is no hard and fast rule about the changing medication needs of adolescents. It used to be thought that adolescents "outgrow" ADHD sometime in their teenage years, and medication was often stopped at that time. We now know that although hyperactivity often becomes less of a problem, impulsive behavior and inattention usually persist. Adolescents do not necessarily need changes in their medication dosage even after the large growth spurts that adolescence brings. Your teenager's dose, however, may need to be increased or lowered on the basis of his ability to function well academically, behaviorally, and socially, not because of his growth.

Medication needs may also change because of increased homework demands, or because of the typically complex schedules of adolescents. If your teenager leaves for school at 7:30 in the morning, has soccer practice after school, and does not get to his homework until 8:00 pm, even a 12-hour preparation of stimulant medication may have worn off by that time. Some teenagers solve this by going back to an 8-hour preparation for the school day, and then synchronizing a shorter-acting (4-hour) dose to cover their homework time.

Your teenager craves autonomy, yet the presence of ADHD means he will probably need extra structure and support from you. Be honest with him about your concerns, and ask for his help in designing a medication routine that will best address his needs as well as your concerns. You might agree, for example, that he will be responsible for remembering to take his medication, unless more than 10% of his pills remain untaken on a weekly pill count. If conflicts arise over the balance between limits and personal freedom, ask your teenager's pediatrician, psychologist, or school counselor to help mediate or contribute ideas.

If your teenager continues to question the effectiveness of stimulant medication, or states a desire to discontinue medication altogether, his pediatrician might help him set up a carefully monitored "trial" or experiment that will include careful teacher observations of relevant academic, behavioral, or social concerns for a specified period on and off medication. The teacher will make these observations without knowing which period is off and which is on. Your son can also keep a careful diary or his own observations. The observations can be reviewed after the trial for any significant differences in homework completion, grades, etc, on and off medication, and then make a better informed decision about whether to continue medication as a part of his treatment plan (see Chapter 4).

Conducting such a trial will also respect your adolescent's need to participate in decision making about treatment. This type of activity can be particularly effective for skeptical teenagers who prefer to "see" before they "believe." Medical professionals can also provide your teenager with books and videotapes about ADHD treatment, and put him in touch with ADHD support groups that can help him understand how other adolescents have learned to manage their ADHD.

Abuse of Stimulant Medication

For a minority of teenagers with ADHD, resistance to taking stimulant medication may be less of a problem than overuse. Stimulants are classified as Schedule II drugs by the US Drug Enforcement Administration, and, sooner or later, adolescents who take stimulant medication usually become aware of its "street value." Your child may be tempted at some point to give or sell her medication to others, or to take more than the pre-scribed dose herself. While it is a fact of life that most teenagers experiment with some form of high-risk behavior, such as a sin-gle episode of alcohol or drug experimentation, the presence of ADHD makes it especially important for you (and, ideally, your child's pediatrician) to discuss the dangers of drug abuse with her and to monitor her medication use. It is felt that teenagers who are doing well on a treatment plan that may include taking stimulant medications are generally less likely to abuse stimu-lants than those who do not have a treatment plan in place and are not taking medication, and because of this are experiencing low self-esteem, are more impulsive, and are more inclined to take risks. If your child has a coexisting behavioral disorder, or has abused or sold medication in the past, develop a system for dispensing medication that prevents these possibilities to the greatest possible extent.

Meeting New Academic Challenges

"Last Thursday I forgot to take my pill," writes Sharon, a high school senior with inattentive-type ADHD. "As the day progressed, I became increasingly observant. By eighth period I could, for the first time, hear the low electrical buzz in the chemistry lab. I noticed the dripping of one of the faucets and the curled corner of a piece of paper peeling off of its poster board backing. I saw the faint streaks of green that lingered on the chalkboard beneath the white chalk equations. As a classmate's wisps of breath lightly touched my hair, I could feel the strands' small movements. Occasionally, I could discern fragments of conversation coming from the hall outside. As my head whirred with this overload of sensations the air seemed to congeal; grow slow. I felt heavy and lethargic; my senses seemed to have thickened and blurred. When class ended, I realized I had neglected to write down any of the directions for the next day's experiment."

Sharon also experienced great difficulty organizing and prioritizing her homework assignments—preventing her from turning in completed work on time. "I would often sit down and start my homework with the best of intentions," she writes. "Two hours later I would look up and discover, to my surprise, that I had spent the whole time reading a 'few' chapters of a novel or staring out the window. I couldn't understand how I had lost that time."

It is easy to understand how a teenager with these types of difficulties could quickly become overwhelmed by the increasing academic demands of middle school and high school. While some students with ADHD—particularly those with milder symptoms, good parental support, strong abilities/ verbal skills—may manage the shorter assignments and the less complex concepts of elementary school, many will have more difficulty in the upper grades in terms of quantity (longer assignments, more homework) and quality of work (increasingly abstract language and manipulating more complex ideas in their minds). Proper medication treatment can go a long way in supporting your child's academic efforts (as it did with Sharon when she remembered to take her pill). A treatment plan with specially targeted academic support at home and in the classroom is essential as well, as you will see. It is also important to understand, however, that certain higher-level academic tasks, especially those requiring multitasking—doing 2 or more things at the same time—may develop more slowly in your adolescent with ADHD. This is not to say that she can never do as well academically as her peers—only that she will probably have to work "harder" with structured individualized systems, strategies, and supports. Because there is no routine "one-size-fits-all" formula for these aids, she may also need to rely on professional advice in designing the best routines and your own support, patience, and commitment.

As students mature, they are expected to be able to carry out more complex learning tasks—tasks that may prove especially challenging to your adolescent with ADHD. These include

- **More consistent and sustained attention** to classroom lectures and deskwork
- **More efficient processing of information** that she encounters through reading or classroom lectures
- **Mature visuospatial skills** that help her interpret and reason about things she sees
- **Complex thinking** that allows for advanced problem-solving and the ability to handle abstract concepts
- **Higher-level language abilities** required for a greater emphasis on abstract language and fluency in written language, as well as for studying a second language in school

- **Fine motor skills** needed for efficient note taking, keyboard use, and speed writing
- **Better self-organization** needed to complete her work each day and turn it in on time
- **Improved sequencing skills** that allow her to schedule enough time for schoolwork every day, plan the steps necessary to complete long-term assignments, prioritize work assignments, and keep up with school demands

This is a heavy menu of new demands for any student—especially those with ADHD and related problems. Delayed development of any of these skills can lead to poorer academic functioning. As your child moves toward adolescence, pay special attention to how well she is managing these types of challenges and plan to focus on them increasingly as she grows.

Reviewing Your Adolescent's Education Program

Overseeing your child's academic career during adolescence is easier in some ways and more difficult in others. As your child matures, she is better able to communicate her school-related problems to you—though, as a teenager, she may be reluctant to do so. The fact that she attends multiple classes with a number of different teachers allows you to compare her performance among classes and therefore more accurately identify problems. Teachers who now see her for just one period a day are less likely, however, to know your adolescent well, and to be able to provide insight into her situation. Finally, while the chances are greater that your child's ADHD and any coexisting conditions have been accurately diagnosed by adolescence, and that a successful education program has been created for her, some problems may have been compounded by earlier failures, a decrease in self-esteem, the development of behavioral or emotional disorders, or an academic or social "reputation" that may be difficult to overcome.

As always, it is better to initially focus on your adolescent's strengths, and only then to begin to tackle the weaknesses. If your child is having significant school problems and you have not already worked with school personnel to create an education program, or have not considered seeking coverage for her under the Individuals with Disabilities Education Act (IDEA) or Section 504, refer to Chapter 7 for information on how to implement these sometimes vital forms of support. Particularly if your child is changing to a new school or you have not previously established contact with her principal or special education coordinator, meet with one of them now to discuss your teenager's diagnosis and any classroom accommodations that might be available if needed. If you feel that you need more support in this, ask your child's pediatrician to contact her school directly, and review Chapter 7 for ideas on other options.

Request a meeting with your child's educational team to help you prepare for the coming academic year. At this meeting (or, if no meeting is scheduled, during early conversations with as many of her teachers as possible once the school year has begun), find out when regular parent-teacher conferences are scheduled, arrange for additional regular meetings or phone conversations if you and the teacher agree that these would be helpful, and decide how to communicate about any issues that arise. Discuss how any special educational services or accommodations will be implemented. Arrange for the completion of a weekly report card, if you have decided to use one. It is also a good idea to understand each teacher's philosophy concerning ADHD, and to tactfully correct any broad misconceptions. Of course, you would be wise to emphasize from the start that you are there to support the teachers' efforts to help your teenager—not to second-guess the teachers or "tell them what to do."

After 2 or 3 months have passed, you, your child, and her teachers will have accumulated enough information about her performance to review a list of academic goals and, if necessary, revise her education program. Pay attention to the special skills she needs to develop to handle her increased adolescent workload, including

- Completing homework and turning it in on time
- Breaking down long-term assignments into manageable chunks and prioritizing daily assignments
- Comprehending and recalling what she reads
- Listening in class and taking adequate notes
- Memorizing facts
- Managing her time
- Organizing her study area, backpack, and class folders
- Writing legibly and quickly, and typing efficiently on a computer keyboard

Behavioral issues in the classroom should also be addressed at this time because they can strongly affect your teenager's ability to learn and the classroom environment in general. Teenagers with inattentive-type ADHD may especially need help in participating in class discussions or seeking extra help when they need it. Those with hyperactive/impulsive-type ADHD or a behavioral disorder are more likely to have problems with disrupting the class, arguing with teachers, getting into fights with classmates, or skipping class. (For more information on behavioral and other coexisting disorders, see Chapter 8.)

Once you have identified the major functioning difficulties experienced by your child, and have prioritized them in order of importance, try to pinpoint exact targets for improvement. Does she have trouble memorizing facts, for example, because she tries to memorize too many in a single session or because having the television on while she studies prevents her from focusing? Does her disruptive behavior occur when quiet deskwork has gone on for longer than her patience allows, when academic pressures (such as test taking) make her anxious, or when she has forgotten to take her medication?

Comparing your child's functioning from one classroom to another may add insight into precisely where a problem lies. If she is making As in math and Ds in history, for example, is it because her math teacher has a knack for keeping her attention, or for limiting her disruptive behavior? (If so, perhaps the math teacher would be willing to share her techniques with others who teach your child.) Is it because special accommodations, such as untimed tests or shorter homework assignments, are provided in math class but not in history? Might she have an undiagnosed reading-related learning disability that is affecting her performance in history? Or is she simply passionate about math and less confident about history? (If so, her passion should be encouraged and her insecurity in other classes specifically addressed.) It is also important to remember that adolescents with more intense needs may continue to qualify for Individualized Education Programs under IDEA and section 504 of the Rehabilitation Act as discussed in detail in Chapter 7.

Creating an Academic Contract

As adolescence progresses, it becomes increasingly important to assign your child more responsibility for implementing her own education program if she is to remain sufficiently motivated to follow it. One way to encourage your child's active participation is to create a "contract," to be signed by you, your child, and her teachers, defining the areas you have agreed to address, stating how they will be addressed and who will be responsible for which actions, and specifying the rewards (use of the family car, a later curfew on weekends) that your child will receive for successfully fulfilling the contract.

A signed contract communicates to your teenager her "adult" role in managing her own academic progress, and

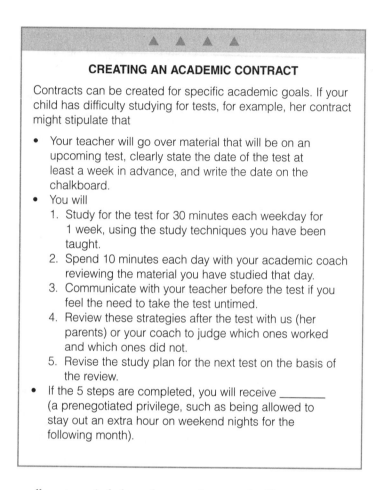

CREATING AN ACADEMIC CONTRACT

Contracts can be created for specific academic goals. If your child has difficulty studying for tests, for example, her contract might stipulate that

- Your teacher will go over material that will be on an upcoming test, clearly state the date of the test at least a week in advance, and write the date on the chalkboard.
- You will
  1. Study for the test for 30 minutes each weekday for 1 week, using the study techniques you have been taught.
  2. Spend 10 minutes each day with your academic coach reviewing the material you have studied that day.
  3. Communicate with your teacher before the test if you feel the need to take the test untimed.
  4. Review these strategies after the test with us (her parents) or your coach to judge which ones worked and which ones did not.
  5. Revise the study plan for the next test on the basis of the review.
- If the 5 steps are completed, you will receive _____ (a prenegotiated privilege, such as being allowed to stay out an extra hour on weekend nights for the following month).

spells out precisely how she can take control of her success. Adolescents who do not see the connection between their own actions and their academic successes or failures (who believe, for instance, that the "winds of fate" control their destiny instead of they, themselves) are more likely to experience school failure. By literally outlining the steps your child can take to change her own situation, and showing her how you and her teachers will support her in getting where she wants to go, you can increase her chances of succeeding.

Specific Schoolwork Strategies

As you have read, one of the best ways to teach your teenager the skills she will need to succeed in school is to break complex processes down into a series of simple steps. In many cases, teenagers with ADHD fail to succeed at school because they simply do not know how to study effectively for tests, keep their school notebooks organized, or manage their assignment notebooks or plan for more complex assignments. These techniques are not always developed naturally. You can certainly share the strategies that you use with your teenager—*but remember* that what works for you will not necessarily work for her. You can also ask your child's teacher or school counselor to refer you to a tutor who can problem-solve with your teenager to find her own most effective ways to memorize material, more fully comprehend what she reads, study for tests, organize her backpack, manage her homework assignments, or accomplish whatever other school-related tasks you have identified. The teacher or counselor may also be able to contribute valuable ideas. Some teenagers with ADHD also find it quite helpful to enroll in peer tutoring programs and study-skills classes if they are available in their schools. Study and time management tips are also available on most ADHD-related Web sites, including www.add.org and www.chadd.org. In most cases, such instruction requires only a few brief sessions. You can then follow up on this instruction at home with your child.

Social and Emotional Challenges in Adolescence

Most teenagers worry about being accepted by their peers, but many adolescents with ADHD have come to expect some social rejection due to their difficulties with controlling their behavior, understanding others' social signals, and being on the socially

GOOD HABITS FOR ACADEMIC SUCCESS

Helping your teenager to discover the tools and motivation to organize her life can make an immense difference in her academic progress and, in turn, her self-esteem. Here are some tips. But remember, study habits need to be individualized, and what works well for one person may not for another.

- **Keep the organization simple.** Consider keeping just one folder for all work that is completed, another folder for all work that still needs to be done, and a third folder for graded work and notes from the teachers to the parents. When the student gets home, she can pull out one folder containing all the assignments she needs to complete. At the end of the evening, all of these assignments will have been placed in the completed work folder. At the end of the next school day the completed work folder should be empty, because all the work has been turned in. Complicated systems like color coding each folder for each subject may seem like a better idea, but can become overwhelming for many students with ADHD.
- **Use a daily planner or handheld computer** to record school assignments, doctor's appointments, and other meetings, and to schedule work on long-term projects. Again, keep it simple. Elaborate systems may be more detailed, but more frustrating to use.
- **Use a backpack as the location for all schoolwork and supplies.** Supplies can be kept in the side pockets, her assignment planner in a separate outside pocket, and her notebook in the main body of the pack. All schoolwork goes into the backpack.
- **Organize her locker** as a place to keep schoolbooks not needed that day—not as a trash can or repository for supplies and papers.

▲ ▲ ▲ ▲

GOOD HABITS FOR ACADEMIC SUCCESS

- **Make lists** of tasks to be accomplished, ideas to be included in a written essay, people to call about a project, etc. The more short-term information your teenager has on paper, the less she has to hold in her head. Keep the lists in a designated place (a backpack, a "note box" at home, etc). Lists scattered throughout the house can be harder to find than remembering the information they contain.

- **Use an outline or flowchart format to take notes.** An outline or flowchart can help your teenager understand the structure underlying the information she hears and can save her from having to write down every word.

- **Preview.** If there are questions in the back of a chapter in a textbook, reading these questions first can help your adolescent know ahead of time what major points the author thinks she should take away from the chapter.

- **Break up tasks into a series of small steps.** Study for tests in a series of relatively brief periods over a number of days instead of cramming the night before. Good study habits can include surveying the topics to be tested; creating questions about the material, then rereading the material to answer her questions; formulating answers in her head or discussing them with you, a tutor, or a "study buddy"; and practicing writing down answers to questions that seem likely to be on the test. She could stage a writing assignment by doing the research one day, thinking about it the next, writing a first draft on the third day, and revising it on the fourth.

- **Set aside a routine time and place for doing homework.** Most teenagers with ADHD can benefit from a routine, non-distracting environment for completing work. This may mean no television or Internet access unless it is required for an assignment.

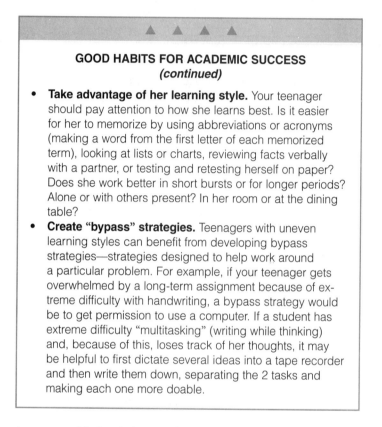

GOOD HABITS FOR ACADEMIC SUCCESS
(continued)

• **Take advantage of her learning style.** Your teenager should pay attention to how she learns best. Is it easier for her to memorize by using abbreviations or acronyms (making a word from the first letter of each memorized term), looking at lists or charts, reviewing facts verbally with a partner, or testing and retesting herself on paper? Does she work better in short bursts or for longer periods? Alone or with others present? In her room or at the dining table?

• **Create "bypass" strategies.** Teenagers with uneven learning styles can benefit from developing bypass strategies—strategies designed to help work around a particular problem. For example, if your teenager gets overwhelmed by a long-term assignment because of extreme difficulty with handwriting, a bypass strategy would be to get permission to use a computer. If a student has extreme difficulty "multitasking" (writing while thinking) and, because of this, loses track of her thoughts, it may be helpful to first dictate several ideas into a tape recorder and then write them down, separating the 2 tasks and making each one more doable.

immature side for their age. This rejection can negatively affect your adolescent's academic performance and emotional health—and can be, in fact, much more troubling to him than making poor grades in school.

As with academic challenges, however, difficulties with social interaction can often be helped by having your teenager learn specific skills. In chapters 5 and 8, you learned a number of ways—including role modeling, role-playing, analyzing interaction, and practicing new techniques—to teach younger children how to interact positively with others. Now, in adolescence, your child is likely to experience new motivation to improve his social life, and advice about social issues is now more often sought from peers than from parents.

Friendships

Teenagers with ADHD are often not the most popular students at school, but they certainly can have the close friendships that are important for their happiness and self-esteem. Your teenager's targeted efforts to increase the accuracy of his social perceptions and monitor his social interactions may make this easier for him. As he develops friendships, support this by allowing his friends to hang out in your home and help to provide the kind of supportive environment that facilitates all friendships. Observe how the friends relate to one another, and provide tactful feedback for your teenager later if you feel that it will be received in a positive and constructive manner. Your adolescent needs to be increasingly aware that friendships take organizational skills, too—returning phone calls, arriving at meeting places on time, and following through on plans.

Conflict Resolution

It is important for your teenager to learn how to resolve conflict without resorting to physical fights, and how to avoid becoming the target of others' aggression. Again, resolving conflict can be difficult for your teenager if his ADHD-related impulsiveness causes him to strike out when he gets upset. An important step in avoiding this problem is to identify his own anger cues and to brainstorm in advance about the kinds of positive solutions he can apply to future conflicts. If this is an issue with your teenager, through discussions with you and peers; post-conflict analysis; and sessions with a counselor, therapist, or social-skills instructor, your child can learn to "talk himself down" when he finds himself in a frustrating clash of wills ("I'm going to take three deep breaths and think about my best choice in this situation before lashing out."). He can also practice such conflict-prevention techniques as "providing an alternative" ("How about if we go bowling first and then see a movie?"), "adding provisions" ("OK, you can drive, but then I get to decide on the restaurant."), or "changing the subject" ("I'm starving. You want to get some pizza?"). Once your teenager has learned a few of these specific techniques, he may be surprised at how effective they are in helping him avoid the crises that used to disrupt his social life.

Working on Social Skills
As with other learning processes, your adolescent can hone his social skills and interaction by

- Developing a list of specific target behaviors to work on
- Outlining a step-by-step plan to address each one
- Receiving consistent, tactful feedback from you, his peers, and his teachers
- Using such techniques as anger-cue identification, analysis of others' social interaction, social role-playing, etc
- Getting training in anger management or social skills, or treatment in individual or group therapy, when appropriate
- Receiving treatment for any coexisting conditions that may affect his social interaction (See Chapter 8.)
- Getting positive feedback for improvement in targeted social skills
- Staying involved in rewarding pro-social activities

That said, it is also true that many people with ADHD continue to have trouble with certain social interaction throughout adolescence and into adulthood. Whether this is the case for your teenager, make it clear that you support him no matter what. Nothing will be more difficult for him than overcoming social rejection. It will mean a lot to your teenager to know that you will always be in his corner. Keep in mind that even teenagers who are socially unhappy in high school go on to find rewarding friendships in college or work situations.

Your Teenager's Emotional Development

It is easy to see how academic, social, and family strains can create a heavy emotional burden for adolescents with ADHD. Low self-esteem caused by academic failure and social rejection can lead to depression, defensiveness, pessimism about the future, hostility, and physical aggression. Combined with ADHD-related impulsiveness, it can pave the way for unsafe sexual activity; alcohol, tobacco, or drug abuse; and other high-risk behavior. Take a moment to consider your teenager's emotional state. Does she spend nearly all of her time alone in her room? Does she seem sad nearly all the time, or irritable? Is her anger starting to get out of hand? Has she been suspended from school more than once this year, or are you receiving reports of inappropriate behavior? If so, discuss these issues with your adolescent and bring them up at follow-up sessions with her pediatrician. Anxiety and depressive disorders (see Chapter 8) are prominent coexisting conditions in teenagers with ADHD, and should be thought of any time your adolescent's social, academic, or behavioral functioning starts to deteriorate without an obvious explanation. The sooner you identify your child's depression, anxiety, anger, substance use, etc, the greater the chances that her situation can be resolved before worse problems develop.

Risk Taking

Adolescence is a time when all teenagers are prone to testing limits and engaging in risk taking. Adolescents with ADHD and an impulsive style are especially prone to taking risks. Surveys have shown that teenagers with ADHD have an earlier age of first intercourse, more partners, less use of birth control, and more sexually transmitted diseases and teenage pregnancy than their peers. Education about these issues in preteen years and continuing guidance now can really pay off. Driving can be a particular area of concern. Teenagers with ADHD receive more traffic citations (especially speeding tickets) and have more accidents and more license suspensions than their peers. As a parent, you may want to consider this area carefully, make sure that your adolescent is at a maturity level appropriate for driving, and set appropriate limits if necessary.

Effective Parenting of Teenagers With ADHD

In chapters 5 and 6, you learned of a number of parenting techniques aimed at helping you interact positively with your younger child. These behavior management techniques can still provide a basis for healthy family relationships, but as your teenager grows increasingly independent you will need to deal with more complex family issues that require some new approaches. A number of these issues are discussed in this section, along with some effective techniques you can use to address them. As when your child was younger, however, you are likely to benefit enormously from sound parenting education information specially designed for families of teenagers with ADHD, or from the supervision of a therapist trained in these techniques.

Helping Your Teenager Become More Independent

As you have learned, achieving independence is every adolescent's primary developmental goal. Your teenager will experience this urge as strongly as his peers without ADHD, but his impulsivity, inattention, and aspects of delayed maturation mean that he may need to move more slowly toward full self-supervision. Specifically, you may need to

- Remove limits at a slower, more staged pace for your teenager with ADHD.
- Work harder at consciously modeling responsible behavior.

- Break down tasks and responsibilities into smaller steps and reward him systematically for accomplishing them.
- Develop a plan for systematically transferring responsibilities over to your teenager as he works on his own independence.

In short, sensitive monitoring and limit setting will be critical as your teenager works her way toward mature self-management and autonomy.

Of course, your teenager will resent a 10:00 pm curfew, for example, if his friends are allowed to stay out until midnight. You should address your concerns directly—talk with him about the reasons you worry about his staying out later. You may be concerned that parties tend to get wilder after about 10:00 pm, a time where you have observed his impulsivity to usually increase, or that driving is potentially riskier late at night because his medication will have worn off by then. If he counters that he is ready to take responsibility for staying out later, and you believe that this may be true and have made the necessary adjustments to ensure success (in this case possibly changing his dosage routine to enhance attention while driving), extend the curfew for 1 hour. If he arrives home on time with no evidence of high-risk activity, praise him and reward him with a continued 11:00 pm curfew. Moving slowly in these smaller steps allows you to continue to systematically build on these successes while giving him the chance to extend the boundaries of his independence. Such triumphs in mutual trust and respect are vital for your teenager's self-esteem and positive attitude.

Providing Structure and Support
During your child's earlier years, you were encouraged to actively monitor his behavior in the classroom and at home, providing frequent rewards, and, when necessary, punishments.

Now that your teenager is growing more independent, you may feel it is time to stop this type of monitoring. However, many teenagers with ADHD continue to need more parental monitoring and structure than their peers without ADHD. While it is best for parents of many other 15-year-olds to back off and let their child manage his own homework production, for instance, your adolescent may need continued monitoring to see that he is completing his work and turning it in on time. While other parents may grow more lax about knowing where their older teenagers are every minute, you may have reason to continue monitoring where your teenager is, with whom, what he is doing, and when he will be home, particularly when you sense that he might find himself in a high-risk situation that may be difficult for him to manage.

Establishing and Enforcing Rules

Teenagers with ADHD typically may have an argumentative style, and your teenager's resistance to your continued monitoring is likely to lead to a great deal of boundary testing, negotiating, and possibly outright rebellion. When warranted, you may feel better—and will be able to save some energy—if you identify 4 or 5 *nonnegotiable* rules based on the issues you consider essential for your teenager and your family. You may decide, for example, that use of illegal drugs of any kind—including marijuana, alcohol, and cigarettes—will not be tolerated in your house, or that driving can only be done at times when stimulant medication still has an active effect. These strict, nonnegotiable rules should be reserved for critical issues of safety or family functioning.

When you have arrived at the 4 or 5 basic rules, write them down and discuss them with your teenager. Explain that the trust built through compliance with these rules can open the door to negotiating the other freedoms he craves. His efforts to respect these few bottom-line demands will improve communication and pave the way toward that greater trust. Finally (and this part can be negotiated), discuss with him the rewards for compliance (extended privileges in other areas) and the consequences (increased restrictions) for breaking these rules, and then enforce these consequences consistently.

Negotiating With Your Teenager

Once your teenager has agreed to follow these few essential rules, you are likely to feel more at ease when negotiating other issues with her. As the parent of an adolescent with ADHD, you will need to become adept at using negotiation to shape your child's behavior and to resolve conflicts as they occur. Negotiation is based on the assumption that, as your adolescent matures, she will take a more active role in creating the rules by which she lives. While your goal should be to gradually lead her toward a thoughtful independence in managing her behavior, it is important to establish the fact that as the parent, right now you assume the final responsibility for rules and consequences.

A good way to negotiate rules or solutions to family conflicts is to use a technique called *problem-solving training*. This technique consists of the following steps:

- Defining the problem and its effect
- Coming up with a variety of possible solutions to the problem
- Choosing the best solution
- Planning how to implement the solution
- Renegotiating a new solution if necessary

Your teenager may resent the fact that she is not allowed to watch television on school nights, for example. To resolve this conflict, you could hold a family meeting to discuss the issue. First, you would *define the problem* and allow your teenager to explain why it upsets her. ("Sara, you want to watch three to

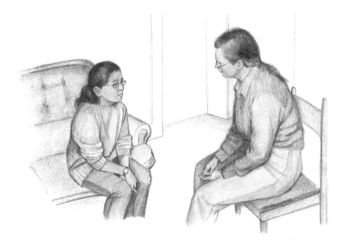

four hours of TV on weeknights like you say all your friends are doing," you might say, "but I see that when you do that you usually only get about half of your homework finished." Sara might add, "Everybody talks about what they watched the night before, and I never have anything to say. It makes me feel left out and like a loser.")

Next, you, your partner, and your teenager would *contribute ideas to resolve this problem.* Usually 6 to 8 ideas are sufficient. No one should express judgment or respond to any of the suggestions in any way, positively or negatively. Each family member should contribute whatever solution comes to mind, even if it seems somewhat unusual or impractical—taking turns if necessary to allow each person to contribute his or her share. Your adolescent or you should write down each potential solution until all suggestions have been recorded.

Next, each family member should take a turn *evaluating* each solution in order. He should consider whether a particular solution would work for him, whether it would work for others in the family, and then assign it a plus or a minus. As the family works down the list of solutions in this way, each solution will accumulate a series of plus and/or minus ratings that can be used to choose the best idea.

To *choose a solution,* you and your family will select any idea that has received all "pluses" and discuss its benefits and weaknesses. If more than one solution has received all pluses, you might be able to pick the one that seems most reasonable to your adolescent. If none has received unanimous approval, choose the one that was best liked and discuss how you might make it acceptable or brainstorm again to find a solution acceptable to everyone. (For a solution to work well, it needs to create a "win-win" situation.) In this way, you will end up with a solution that you can all live with—even if none of you consider it perfect.

Once you have chosen the best solution, you will need to agree on *how it will be implemented.* Who will be responsible for seeing that rules are followed? Who will remind your teenager to comply with the rules when necessary? What are the consequences for breaking the rules and the rewards for complying? If you have agreed, for example, that Sara can watch television for 1 hour each school night as long as she has completed her homework, you must decide how late at night she can watch television, who will be responsible for reminding her that her homework needs to be finished first, who will check to make sure it is done, what privileges she will lose if she breaks these rules, and what rewards she will enjoy if she follows them. The more airtight you can make this part of the agreement, the less time and energy you will spend arguing about the rules later. The entire agreement should be written down and, if appropriate, signed by everyone present.

When first attempting to solve problems in this way, it is best to start with issues that are important but not emotionally intense for your teenager or for you. Once you have practiced these new techniques with one or more easier topics, you can move toward resolving more volatile conflicts. Eventually you may become so adept at this rational form of problem-solving that you and your teenager will be able to resolve arguments on the spot in most cases, using informal versions of this technique.

Providing Appropriate Consequences

Throughout this book, we have emphasized the importance of providing positive reinforcement whenever possible, ignoring negative behaviors that are not dangerous or destructive, and punishing only the few intolerable behaviors on which you and your child are currently focusing. This practice should continue throughout adolescence—with the reminder that the more positive feedback you can offer your child during these difficult years, the more competent he is likely to feel. It is also a fact that you will need to save consequences or other negative feedback for the times when you really need them. Constant criticism or punishment will desensitize your child to your reactions, so that he may not respond if you ever get truly angry or concerned.

You will need to "stick to your guns" in enforcing the rules and procedures on which you and your teenager have agreed. Provide rewards and consequences consistently, and as soon as possible after the behavior has occurred. Measures such as time-out are no longer age-appropriate for adolescents. More appropriate consequences include pre–agreed-on losses of privileges, such as temporarily losing car key rights for coming home late. Try to let these negotiated consequences take the place of argument, recrimination, yelling, or nitpicking. Keeping the conflicts and emotions out of it, and simply providing the appropriate response, is one way to keep family life relatively pleasant and upbeat.

Fostering a Positive Attitude and Giving Each Other Breaks

As you have read repeatedly throughout this book, a positive attitude and an emphasis on strengths is the best approach for your adolescent and for the family as a whole. Your support and sensitive parenting can make all the difference to an adolescent who may meet with rejection, frustration, or even failure at school. Research suggests, in fact, that the presence of one fully supportive adult in the life of a child with ADHD is one of the key factors in determining that child's future success. Be sure to invest plenty of quality time in your teenager—and make it fun and rewarding for both of you. Sometimes, when things get too tough at home, it is a good idea to take a break from one another. A weekend away can restore your awareness that your problems at home can be solved, and can give you and your teenager the space you need to maintain a viable relationship. Parents need support too!

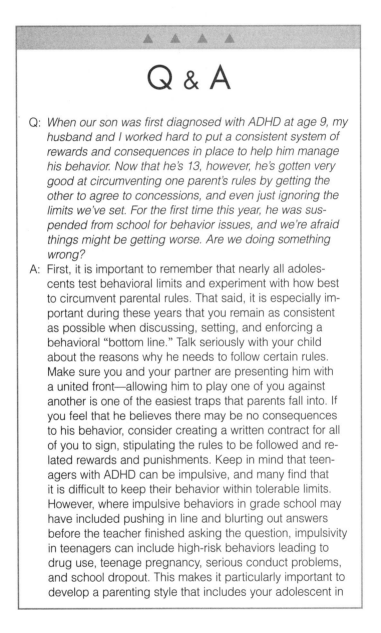

Q & A

Q: *When our son was first diagnosed with ADHD at age 9, my husband and I worked hard to put a consistent system of rewards and consequences in place to help him manage his behavior. Now that he's 13, however, he's gotten very good at circumventing one parent's rules by getting the other to agree to concessions, and even just ignoring the limits we've set. For the first time this year, he was suspended from school for behavior issues, and we're afraid things might be getting worse. Are we doing something wrong?*

A: First, it is important to remember that nearly all adolescents test behavioral limits and experiment with how best to circumvent parental rules. That said, it is especially important during these years that you remain as consistent as possible when discussing, setting, and enforcing a behavioral "bottom line." Talk seriously with your child about the reasons why he needs to follow certain rules. Make sure you and your partner are presenting him with a united front—allowing him to play one of you against another is one of the easiest traps that parents fall into. If you feel that he believes there may be no consequences to his behavior, consider creating a written contract for all of you to sign, stipulating the rules to be followed and related rewards and punishments. Keep in mind that teenagers with ADHD can be impulsive, and many find that it is difficult to keep their behavior within tolerable limits. However, where impulsive behaviors in grade school may have included pushing in line and blurting out answers before the teacher finished asking the question, impulsivity in teenagers can include high-risk behaviors leading to drug use, teenage pregnancy, serious conduct problems, and school dropout. This makes it particularly important to develop a parenting style that includes your adolescent in

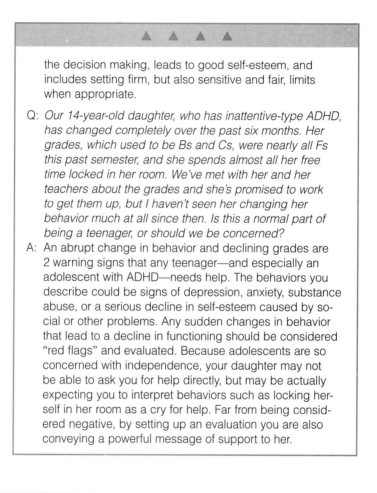

the decision making, leads to good self-esteem, and includes setting firm, but also sensitive and fair, limits when appropriate.

Q: *Our 14-year-old daughter, who has inattentive-type ADHD, has changed completely over the past six months. Her grades, which used to be Bs and Cs, were nearly all Fs this past semester, and she spends almost all her free time locked in her room. We've met with her and her teachers about the grades and she's promised to work to get them up, but I haven't seen her changing her behavior much at all since then. Is this a normal part of being a teenager, or should we be concerned?*

A: An abrupt change in behavior and declining grades are 2 warning signs that any teenager—and especially an adolescent with ADHD—needs help. The behaviors you describe could be signs of depression, anxiety, substance abuse, or a serious decline in self-esteem caused by social or other problems. Any sudden changes in behavior that lead to a decline in functioning should be considered "red flags" and evaluated. Because adolescents are so concerned with independence, your daughter may not be able to ask you for help directly, but may be actually expecting you to interpret behaviors such as locking herself in her room as a cry for help. Far from being considered negative, by setting up an evaluation you are also conveying a powerful message of support to her.

CHAPTER ELEVEN

A Look at Your Child's Future

▲   ▲   ▲   ▲

Most children and adolescents with attention-deficit/hyper-activity disorder (ADHD) find the elementary school and high school years difficult in one way or another, and as your child reaches the end of adolescence she probably looks forward to a more independent life of her own. However, whether she goes straight from high school into a job or attends college, she will need to continue to monitor her ADHD-related functioning problems, advocate effectively for her needs, and structure her life in ways that will help her succeed. Why? Because between one half and two thirds of children with ADHD will continue to have some significant symptoms as adults. However, these find-ings are based on adults who did not grow up with the diag-nosis and treatment methods outlined here. So perhaps these statistics will not hold true for your child with ADHD. It is like-ly instead that your child will have an increasingly better future handling her ADHD as an adult, as even more becomes known about state-of-the-art assessment and treatment for ADHD.

In this chapter, you will find helpful information on

- How to help your child research and apply to colleges and universities that can satisfy her interests and needs
- How she can best transition to life as a young adult in college or in a job
- Health and safety issues of special importance to adults with ADHD

- Relationship challenges and family responsibilities that your grown child will need to learn to manage

After High School: College and Work

Your teenager can best prepare himself for this giant step toward independence by thinking about what sort of adult life he hopes to have. Has he been frustrated by the work demands of his high school environment and longed for the time when he can run his own life and be his own boss? Does he have a special passion or talent that occupies much of his energy and attention? This may be the time to explore his interests more deeply through an internship, apprenticeship, or entry-level job. Are higher education and professional job prospects important to him? Then he should consider attending college—and may want to take advantage of special programs designed to help students with ADHD. Of course, no high school student can

be expected to come up with a definitive answer to all of these questions right away, but it is important to at least start to consider them before jumping into a first job or higher-education experience. Frequent job and career changes are one reason why some adults with ADHD lag behind their peers in career success. Thinking things out carefully and resisting the impulse to "act first and think later" may save your adolescent time and effort in the long run.

Once your teenager has begun thinking about these issues, his high school counselor can be a valuable resource. A good counselor can provide him with an objective picture of his school profile and discuss with him how his interests best match different jobs and occupations, where their typical stresses and satisfactions lie, and how he might find a satisfying path toward his career goal. If he has had an ongoing Individualized Education Program, the counselor can also help see that the types of post–secondary-school transition steps mandated by the Individuals with Disabilities Education Act (IDEA) (see box on page 302) are being carried out effectively for him. Your teenager should also discuss his plans for the future with his pediatrician, psychologist, or other medical advisor, particularly in terms of how his ADHD symptoms may affect his experiences in various jobs and professions, and how he can continue to effectively monitor and self-manage his symptoms.

Getting Into College
Choosing an appropriate school is difficult for most college-bound students, but it can become an even more complicated process, and more crucial, for a teenager with ADHD. Not only must he find a college that suits his academic, social, and geographical preferences, but he also must decide whether the education format and any special services provided by the institution will be sufficient to support his needs. Your adolescent, even more than many of his peers, may need to add to the

PREPARING FOR THE FUTURE

The Individuals with Disabilities Education Act (IDEA) stipulates that, from about age 14 years, when a child with ADHD enters high school, his Individualized Education Program (IEP) team should start to discuss and consider his goals for post-school adult life. By age 16 years or even earlier, if appropriate, the IEP must include a statement of the transition services your child will need—that is, services that will facilitate his progress toward his career, academic, or other aspirations. Such services may include preparation for Scholastic Aptitude Tests or other proficiency tests necessary when applying for college admission, as well as training in self-advocacy and self-sufficiency skills.

During your child's junior and senior years of high school, he should be reassessed for specific functioning problems related to his ADHD, learning disabilities, and any other coexisting conditions—particularly if he plans to attend college. He will need to provide detailed documentation of these disabilities to qualify for untimed or other special college-entry testing accommodations and for special support services at college. His IEP alone, or a general diagnosis of ADHD, will not be sufficient to obtain these services.

Once your child graduates from high school, he will no longer receive services provided by the school system. However, if he has been receiving "rehabilitation services," such as counseling and vocational evaluation and assessment, as part of his transition plan, he can continue to receive them. An Individual Written Rehabilitation Plan will be created for him, allowing him to take advantage of such services.

For more information on this and other aspects of preparing for life after graduation, consult your child's school guidance counselor, as well as www.add.org, www.chadd.org, and other Web sites serving students and adults with ADHD.

universal cry of high school seniors: "Will I be accepted?"; and the more important question, "Is this the right place for me?"

What to Look For

Location, size, and academic offerings are 3 important elements for all prospective students to consider when choosing among the many colleges available to them—and these are vital areas of concern for your teenager as well. He will need to think about whether he prefers to attend school near home, allowing him to take advantage of familiar resources if he needs help, or farther away where he can "start his own life with a clean slate"—understanding that he may have to identify and make contact with a new set of medical and support services. He must consider which is better for him: a small college, where personal attention may be easier to obtain, or a large university with possibly better funding and more options for support services. He must also decide whether the institution's academic demands and supports will match his learning style and needs.

Because the transition to a self-structured life outside the home can be especially challenging for teenagers with ADHD, the presence and effectiveness of a college's ADHD support program is a prime consideration. A few colleges specialize in educating students with learning disabilities. Others offer comprehensive support systems with trained, experienced staff and many specialized services for students with ADHD. Most offer limited specialized services and accommodations for students with ADHD, while some provide only a single learning center serving all students with disabilities and students who need temporary tutoring. The quality of support services offered by a college or university may outweigh your teenager's preferences in other areas. He may decide, for example, that a large or geographically distant university may work as his first choice if its support services are stronger than those of a college closer to home.

▲ ▲ ▲ ▲

COLLEGE SUPPORT SERVICES AND ACCOMMODATIONS

Before she can choose an appropriate college, your adolescent will need to consider—ideally with you and her guidance counselor, teachers, pediatrician, and/or psychologist—which services or accommodations she may need in her new life as an undergraduate. Services and accommodations for college students with ADHD may include

- **Special orientation programs** to introduce students to the institution's academic structure and available services
- **Specialized academic advising** to help students identify the classes, professors, class load, and even the major best suited to their interests and needs
- **Priority scheduling** to allow students to sign up for the most appropriate classes at the most appropriate times of day
- **Reduced course load** that prevents students with ADHD from becoming overwhelmed (A reduced course load may mean that the student will have to make up credits during summer school or a fifth year.)
- **A private dormitory room** for students who may find the presence of a roommate too distracting or disruptive
- **Math laboratories, writing workshops, computer laboratories, and reading courses** to supplement and improve basic academic skills
- **Specialized tutoring** for students with ADHD—emphasizing organizational and planning skills and effective study techniques, as well as help with specific coursework and examination preparation
- **A "personal coach"** to check in with the student each day, reviewing her schedule for the day and the work she expects to accomplish
- **Classroom technology** such as laptop computers, tape recorders, videos, and other recording aids to facilitate students' ability to retain and review the information in classroom lectures

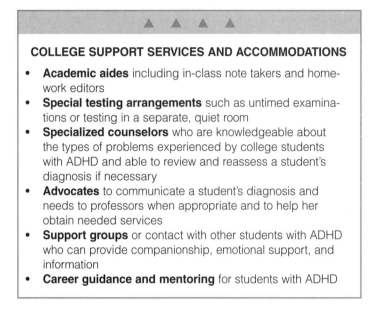

COLLEGE SUPPORT SERVICES AND ACCOMMODATIONS

- **Academic aides** including in-class note takers and home-work editors
- **Special testing arrangements** such as untimed examinations or testing in a separate, quiet room
- **Specialized counselors** who are knowledgeable about the types of problems experienced by college students with ADHD and able to review and reassess a student's diagnosis if necessary
- **Advocates** to communicate a student's diagnosis and needs to professors when appropriate and to help her obtain needed services
- **Support groups** or contact with other students with ADHD who can provide companionship, emotional support, and information
- **Career guidance and mentoring** for students with ADHD

Once your teenager has identified the services that are high priorities for him, he can look for institutions that provide those services. Support services are not always described in college catalogs and brochures, so you and your teenager will need to do some extra research to find out exactly what is available at each institution. The first step for you or your teenager is to call or visit the special services office of each institution that interests him to determine which services may be available at that college or university. (The actual name of the services office tends to vary by institution. It may be listed as "student disability services," "learning support services," or something similar.) Early contact and familiarization with the student support office is important because this office is most often responsible for notifying professors of any classroom accommodations to which a student is entitled. Once enrolled at the college, students must register with the office and provide documentation of their disability to receive special services.

Some students, however, may choose to start college without ever disclosing their ADHD diagnosis, or disclose it to the special services office only when they feel they would benefit from the types of services described previously. The choice of whether and when to disclose this information is highly individual, but deserves thought and discussion as your adolescent begins his college search. There is certainly no right or wrong approach, but students with obvious and ongoing support needs might more strongly consider exploring support services at the time that they begin thinking about college.

Following is a list of general questions that your teenager may want to present to the representative of each college's special services office. Of course, he will want to tailor the questions to apply to his particular anticipated needs. He may obtain more helpful information by also providing the representative with a list of the accommodations or services he hopes to obtain, along with documentation supporting his diagnosis of ADHD and his need for particular aids.

- What services or accommodations does the university or college routinely provide for students with ADHD—specialized academic advising, early registration, a private dormitory room, untimed testing, or any of the other services listed previously? Is there an extra charge for any of these services? If the college does not provide them, are they conveniently available off campus?
- How long has the support services office existed? How many, if any, staff members are specially trained to work with students who have ADHD?
- How many students with ADHD does the office serve?

- Does the university provide other services for all students that may especially benefit students with ADHD—such as Web-based courses that provide lecture notes or videos online, small seminars to review material covered in classroom lectures, and a willingness to work with new instructional techniques or technology?
- Are counselors or psychologists available on an ongoing basis to help students with ADHD adjust to college life and help with any problems that arise?
- Do counselors help connect students with faculty who are knowledgeable and supportive regarding the needs of students with ADHD? Is there a program in place to educate faculty members about ADHD?
- Do support groups for students with ADHD exist on campus? Can the office provide your child with the names of other students with ADHD who are willing to be contacted?

How to Apply

Once your adolescent has created a short list of colleges that best suit his interests and needs, he will begin the application process. Most colleges and universities require applicants to take Scholastic Aptitude Tests (SATs) or American College Testing (ACT) examinations. Your teenager can apply to take these tests under extended time conditions or with other special accommodations. To do this, he must present a written diagnosis of his condition, signed by a qualified, appropriate professional (dated or updated within the past 3 years) along with evidence of early impairment, current impairment, and specific problems. In addition, he will need a copy of his Individualized Education Program (IEP) at school and proof that he receives testing accommodations at school similar to those he is presently requesting. Because further documentation may be required, and specific dates are reserved for special testing, your teenager should contact the Web sites of the Educational Testing Service, the organization that administers the SAT examinations, at www.ets.org, or the ACT Web site at www.act.org, before registering to take either test.

Your teenager does not have to be concerned that revealing his ADHD diagnosis will negatively affect his chances for admission. The Americans with Disabilities Act (ADA) bars discrimination against students with disabilities in the college application process, and admissions committees cannot legally discriminate against students with ADHD. The fact that a student has ADHD is less important than his demonstrated ability to manage his schoolwork sufficiently to meet his school's academic standards. If your adolescent's high school academic record has fallen short of his potential, a personal interview with an admissions officer can provide a key format for discussing the reasons for his past difficulties and his plans for addressing them in the future. Meanwhile, an open attitude toward his academic strengths, weaknesses, and support needs may help him start his new life with a healthy attitude and greater success.

Your teenager's acceptance into a college or university is an important landmark in the challenging process of transitioning from adolescence to independent adult life. To help smooth the way, some colleges offer summer programs prior to the beginning of the freshman year. These programs can be especially helpful for students with ADHD. Your teenager can further prepare for his freshman year by exploring his future college's library facilities, social opportunities, academic services, and other offerings on the Web; contacting his future roommate; talking with older students who can tell him more about the school; and talking with you about the challenges and joys he is likely to encounter next year.

▲ ▲ ▲ ▲

YOUR COLLEGE STUDENT'S RIGHTS

Attention-deficit/hyperactivity disorder, when it substantially limits a major life activity (such as learning), is legally categorized as a disability under Section 504 of the Rehabilitation Act of 1973 and the Americans with Disabilities Act. Section 504, which applies to all colleges that receive federal funds—all public and most private colleges—prohibits discrimination against students with this type of disability and requires the colleges to provide the academic accommodations and services necessary to make courses, examinations, and activities accessible to these students.

Americans with Disabilities Act provisions apply generally to public and private colleges, whether they receive federal funds. This act prohibits discrimination against otherwise qualified students with ADHD-related problems that substantially limit their learning, and requires those students to be provided with reasonable accommodations.

A student with ADHD may or may not choose to disclose her diagnosis when applying to college. If she does not want special accommodations during the Scholastic Aptitude Test, American College Testing, or other testing, or during other aspects of the application process, she may decide to disclose her disability only after admission. Disclosure after admission, and registration with the college's special services office, is necessary to receive services and accommodations to meet her ADHD-related needs.

Coping With College Life

Social Life

From the day she moves into her college dormitory room, your adolescent will be confronted with an array of choices that can challenge any new college student, but particularly those with ADHD. Her most immediate concern may involve finding her place within the social network. In some cases, the effort to fit in at social gatherings and to form new friendships may lead to overindulging in alcohol or experimenting with illicit drugs. While this is the case for many students who then move on to a more balanced academic and social life, students with ADHD may be more likely to consider using dangerous substances to ease their social discomfort, diminish general anxiety, or "numb" their ADHD-related symptoms. A family history of substance abuse, failure to use the college's academic and social support services, lack of confidence regarding the ability to succeed at school, or a treatment plan that has not prepared the student to manage her symptoms in healthy ways can all increase the risk for drug or alcohol abuse. (It is important to note that the use of stimulant medication as prescribed should not increase this risk and may, in fact, diminish it as it helps to diminish impulsive behavior.)

Before your teenager leaves for college, it can help to have a frank discussion about the high risk of early derailment through alcohol or drug abuse at college. Acknowledge the fact that growing up involves a great deal of experimentation, and that the temptation to go along with what others are doing will be high. At the same time, lack of sleep, poor diet, and constant partying (or a lack of social activity) can throw your teenager off balance, intensifying her anxiety or ADHD-related symptoms so that she may be tempted to "self-medicate" with alcohol or drugs. Certainly, everyone makes mistakes during the difficult transition from adolescence to adulthood. The important thing for your teenager is to maintain awareness of how well she is doing in all areas of functioning and to get help early if she finds herself in trouble. This is not the time for her to take a wait-and-see approach or to try to solve such problems on her own. If she will be taking medication or need to make use of counseling services, it would be best to get a referral to an appropriate physician or psychologist (in or out of the student health service) before classes begin and to have the names, phone numbers, and e-mail addresses of key personnel in an appropriate place. If the need arises, the sooner she seeks help from a psychologist, counselor, residential advisor, or other university support person with whom she has familiarized herself when applying to the school, the sooner she can maintain control over her life and the fewer academic, social, and emotional setbacks will have occurred.

Emotional Changes

Some students with ADHD welcome college life as a chance to "start over" in a place where no one knows that they have a disability. However, if they neglect to attend to their study habits, carefully plan their study time, take medication, or attend counseling sessions, their old ADHD-related problems may start to resurface or increase. This experience can be extremely demoralizing to a young adult just beginning an independent life. Again, the college students most able to avoid these setbacks are those who consciously balance out their activities, study habits, sleep patterns, social lives, and limits on drug and alcohol experimentation within the framework imposed by their ADHD-related needs and limitations. Obtaining support in this area, such as joining a college support group for students with ADHD, may help her with this type of healthy self-monitoring and encourage her in her efforts to integrate ADHD interventions into her adult life.

Academic Concerns

Social and emotional concerns may take center stage at first for your college freshman, but academic issues may soon become more urgent. Ideally, your child arrived at college with a good idea of her academic strengths and weaknesses and some tested strategies for dealing with them. If she has already presented the documentation necessary to register with the college's special services office, she will have had the opportunity to learn about available services and accommodations and meet members of the services staff. Through early registration, online research, appointments with professors, and conversations with older students, your child can also start to learn which professors and classes may be most appropriate within her range of choices. Some college students with ADHD have trouble advocating for themselves—asking a professor to allow them to take tests untimed or in a private room (if that has proved helpful in the past), getting permission to use a laptop computer or a human aide to take notes in class, requesting early registration, etc. Counselors in the special services office are usually available to help these students obtain the services or accommodations they need. It is important to request such modifications well ahead of time, rather than expecting a professor to agree to an accommodation on the day of the test or lecture.

College students with ADHD may find it useful to arrange for a "personal coach" (see Chapter 7) who serves as a daily monitor—checking in briefly with her each day, asking her what her most important tasks are for that day and how she plans to accomplish them, and providing positive feedback and support for working toward her goals. While such coaches can help younger children with ADHD learn healthy habits of self-awareness and self-monitoring, they can be especially helpful in helping college students bridge the gap between parental monitoring and full independence. Some special service offices at colleges and universities are beginning to provide such coaches, or references to off-campus coaching services, to students with ADHD. Almost always, there is an extra charge for this service. However, for a student who is struggling to stay on track as she adjusts to college life, a "coach" can make a big difference.

Again, your child should be strongly encouraged and re-
minded to seek help early if she encounters problems with
schoolwork, testing, or other academic issues. (See Chapter 10
for academic strategies that may improve her college performance.) In addition, academic and special supports available on
campus are likely to include a freshman orientation, freshman
experience course, residential advisor, freshman advisor, tutoring network, writing center, computer laboratory, counseling
center, career counselor, health center, and fitness center. All
of these services are paid for as part of her tuition, so they are
readily available to her—and the sooner and more frequently
she takes full advantage of them, the more on-track her college
experience is likely to be.

Employment and the Workplace

College life is a challenge for any adolescent, but life at work can
be just as formidable for a young adult with ADHD. Not only is
he exposed to the same social and emotional pressures as his
peers on college campuses, but he also must perform in a work
environment that typically provides no supportive services and
where no one may know he has ADHD. He may find it more
stressful than he had expected to arrive at work exactly on time,
manage paperwork or other detail-oriented work, attend frequent meetings, meet deadlines, and otherwise conform to
what can often be a noisy, stressful, and, in some cases, physically inactive environment. While teenagers with ADHD
can often perform as well as their peers without the condition,
adults with ADHD who are employed full-time tend to switch
jobs more frequently and earn less money than their colleagues.

Your teenager will certainly start off on the right foot if he
spent time during high school considering what types of jobs
might best suit someone with his particular strengths and weaknesses. Career counseling services are often available through
the high school guidance office, and may be mandated under

the IDEA. Any job can be made more "ADHD-friendly" if the employee knows how to alter his environment to better suit his needs and to advocate effectively for appropriate accommodations.

Coping With the Workplace

If your teenager has joined the workforce but finds his job too difficult, he should get some help in analyzing where his job-related challenges lie. Is he overwhelmed by paperwork? Does he get in trouble for arriving late on too many days? Does he put off tasks and thus fail to complete them? Does he forget his employer's instructions? Does he find it impossible to concentrate with all the noise around him? Is it hard for him to get along with coworkers or his boss?

Once he has identified his problem areas, he can brainstorm on his own or with coworkers, a job coach, a counselor or psychologist, or you or members of his treatment team about ways to address them. He may decide to use a daily planner or computer software to manage daily tasks and appointments. A watch with alarms or a timer can help him keep track of work arrival time or deadlines, and a tape-recording device or hand-held computer can be used to record tasks to be accomplished. He may choose to carpool with a coworker to help him get to work on time, and to take regular, brief "exercise breaks" to work off excess energy. Many more such ideas are available on online support sites for adults with ADHD, such as www.add.org and www.chadd.org, and in books for adults with ADHD listed in this book's Resources section. Remember, there is no "one–size-fits-all" approach to these problems.

Asking Your Employer for Help

If these self-help techniques prove insufficient, and if your teenager feels comfortable disclosing that he has some functional issues related to ADHD, he should consider asking his employer about accommodations she might provide that could help him

work at his best level. Accommodations might include a less
distracting office or workspace, a daily review each morning
of work to be done, help with breaking complex jobs into
smaller tasks, or even flex-time or a transfer from a heavily
detail-oriented, time-pressured job to one that better matches
his strengths. It may be difficult for him to work up the courage
to ask for such help at first, but chances are that his employer
will make at least some effort to cooperate. His problems at
work may have puzzled or displeased her if she did not previously understand their cause, and she will probably appreciate
and respect his effort to improve his performance. As is the case
in any aspect of his life, he is likely to meet with greater success
on the job as he focuses on his strengths rather than his weaknesses. Adults with ADHD are often among the most creative,
imaginative, energetic members of society. The more successfully
he can understand and communicate to his employer his talents,
strengths, and needs, the harder she may work to help him. The
better his self-esteem coming out of high school, the more likely
that he will feel empowered to effectively advocate for himself in
a present or future job.

As was pointed out earlier in this chapter, your adolescent
may be entitled to continued counseling services and assessment under an IDEA-mandated Individual Written Rehabilitation Plan. If this is not the case, however, he will need to be
extra-vigilant regarding any ADHD-related symptoms that are
beginning to get out of hand because routine accommodations
are rarely provided by an employer. Make sure that your teenager has the names and phone numbers of physicians, job counselors, therapists, and other community resources who can help
him with a variety of potential difficulties and try to provide
nonjudgmental help or "reality checks" if he approaches you
about these issues. If he is older than 19, he will probably need
to have his own health insurance policy and should review it

along with his job-related benefits to learn in advance what counseling or other support services can be obtained. He may also consider the possible benefits of using a "coach" to help with some of these transitions from adolescence to adult life. Again, a thorough understanding of his ADHD-related strengths and weaknesses, coupled with a determination to monitor and manage his symptoms, is the best way for your growing adolescent to join the ranks of young adults with ADHD who enjoy stimulating, fulfilling, and successful careers.

Health and Safety

Recent studies have shown that adults with ADHD may be at greater risk for health- and safety-related problems than their peers without ADHD. Their greater risk-taking behaviors and frequently erratic driving practices (inability to follow driving rules, inconsistent operation of vehicles) increase the chances of injuries. During adolescence and young adulthood, they may also have more unprotected sex with a greater number of partners than those without ADHD, and are therefore at greater risk for acquired immunodeficiency syndrome (AIDS) and other sexually transmitted diseases.

It is important that your child be informed as early as the preteen and early teen years about these areas of increased risk. Be sure she understands that, because she has ADHD, she may have to monitor her risk-taking behavior more closely than others her age. In general, the more fully she understands as a young adult that her health and safety are her own responsibility, and that monitoring her risk-taking behavior will always be an important part of her life, the better prepared she will be to meet these challenges.

Family Life

Particularly if your child has experienced social rejection or problems with relationships earlier, he may be concerned about how his ADHD will affect his ability to enjoy a happy, fulfilling adult family life. In the past adults with ADHD have tended to experience more problems than their peers in the areas of long-term personal relationships and parenting. Such ADHD-related symptoms as impulsiveness, inattention, and lack of organization can disrupt family functioning—shifting most of the responsibility to other family members and thus generating a great deal of resentment and anger. Frequent job changes or the highs and lows of entrepreneurial life can also take their toll. Because ADHD tends to run in families, adults with the condition may find that some of their children share many of their own symptoms. Managing a child's ADHD-related behavior and consistently implementing such treatment approaches as behavior therapy can be particularly challenging for a parent with ADHD.

Again, however, the extent of the problems in today's families may have been intensified to some degree by the less effective treatment the adults with ADHD are likely to have received while growing up. In addition, some adults with ADHD were not even diagnosed until adulthood, when their behaviors had already caused a great deal of damage to their family lives and built up a daunting store of personal resentment, self-esteem issues, and other problems. Hopefully, a newer generation of adults—having received careful evaluation, treatment, and monitoring throughout childhood and adolescence, and having been taught sound principles of behavior management as adults—will also find increasing success in family life and parenting.

As in academic life and on the job, a direct, forthright approach is often best when trying to minimize any effects of ADHD on personal relationships. Partners and children of an adult with ADHD are far more likely to accept and try to work around the lack of attention to their feelings and ideas, for example, if they understand that he is unable to restrain his need to "cut to the chase." The typical complaints of family members—that the person with ADHD is selfish, unperceptive, disorganized, forgetful, dangerously impulsive, and excessively risk-taking—are all aspects of ADHD, not a personality defect or an indication that he does not love them. Efforts to communicate this fully to his partner and children—if necessary with the help of a counselor or family therapist—can go a long way in putting his family life on the right track.

Once the entire family understands how ADHD can affect behavior and influence personal interactions—once family members understand that the parent's or spouse's inattention or impulsiveness is not his "fault"—they can begin to identify problem areas in their daily lives and experiment with the best ways to address them. Typical relationship-enhancing approaches include

- **Understanding the need for structure.** Because adults with ADHD often lack structure in their inner lives, they may need more external structure if they are to function well. Partners of adults with ADHD often find that life goes more smoothly when family members routinely make lists of tasks to be done, maintain a family calendar to which everyone can refer, clarify which family member is responsible for which chores, and remind the person with ADHD, if necessary, of time constraints.
- **Breaking down tasks into manageable steps.** It may be possible to get through a mortgage application together or to plan a daughter's wedding without major setbacks—as long as partners agree to take it one step at a time.
- **Playing to each other's strengths.** If one partner is a more organized bill payer and the other can commit to driving the kids to their after-school activities, there is no reason why these tasks cannot be divided in the most acceptable

and effective way. Taking on too much responsibility for daily chores is a major complaint of partners of adults with ADHD, so it is important to make sure that, even if the adult with ADHD is better off not being assigned deadline-oriented duties, he makes up for it by taking on other chores that are viewed by his partner as having an equal payoff value.

- **Learning how to communicate effectively.** Despite best efforts, ADHD-related behaviors can still cause resentment in family members. Rather than expressing anger in non-productive ways, or risk intensifying the resentment by trying to talk about the issue with an inattentive partner, it may be better to agree ahead of time on a more effective way to communicate—over the phone, via e-mail, using a timer to ensure that each person has a chance to speak or, in times of major conflict, with the help of a family or couples therapist.

- **Maintaining realistic expectations.** Just as some adults without ADHD will always be inept at preparing meals, some adults with ADHD may never be able to handle the family's finances as well as their partner. If the non-ADHD partner is unwilling or unable to take over responsibilities, it may be better to hire outside help than to blame a partner for his inadequacies.

- **Understanding that relationships are a 2-way street.** Couples and families need to take care that the entire burden to solve ADHD-related problems is not placed on the person with ADHD. Just as the adult with ADHD must work to manage his problems with organization or impulse control, his partner should try to support and facilitate his efforts. Mutual respect will help motivate all family members to continue doing their best.

- **Learning to forgive each other.** Attention-deficit/
hyperactivity disorder–type behaviors can create a great
deal of resentment, which when expressed can cause the
adult with ADHD to withdraw further, creating more
resentment. Partners need to learn to break through this
negative cycle by forgiving each other for behavior lapses,
and forgiving themselves for their imperfections.
- **Celebrating the joys of the partnership.** Adults with
ADHD typically bring a great jolt of energy, spontaneity,
inspiration, and excitement to marriage and family life.
Couples should remember to take a break from problem-
solving now and then to remember why the got together
in the first place, and to appreciate what they have accomplished together and who they have become.

Specific techniques for addressing problems as they arise
can be adapted from the earlier education and treatment experiences of the adult with ADHD, or both partners may be
able to create new ones together and on their own. Ideas are
also available on ADHD-support Web sites and in books for
adults with ADHD (see Resources).

Successful Arrival at Young Adulthood

Adults with ADHD are much more likely to enjoy successful
and satisfying lives if they were properly prepared during childhood and adolescence to monitor and manage their symptoms
on their own. Throughout this book, you have been encouraged
as a parent to give your child the gift of self-empowerment—to
include her in the process of understanding her symptoms; all
decisions relating to her evaluation and treatment; discussions
of the ways in which ADHD is affecting and may later affect
her daily life; and planning for her future as a student, a family member, and a productive member of the adult world. By
parenting to your child's strengths, continually building her

knowledge base, taking care to applaud her efforts, and otherwise nurture her self-esteem through childhood and adolescence, you have taught her to think of herself not as an
"ADHD adult" but as an "adult who has ADHD."

Now, as your adolescent enters adulthood, armed with the
knowledge, experience, and practiced ability to manage her
ADHD-related symptoms, she will begin independent life in a
stronger position than that of the generations who preceded
her. Of course, every young adult with ADHD is different, and
no individual outcome can be predicted. But by incorporating
the guidelines presented in this book, and empowering her to
use this information as you watch her proceed from childhood,
through adolescence, to young adulthood, you will have helped
your child take advantage of her unique strengths and take
charge of her vulnerabilities as she begins her adult life.

Afterword

▲ ▲ ▲ ▲

Future Directions

All recent clinical advances that you have read about in this book still leave much unanswered about what causes attention-deficit/hyperactivity disorder (ADHD). Fortunately, we have recently learned a great deal about treating ADHD and coexisting conditions, and have shared it with you in these chapters—but you can look forward to many exciting and helpful advances in the near future.

Theories About ADHD

Currently only theories exist regarding the underlying causes of ADHD, and these theories abound. A recent theory proposed by Dr Russell Barkley suggests that the problems children with ADHD have stem not so much from difficulties in paying attention as from having trouble inhibiting behavior—that is, stopping the urge to do something more engaging than the task at hand. He describes the problems stemming from the ADHD core symptoms—inattention, hyperactivity, and impulsivity—as due to this delay in the development of inhibition of behavior. Another theory, proposed by Dr Allan Mirsky, divides attention into a number of elements (such as difficulty sustaining attention, focusing, shifting attention from one task to another, etc) and relates them to structures in distinct regions of the brain. This model suggests that a number of aspects of attention are impaired in children with ADHD, and that the deficits in attention cannot be accounted for by learning disabilities.

Advances in Basic Research—Brain Imaging, Brain Chemistry, and Genetics

Regardless of which of the many theories about the cause of ADHD prevails, your child with ADHD is coming of age at an exciting time in the history of ADHD research. Over the next several years, children may begin to benefit from new brain-imaging technology, as well as genetics and clinical research that are daily revealing more information about the biological bases of ADHD and related disorders, as well as about which treatments are most likely to lead to the best outcomes. Longer-term studies of children with ADHD are beginning to show that those who receive the types and quality of ADHD treatment described in this book have fewer problems with their functioning at home and school compared with those who do not receive this level of treatment. As research affords scientists with more insight into the causes and effects of ADHD, they will be able to devise more precise diagnostic processes and fine-tune existing treatments to better target the needs of children with specific subtypes of ADHD and related conditions.

Brain-imaging technologies, including positron-emission tomography (PET) scans and functional magnetic resonance imaging (fMRI) studies, provide images of the brain as children perform learning tasks, and continue to give us more and more information about actual brain functioning in children and adolescents with ADHD. This research suggests that several different brain areas are involved in the collection of behaviors categorized as ADHD. Future fMRI studies and new brain wave analysis techniques like quantitative electroencephalograms will help experts more clearly document the neurologic and behavioral nature of ADHD, paving the way for better understanding and treatment.

Current research is also helping us to understand how genes help regulate aspects of attention and behavior through interactions with brain chemicals called neurotransmitters. These neurotransmitters are essential for optimal brain functioning. Changes in the amounts of these neurotransmitters and in the brain's sensitivity to them may lead to differences in a child's attention and behavior. Identifying the specific genes responsible for ADHD would allow experts to categorize ADHD into more accurate subgroups and to develop objective tests for diagnosing ADHD. Increased knowledge about brain functioning and gene and neurotransmitter interactions would also allow experts to develop medications targeting specific brain areas and behaviors.

Advances in Clinical Research—Fine-tuning the Diagnosis and New Treatments

Future clinical research with groups of children with ADHD may prove helpful on a number of fronts related to diagnosis and treatment. Studies are needed, for example, to better validate the 3 subtypes of ADHD—inattentive, hyperactive-impulsive, and combined. More information is also needed on how applicable the current diagnostic criteria are for very young children and older adolescents, along with a better understanding of how ADHD-related symptoms and problems change over the course of a child's development. The question of how much of a behavior is too much also needs to be better answered. The point at which a behavior at the upper limits of normal crosses the line to meet the criteria for ADHD is central to the issue of which children should be diagnosed with and treated for ADHD versus children whose families just need education, support, and careful monitoring. Present research is also being directed toward refining the current diagnostic process because there is still no set of laboratory findings to verify a diagnosis. We need to know more about how reliable and valid parent and teacher rating scales really are. Researchers are also working to better understand specific ways in which ADHD interferes with children's functioning so that more effective treatment planning can take place.

As you have read in this book, there is now a burst of research into medication management, and new medications for ADHD are rapidly becoming available. It is particularly exciting that classes of medications that are not stimulants are presently being researched and developed. Much more needs to be known about which behaviors are most likely to respond to which types of medications in which individuals. More research on the effects of specific types and the intensity and frequency of treatments on people with different characteristics (age, gender, subtype of ADHD, coexisting conditions) could reduce some of the necessary trial and error work involved in the current treatment process. Identifying how specific treatments affect specific behaviors or components of ADHD, rather than the whole cluster of behaviors, and which are best for unique combinations of ADHD and other conditions, would allow pediatricians to better tailor treatment to each individual with ADHD. In addition, much more needs to be learned about behavioral and other non-medication approaches to treatment.

Finally, most studies about ADHD and its treatment have taken place over periods of weeks or months instead of years. The long-term outcome of those in your child's generation—children who typically received better treatment than their predecessors with ADHD and have been treated with state-of-the-art medication and/or behavior therapy for years—is not yet fully known. Clearly, your child and your family will benefit from new research into the long-term effects of these treatments, including changes over time in the core symptoms of ADHD and in coexisting conditions; the obstacles imposed by them; and how treated individuals' academic careers, work experiences, and family lives can be improved.

Knowledge Is Power

Clearly, the better informed you and your child, as an adolescent and adult, are about new ADHD-related research and about ADHD across the life span, the more likely it is that he will benefit from these increases in our understanding of future treatment innovations. As your child makes the transition to adulthood, he should remain allied with professionals familiar with the latest studies regarding ADHD and coexisting conditions. He should also be familiar with the names and Web site addresses of the major national ADHD support and advocacy groups, such as Children and Adults With Attention-Deficit/Hyperactivity Disorder (CHADD), and encouraged to check in with them and other reliable sources regularly for updates on recent ADHD-related research, as well as new legislation and sources of support. Thanks to CHADD and similar organizations, children and adults with ADHD are much better served in the community than they were scant decades ago. As an adult, your growing child could benefit enormously from adding his own time and energy to these advocacy efforts.

Knowledge is power for children, adolescents, and adults with ADHD, and the "gold standard" to which you and your child should apply any new information is whether it will improve his functioning and enhance his self-esteem, relationships, school and job performance, happiness, and health. As a self-aware, self-monitoring, and self-confident individual, he will be well equipped to take advantage of the advances in ADHD-related knowledge, treatment, and practical support that are sure to come his way. As we stated in the introduction to this book, we remain optimistic that by using the approaches described here, and by updating your knowledge periodically from reliable sources, you will remain on the cutting edge of the most proven effective paths to an optimum outcome for your child.

Resources

Organizations and Educational Resources

Attention-Deficit Disorder Association (ADDA)
1788 Second St, Suite 200
Highland Park, IL 60035
847/432-ADDA
www.add.org

Children and Adults With Attention-Deficit/Hyperactivity Disorder (CHADD)
8181 Professional Place, Suite 150
Landover, MD 20785
301/306-7070
800/233-4050
www.chadd.org

Learning Disabilities Association of America (LDA)
4156 Library Rd
Pittsburgh, PA 15234
412/341-1515
www.ldanatl.org

Parent Advocacy Coalition for Educational Rights (PACER)
PACER CENTER, Inc.
8161 Normandale Blvd
Minneapolis, MN 55437
952/838-9000
www.pacer.org

Tourette Syndrome Association, Inc. (TSA)
42-40 Bell Blvd, Room 205
Bayside, NY 11361
800/237-0717
www.tsa-usa.org

ADHD Resources Available on the Internet

About Our Kids
www.aboutourkids.org/articles/about_adhd.html

ADDitude Magazine for People With ADHD
www.additudemag.com

ADDvance Online Resource for Women and Girls with ADHD
www.addvance.com

American Academy of Family Physicians (AAFP)
www.familydoctor.org/
Professional site with a parent information component.

American Academy of Pediatrics (AAP)
www.aap.org
Professional site with parent information component.

Attention-Deficit Disorder Association (ADDA)
www.add.org

Center for Children and Families
http://wings.buffalo.edu/psychology/adhd
Includes a list of summer treatment programs in the United
States and Canada.

**Children and Adults with Attention-Deficit/Hyperactivity
Disorder (CHADD)**
www.chadd.org

Comprehensive Treatment for Attention Deficit Disorder (CTADD)
www.CTADD.com
A site for parents and professionals.

Intermountain Health Care
www.ihc.com/xp/ihc/physician/clinicalprograms/primarycare/adhd.xml
Professional site with parent information, including *ADHD: A Parent's Guide.*

National Institute of Mental Health (NIMH)
www.nimh.nih.gov/publicat/adhdmenu.cfm
Site devoted to children and use of psychotropic medication.
301/443-4313 (NIMH Information Center)

One ADD Place
www.oneaddplace.com

Pediatric Development and Behavior
www.dbpeds.org/handouts/
Professional site with handouts of interest to parents.

San Diego ADHD Web Page
www.sandiegoadhd.com

Internet Sites With Further Educational Resources and Information

All Kinds of Minds Institute
www.allkindsofminds.org
Institute for the understanding of differences in learning.

Educational Resources Information Center (ERIC)
http://ericir.syr.edu
Information network on educational topics.

Federal Resource Center for Special Education
www.dssc.org/frc
Nationwide technical assistance network to respond to the
needs of students with disabilities.

Internet Resources for Special Children
www.irsc.org
Resources and online communities for children with disabilities
and other health-related disorders.

National Information Center for Children and Youth with Disabilities (NICHCY)
www.nichcy.org
Information on disabilities and disability-related issues.

SandraRief.com
www.sandrarief.com
Provides educators and parents with guidance, strategies, and
resources to raise achievement and ensure educational success.

Teaching LD
www.dldcec.org
Trustworthy and up-to-date resources about teaching students
with learning disabilities.

US Department of Education
www.ed.gov
Includes the No Child Left Behind Web site.

Books for Parents, Teachers, and College Students
General

Barkley RA. *Taking Charge of ADHD: The Complete, Authoritative Guide for Parents.* 2nd ed. New York, NY: Guilford Press; 2000

Fowler M. *Maybe You Know My Teen: A Parent's Guide to Helping Your Adolescent With Attention Deficit/Hyperactivity Disorder.* New York, NY: Broadway Books; 2001

Hallowell EM, Ratey JJ. *Driven to Distraction: Recognizing and Coping with Attention Deficit Disorder from Childhood through Adulthood.* New York, NY: Touchstone; 1995

Jones CB. *Sourcebook for Children with Attention Deficit Disorder: A Management Guide for Early Childhood Professionals and Parents.* San Antonio, TX: Psychological Corp; 1999

Jones CB. *Attention Deficit Disorder: Strategies for School-Age Children.* 2nd ed. San Antonio, TX: Psychological Corp; 1998

Nadeau KG. *ADD in the Workplace: Choices, Changes, and Challenges.* Philadelphia, PA: Brunner/Mazel Inc; 1997

Nadeau KG. *Survival Guide for College Students with ADD or LD.* Washington, DC: Magination Press; 1994

Nadeau KG. *Adventures in Fast Forward: Life, Love and Work for the ADD Adult.* Philadelphia, PA: Brunner/Mazel Inc; 1996

Nadeau KG, Littman EB, Quinn PO. *Understanding Girls with AD/HD.* Silver Spring, MD: Advantage Books; 2000

Parker HC. *The ADD Hyperactivity Workbook for Parents, Teachers and Kids.* 3rd ed. Plantation, FL: Specialty Press; 1999 A practical, how-to guide with charts and stickers. Available in Spanish.

Quinn PO, ed. *ADD and the College Student: A Guide for High School and College Students with Attention Deficit Disorder.* Washington, DC: Magination Press, Brunner/Mazel Inc; 2001

Robin AL. *ADHD in Adolescents: Diagnosis and Treatment.* New York, NY: The Guildfor Press; 1998
A book written for clinicians that parents familiar with psychological concepts may also find valuable.

Wilens TE. *Straight Talk about Psychiatric Medications for Kids.* New York, NY: Guilford Press; 2002

ADHD and School

Anderson W, Chitwood S, Hayden D. *Negotiating the Special Education Maze.* 3rd ed. Bethesda, MD: Woodbine House; 1997

Levine M. *A Mind At a Time.* New York, NY: Simon & Schuster; 2002

Levine M. Educational Care: A System for Understanding and Helping Children With Learning Disabilities at Home and in School. 2nd ed. Cambridge, MA: Educator's Publishing Service; 2002

Reif S. *How to Reach and Teach ADD/ADHD Students: Practical Techniques, Strategies, and Interventions for Helping Children with Attention Problems and Hyperactivity.* San Francisco, CA: Jossey-Bass; 1993 (Available in Spanish.)

Smith C, Strick L. *Learning Disabilities from A to Z.* New York, NY: Simon & Schuster; 1999

Zentall S, Goldstein S. *Seven Steps to Homework Success: A Family Guide to Solving Common Homework Problems.* Plantation, FL: Specialty Press; 1999

Behavior Management and Social Skills

Barkley RA. *Your Defiant Child: Eight Steps to Better Behavior.* New York, NY: Guilford Press; 1998
Helpful with children with oppositional behaviors and oppositional defiant disorder.

Frankel F, Wetmore B. *Good Friends Are Hard to Find: Help Your Child Find, Make and Keep Friends.* Glendale, CA: Perspective Publishing; 1996

Garber SW, Garber MD, Spizman RF. *Beyond Ritalin: Facts about Medication and Other Strategies for Helping Children, Adolescents and Adults with Attention Deficit Hyperactivity Disorder.* New York, NY: Harper Collins; 1997

Greene R. *The Explosive Child: A New Approach for Understanding and Parenting Easily Frustrated, Chronically Inflexible Children.* New York, NY: HarperCollins; 2001

Heininger JE, Weiss SK. *From Chaos to Calm: Effective Parenting of Challenging Children with ADHD and other Behavioral Problems.* New York, NY: Perigree Books; 2001

Coexisting Conditions

Attwood T. *Asperger's Syndrome: A Guide for Parents and Professionals.* London, England: Jessica Kingsley Publishers; 1998

Haerle T, Eisenreich J. *Children with Tourette Syndrome: A Parent's Guide.* Bethesda, MD: Woodbine House; 2003

Koplewicz H. *More Than Moody: Recognizing and Treating Adolescent Depression.* New York, NY: Putnam Pub Group; 2002

Waltz M. *Bipolar Disorders: A Guide to Helping Children and Adolescents.* Sebastopol, CA: O'Reilly; 2000

Books for Children and Adolescents With ADHD

Younger Children

Corman C, Trevino E. *Euklee the Jumpy Jumpy Elephant.*
Plantation, FL: Specialty Press; 1996
An entertaining way for your young child to learn about
ADHD.

Galvin M. *Otto Learns About His Medicine: A Story About
Medication for Children with ADHD.* 3rd ed. Washington, DC:
Magination Press; 2001
An illustrated introduction for children about taking
medication for ADHD.

Gordon M. *Jumpin' Johnny Get Back to Work! A Child's Guide to
ADHD/Hyperactivity.* DeWitt, NY: Gordon Systems; 1991
Available in Spanish. Available as a video.

Roberts B. *Phoebe Flower's Adventures: That's What Kids Are For.*
Bethesda, MD: Advantage Books; 1998
Series for children starring a young girl with ADHD—one of
the few stories that features a girl.

Older Children

Gehret J. *Teaching with I'm Somebody Too.* Fairport, NY: Verbal
Images Press; 1996
Novel told by the sister of a boy with ADD. Explains ADD and
how it affects a family.

Gordon M. *I Would If I Could.* DeWitt, NY: Gordon Systems;
1992
Acknowledges the unique experience of a child with ADHD,
offering the reader a humorous, empathetic forum for exploring
his own feelings.

Gordon M. *My Brother's a World Class Pain.* DeWitt, NY: Gordon System; 1992
A book for siblings of children with ADHD.

Ingersoll BD. *Distant Drums, Different Drummers: A Guide for Young People with ADHD.* Bethesda, MD: Cape Pubns; 1995
Stresses a positive perspective and the value of individual differences.

Levine M. *All Kinds of Minds: A Young Student's Book about Learning Abilities and Learning Disorders.* Cambridge, MA: Educators Publishing Service; 1992
Written for middle-school and older children, this book explains the nature of attentional disorders and a variety of learning disorders while reminding readers of their related strengths. Includes discussions of social challenges, motor problems, and difficulties with self-esteem. An audio version is also available.

Quinn P, Stern J. *Putting On the Brakes: Young People's Guide to Understanding Attention Deficit Hyperactivity Disorder.* Washington, DC: Magination Press; 2001
A guide to ADHD written about entering adolescence.

Adolescents

Nadeau KG. *Help4ADD@High School.* Bethesda, MD: Advantage Press; 1998
A book written in an entertaining "Web site" format, providing useful information on how students can help themselves in school.

Quinn PO. *Adolescents and ADD: Gaining the Advantage.* Washington, DC: Magination Press; 1995

Magazines and Newsletters

The ADHD Report
Russell Barkley and Associates
Guilford Press
72 Spring St
New York, NY, 10012
800/365-7006
A newsletter for practitioners reviewing current scientific research as well as controversial issues regarding ADHD. Parents may also want access to some of this information.

ADDitude Magazine
2476 Bolsover, Box 421
Houston, TX 77005
888/762-8475
www.additudemag.com
A commercially produced magazine focused on living with ADD. "The happy, healthy lifestyle magazine for people with ADD."

ADDvance On-line
www.addvance.com/
Monthly e-newsletter for girls and women with ADHD with current ADHD information by Patricia Quinn, MD, and Kathleen Nadeau, PhD. Available with membership to The National Center for Gender Issues and ADHD.

ATTENTION!
CHADD
8181 Professional Place, Suite 201
Landover, MD 20785
800/233-4050
www.chadd.org
A magazine for parents of children with ADHD, as well as adults with ADHD, informing readers of recent developments relating to the condition. Available with membership to CHADD.

ADHD Book and Video Resources

ADD WareHouse
300 Northwest 70th Ave, Suite 102
Plantation, FL 33317
800/233-9273
http://addwarehouse.com

Childswork Childsplay
135 Dupont St
PO Box 760
Plainview, NY 11803-0760
800/962-1141
www.childswork.com

INDEX

▲ ▲ ▲ ▲

A

Abuse of stimulants in adolescent ADHD, 273
Academic advising in college, 304
Academic aides in college, 305
Academics
    ADHD and, 182, 183–185
    in adolescent ADHD, 274–281
        creating contract for, 279–281
        habits for success in, 282–284
    at college, 311–313
    disorders that interfere with, 220
    problems in, 229–230
    in school management, 158–160
Acquired immunodeficiency syndrome (AIDS), 316
Active ignoring in parent training, 137
Adaptive physical education, 226
Adderall XR, 195. *See also* Amphetamines
ADDitude Magazine, 338
ADDvance On-line, 338
ADHD Report, 338
Adolescent ADHD, 261–297
    academic challenges in, 274–281
    changing treatment needs in, 270–271
    conflict resolution in, 285–286
    creating academic contract in, 279–281
    dependence issues in, 268

difficulty focusing and organizing in, 266
education program for, 276–279
effective parenting and, 288–295
emotional challenges in, 281, 284–288
establishing and enforcing rules in, 290–291
fostering positive attitude in, 295
friendships in, 285
hyperactivity/impulsivity in, 33–34
impulse control in, 264–266
inattention in, 32
involvement of adolescent in treatment plan, 50, 65, 89–90
long-term planning in, 266–267
medication management in, 271–273
negotiating with your teenager, 291–294
predictors of success during, 269
providing appropriate consequences for, 294
risk taking in, 287–288
schoolwork strategies in, 281
self-esteem in, 267–268
social challenges in, 281, 284–288
social skills in, 286–287
stimulant abuse in, 273
teenager development and, 262–264
testing of behavioral limits in, 296–297
treatment plan for, 268–269